Marketing: An Integrated Approach

Marketing: An Integrated Approach

Dolores Brown

STATES
ACADEMIC PRESS
www.statesacademicpress.com

States Academic Press,
109 South 5th Street,
Brooklyn, NY 11249, USA

ISBN: 978-1-63989-342-3

Cataloging-in-Publication Data

Marketing : an integrated approach / Dolores Brown.
p. cm.
Includes bibliographical references and index.
ISBN 978-1-63989-342-3
1. Marketing. 2. Selling. 3. Industrial management. I. Brown, Dolores.
HF5415 .M37 2022
658.8--dc23

For information on all States Academic Press publications
visit our website at www.statesacademicpress.com

Contents

Permissions

Index

Preface

The term marketing refers to the processes that communicate, deliver and exchange offerings that have value for customers, partners and society. The main objective of any marketing strategy is to create a relationship with the customer. Every new product is brought to the consumers through the process of marketing which involves steps such as market research, market targeting, distribution, pricing, promotion and communication strategies. The two major types of marketing are business-to-business (B2B) and business-to-consumer (B2C) marketing. In a B2B approach a business sells to another business while in a B2C type of marketing an organization sells to individual people. Any major marketing decision is based on either the 4P or 4C marketing mix. 4P are conventional in nature and refers to product, pricing, place and promotion. The 4C are defined as consumer, cost, convenience and communication. This book unfolds the innovative aspects of marketing which will be crucial for the holistic understanding of the subject matter. Its extensive content provides the readers with a thorough understanding of the subject. Coherent flow of topics, student-friendly language and extensive use of examples make this book an invaluable source of knowledge.

To facilitate a deeper understanding of the contents of this book a short introduction of every chapter is written below:

Chapter 1- Marketing is the collection of activities undertaken by a business or company in order to promote their product and services to the target audience. The process of gathering strategies and tactics to achieve the marketing aims of a company is known as a marketing plan. This chapter introduces the reader to the field of marketing.

Chapter 2- Marketing is a broad term which encompasses many smaller niches of marketing. Business marketing, social marketing, service marketing, rural marketing, green marketing, relationship marketing and international marketing are some sub-disciplines of marketing which are thoroughly discussed in this chapter.

Chapter 3- The development of a new product, pricing, profitability, demand, launch, marketing and any other related research falls under product management. A brand is a unique name, term, design or symbol that sets apart a business product from other similar products. The techniques that go into positive enhancement of the image and value of a particular brand over time are called brand management. This chapter provides a comprehensive summary of product and brand management.

Chapter 4- No two strategies of marketing are alike. Businesses often aim to outdo the other in marketing their products leading to an assortment of marketing strategies. This chapter's focus is on the diverse marketing strategies like promotional merchandises, sales promotions, advertisements, branding and publicity stunts employed by companies to promote their respective products and services.

Chapter 5- Marketing environment is a term that refers to the different factors and forces that are in play and influence the marketing operations of businesses. It can be further grouped into specific categories like internal environment, external environment, macroenvironment, microenvironment, etc. This chapter provides the reader with detailed explanations of each sub-type of marketing environment and their particular components.

I would like to share the credit of this book with my editorial team who worked tirelessly on this book. I owe the completion of this book to the never-ending support of my family, who supported me throughout the project.

Dolores Brown

Marketing: An Introduction

Marketing is the collection of activities undertaken by a business or company in order to promote their product and services to the target audience. The process of gathering strategies and tactics to achieve the marketing aims of a company is known as a marketing plan. This chapter introduces the reader to the field of marketing.

Marketing is a widespread phenomenon. With the advances in information & technology and rising competition, the business organizations are finding forces that help them survive and succeed. Due to the impacts of globalization, deregulation, industry convergence and increasing customer sophistication, marketing has become an inescapable reality.

In this era of heightened competition coupled with dynamic customers, firms find it challenging to establish their foothold in the marketplace. Across the globe, marketing has been well accepted and practiced extensively to meet the demands of the compelling environmental forces. Marketing as a discipline is used by profit as well as non-profit organizations. Marketing is practiced everywhere and anywhere be it products, services, ideas, events, place, people or social cause. The term marketing is derived from the term market which refers to a place of exchange between the buyers and sellers. The process of marketing evolves from the interplay of demand and supply functions in the market which define the buyer's and seller's side respectively. The following definitions of marketing highlight how marketing relates to markets:

> "Marketing is a social and managerial process by which individuals and groups obtain what they need and want though creating and exchanging products and value with each other" – Kotler.

> "Marketing is the managerial process through which products are matched with markets and through which transfers of ownership are affected" – Cundiff, Still and Govoni.

The process of exchange generates value for both the parties: goods and/or services for the consumer and profits for the marketer. The marketer aims at providing satisfaction to customers and in return earns the profits leading to its success in the marketplace. The various marketing decisions taken by the marketer are defined from customer's point of view with all the activities of the organization beginning with the customer and ending with the customer.

Marketing recognizes that business cease to exist without customers and therefore understanding of customers is essential for a firm to thrive in the competitive scenario. Marketers must first comprehend the needs and wants of customers. The definitions of marketing below reflect how marketing is seen as a response to customer needs:

> "Marketing is an organized system of behavior that functions for the purpose of evaluating and facilitating the satisfaction of consumer need" – Arnold R. Weinstein.

"Marketing is a total system of interacting business activities designed to plan, price, promote and distribute want satisfying products and services to present and potential customers" – William J. Stanton.

The needs/wants/desires of customers must be backed by the ability of the customers to purchase for these customer requirements to turn into demand. Marketing strives to fulfill this demand by integrating the various organizational functions towards the achievement of customer satisfaction and happiness. The definitions given below resonates the process of marketing with the gratification of customer demand.

"Marketing is the process of determining consumer demand for a product or service motivating its sale and distributing it into ultimate consumption or profit" – E.F.L. Brech.

"Marketing is the response of the businessmen to the need to adjust production capabilities to the requirement of consumer demand" – E.J. McCarthy.

Recognition of human needs and wants and its translation into desirable products is the job of the marketer. However, the term product in marketing has a wider scope and it covers varied range of products in the form of tangible products, intangible services, people, places, organizations, events, causes and ideas.

Marketing Management

Markets are mosaic in nature and are scattered geographically as well as demographically. The diverse groups of customers with distinct requirements call for effective marketing to take place. This requires the marketers to base the marketing programs and decisions on the principles of management. Marketing management is the process of analyzing, planning, implementing and controlling the marketing activities and programs efficiently and effectively.

The process of marketing management begins with market analysis which involves the recognition of customers which the marketer would like to serve. This involves decomposing the whole market into various parts and then selecting the part(s) which appear feasible to the marketer.

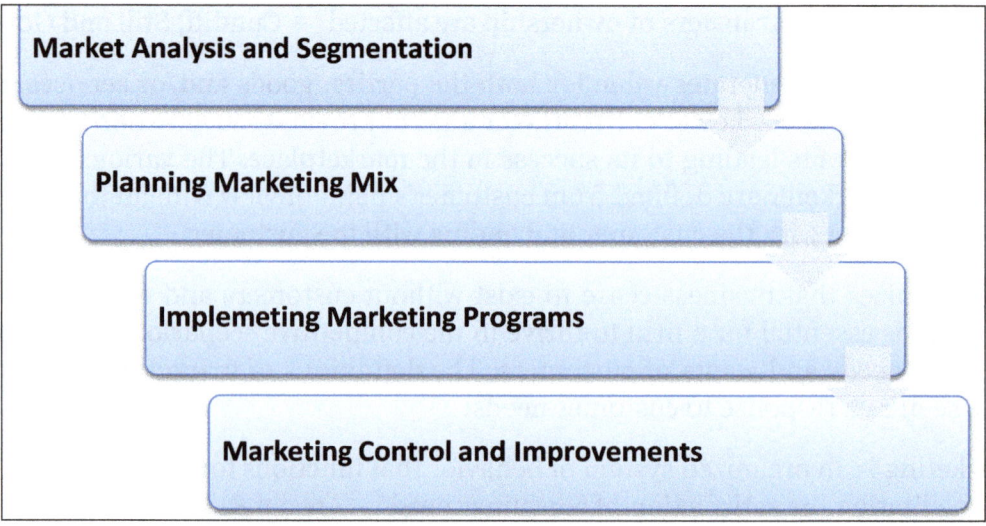

Figure: The Marketing Management Process.

The next step is to decide upon the course of actions with respect to the various marketing tools which are integrated towards the fulfillment of predefined objectives. This involves taking decisions with regard to the product design and development, branding, packaging and labeling, setting price levels, channels of distribution, communication mix elements etc. This comprehensive planning is followed by the execution of marketing programs and finally, control is being exercised by ensuring that the marketing activities are in accordance with the plans and deviations, if any are taken care of by taking corrective action.

Features of Marketing

- Customer Focus: The marketing function of a business is customer-centered. It makes an attempt to study the customer needs, and goods are produced accordingly. The business existence depends on human needs. In a competitive market, the goods that are best suited to the customer are the ones that are well-accepted. Hence, every activity of a business is customer-oriented.

- Customer Satisfaction: A customer expects some services or benefits from the product for which payment is made. If this benefit is more than the amount paid, then the customer is satisfied. In the long run, customer satisfaction helps to retain market demand. It helps achieve organizational objectives. Customer satisfaction can be enhanced by providing value-added services, which includes providing additional facilities at little or no extra cost.

- Objective-Oriented: All marketing activities are objective-oriented. Different objectives are fixed at different levels, but the main objective is to earn profit from business along with the satisfaction of human wants. Marketing activities undertaken by sellers make an attempt to find out the weaknesses in the existing system, and measures are taken to improve the shortfalls so that the objectives are achieved.

- Marketing is both Art and Science: Art refers to a specific skill that is required in marketing activities of any type of business. Science refers to a systematic body of knowledge, based on facts and principles. The concept of marketing includes a bunch of social sciences such as economics, sociology, psychology and law. It indicates market operations based on some principles. Hence, marketing is an art as well as a science.

- Continuous and Regular Activity: Marketing is an activity designed to plan, price, promote and distribute products. At the same time, it also addresses both the current and future consumers. Thus, it is a continuous process. A marketer has to consistently monitor environment. This helps in coming up with new products.

- Exchange Process: Marketing involves exchange of goods, services and ideas with the medium of money. Exchange takes place between sellers and buyers. Most of marketing activities are concerned with the exchange of goods. Functions such as distribution, after-sale services and packaging help in the exchange process. Channels of distribution and physical distribution play an important role in the exchange process by creating place utility.

- Marketing Environment: Economic policies, market conditions, and environmental factors, such as political, technological, demographic and international, influence marketing activities. Marketing activities are inseparable from such environmental factors. A successful marketer needs to adapt to these changing factors and adjust marketing strategies to suit new market developments.

- Marketing Mix: A combination of four inputs constitutes the core of a company's marketing system—product, price, place, and promotion. Marketing mix is a flexible combination of variables. They are influenced by consumer behaviour, trade factors, competition and government regulatory measures.

- Integrated Approach: The marketing activities must be co-ordinated with other functional areas of an organization. Functions such as production, finance, research, purchasing, storekeeping and public relations (PR) are to be integrated with marketing. This will help in achieving organizational objectives. Otherwise, it will result in organizational conflicts.

- Commercial and Non-Commercial Organizations: With the societal marketing concept gaining importance, social marketers are finding useful new ways of applying marketing principles. Commercial organizations are also adopting cause-related marketing to strike long-term relations with consumers. Business organizations such as educational institutions, hospitals, religious institutions and charitable trusts have also found meaningful applications of marketing. Thus, marketing is applicable to both business and non-business organizations.

- Precedes and Follows Production: Identifying consumer needs and wants is the primary task of a marketing manager. Production activities are adapted to these consumer needs. Thus, marketing precedes production. Marketing helps in the distribution of the goods which follows production. Hence, production and marketing activities are closely related to each other.

Marketplace Orientations

Evolution of Marketing Concept

Every organization differs in terms of their conduct and reflections. The sense of direction of an organization defines an organization's attitude towards the marketplace, this being known as the firm's orientation. It explains the manner in which the organization addresses its goals, plans and activities. The philosophies that govern the behavior of the organizations can be categorized into five concepts belonging to five eras:

The Production Concept

The production concept is the earliest concepts originating with the industrial revolution in the last of the 18th century. Belonging to the production era, it covers the time when the company produced only a few products. The organizations with the production orientation provided the goods to the market based on the principles of availability and affordability. This concept was practiced in times when there were not much products in the market to satisfy the unfulfilled needs and wants of consumers. Whatever the firms produced was supplied to the markets as the manufactures were sure that in a scenario of less supply, the products would get sold. The processes of production and distribution were central to the firm's strategy. A business organization was governed by the objective of ensuring that the product was available in abundance and was not expensive. This objective was realized through achieving economies of scale in production and through having effective channels of distribution. This strategy helped firms to expand their market.

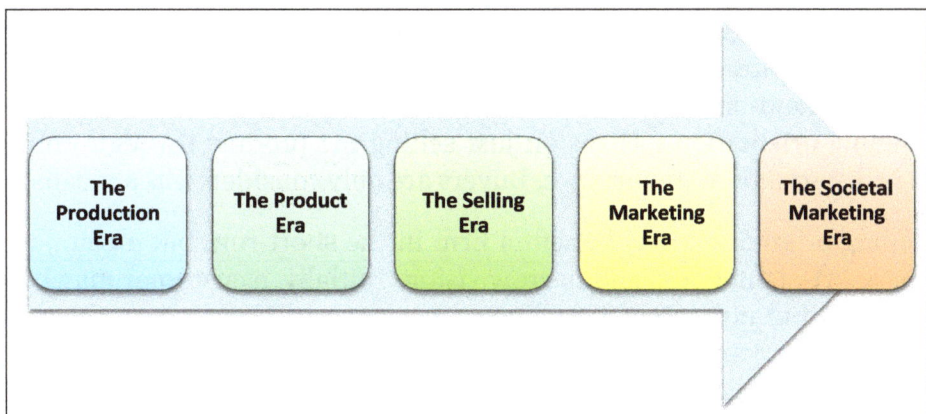

Figure: Evolution of the marketing concepts.

The Product Concept

With the increase in competition and changing customer needs, the production concept could not sustain in the marketplace. Business organizations needed to alter their orientation as the market was flooded with a number of products. This saw the emergence of the product concept wherein the focus was on the quality of products. The firms strived to succeed in the marketplace by providing good quality products to the consumers as the marketers perceived that the consumers would prefer and purchase products that are synonymous with quality. The organizations focused on quality improvement, production again being central to the efforts towards achieving success in the marketplace. The production managers were entrusted with the task of ensuring the best quality products with no consideration being given to the customers and therefore, this concept did not turn out to be a guarantee to the business organizations to build customers.

The Selling Concept

Until now, it was the seller who was the dominant player in the process of exchange. With passing times, competition began to increase. Organizations built up excess production capacity and there was a constant pressure on the firms to produce quality products. The buyer started emerging as the decision maker in the exchange process. This prompted the marketers to find ways to succeed in the marketplace. Persuasion was found as a tool to sell to customers. This concept came to be known as the selling concept wherein the emphasis was to sell to customers through aggressively influencing and inducing them to purchase the products. The selling orientation was based on the notion that the efforts are required to create customers interest in the product and motivate them to buy.

In a market with a number of products and services, customers are not motivated to buy each product. While some of the products may be demanded and searched for by the consumers; some products may be unsought for. The unsought goods are the ones which the consumers do not find important to purchase unless they are made to feel its need such as security products, family planning products. These goods for which consumers are unconcerned need to be pushed towards consumers through persuasive selling efforts as the consumers would not purchase these products on their own.

Organizations guided by the selling orientation educate customers and thereby win customer confidence in the products through hard selling strategies. The aim is to entice customers by effective salesmanship and advertising. Customers have to be motivated towards product purchase making the use of manipulative communication skills. Efforts are made to translate customer defiance into a positive behavioral intention. Without any consideration being given to the customers' needs and requirements, selling orientation focuses on just selling the product through impressive selling. Seller's interest is of paramount importance. Buyers are only considered as a means to earn profits.

Although the selling orientation may benefit a firm in the short run, but a company cannot sustain through this short-sightedness and narrow vision. Initially, a customer may be sold products through manipulation but ultimately, it will be customer's satisfaction with the product that will decide the future of the organization. In situations where the company generates revenues from new customers each time, selling strategy can work but in today's competitive scenario, customer retention is equally important. Loyal customers not only assure a stream of revenue to the business but also help in attracting newer customers for the organization. A dissatisfied customer of a particular product may cease to be a customer of that product in the future and may also affect the potential customers of the business negatively by spreading negative word of mouth.

The Marketing Concept

A business cannot survive by attracting new customers every time. Repeat sales are essential for a business to stay in the marketplace. This renders the selling concept incompetent and thereby necessitates the need for the organizations to reorient their strategy. The business organizations have to design powerful marketing practices capable of retaining the customers for an enduring business. The concept of marketing emerged in the 1950s as a consequence of the changing realities in the marketplace. Customer was placed at the center stage in tune with the demands arising out of fierce competition and market saturation. The earlier orientations were based on an inside-out approach with emphasis on internal organizational elements such as production, technology and sales effort, the marketing concept was an inside-out approach where customers assumed greater importance than the organization and its elements.

The concept of marketing is based on the premise that to compete and win successfully in the marketplace, identification of the needs and wants of customers is required. In order to achieve the goals, an organization should focus on satisfying its customers as customers are the main influential determinant of an organization's stay in the market. It is the customer who pays the price of the product and thereby revenue is generated for the business. Without customer satisfaction, an organization is not able to sell and thereby earn. Products and services should be created in accordance with the customer requirements. The topmost priority for a business is to ensure that the customers feel contended through their product.

Markets today are characterized by a variety of products and services. Customers have a wide choice to exercise in today's highly competitive market. An organization that does not deliver to customers' expectations is made to move out of the market. Customer satisfaction is the key to succeed in present day dynamic business environment.

The concept of marketing created a shift of power from managers to customers as all the marketing decisions are answered in response to the customers' needs and requirements. Whereas earlier the marketers ruled the market with products and services being forced upon the customers, it is the customers now who significantly affect the market forces. Customers have now become the driving force behind organizational efforts. The dynamic customer behavior affects the organizational plans and policies. By satisfying the customers, an organization is able to competently realize its objectives. Customer is the primary element of business with all other elements being defined in terms of customers' needs and wants. Success of business depends on customer happiness. And therefore, under the concept of marketing, managerial and marketing decisions are oriented towards customer's satisfaction. A business gets shape and direction from its customers. There are different products and services available in the marketplace but only those are able to create their position which reflects a manifestation of customers' desire. In order to compete in fierce competition and emerge as a winner, the various marketing mix decisions need to be taken form customer's point of view.

The concept of marketing revolutionized the way business is carried out by reorienting the organizational systems and its aspects from customers' perspective. It is a utilitarian based approach to ensure an organization's stability in the face of fierce competition. The implementation of marketing concept is based on creating value for customers. Marketing as a process begins with the identification of the market for the product or service. Next is the selection of the customer segment which the company wants to target. Once the target customer group is determined, it is analyzed in terms of needs and wants, more specifically the desirable characteristics the customer is looking in a product or service. This is followed by developing the product or service as per customers' expectations and creating a unique positioning for the product in terms of how it differs from competitors offerings.

The Holistic Marketing Concept

The holistic marketing concept views marketing as a system comprising of inter-connected sub systems. Harmony among the marketing components is essential for achieving efficiency and effectiveness. This concept advocates following an integrated approach in pursuance of marketing activities. Marketers need to broaden their thinking in framing and implementation of marketing plans and policies. Satisfaction of customer needs and wants needs competency across varied marketing elements.

The holistic marketing concept takes into account the needs of different stakeholders. The effects of marketing can be felt either directly or indirectly on the various stakeholders. A marketing decision must be analyzed with respect to its far reaching effects. Also the concept postulates, recognizing the interdependencies among the different departments in the organization. The marketing department must act in conjunction and coordination with the other departments. Although different departments differ in terms of their tasks and responsibilities, they should be oriented towards a common goal of achieving customer satisfaction. A comprehensive outlook imbibing different departments, different stakeholders and different activities within the framework of customer value would enable the accomplishment of organizational objectives. The elements of holistic marketing concept are: internal marketing, integrated marketing, relationship marketing and societal marketing.

Internal Marketing

While customers in the market place/space are external to an organization, the employees are the internal customers of an organization. The workforce of an organization plays a crucial role in realizing the objective of customer satisfaction. This necessitates building an efficient workforce with adequate knowledge, skills and dedication towards the realization of the goals of the organization. Also, the internal environment of an organization consists of organizational objectives, plans and policies, resources, procedures and departments. Internal marketing aims at achieving internal efficiency. This requires competent plans and policies to be prepared, optimum utilization of resources, cooperation and coordination among departments and a talented and motivated workforce.

Integrated Marketing

Marketing is a term encompassing several functions and elements that need to be executed in an integrated manner. An effective mix is to be created for the achievement of marketing objectives. The marketing mix comprises of various significant aspects that need to be focused upon. The various marketing activities should be carried out in a coherent manner to create synergy. Marketing cannot succeed in isolation. Marketers must realize that attracting and retaining customers requires various marketing activities to be linked with each other lending complementarity and thereby greater proficiency.

Relationship Marketing

In order to succeed in the hyper competitive marketplace, marketers need to develop healthy relationships with all the stakeholders. Sustained stay in the market requires investment in relationships. Long lasting bonds must be created and maintained with the customers to secure the future of the organization. Organizational key to prosperity lies in customer loyalty. The marketing activities must not only satisfy current needs and wants of the customers but also make consistent effort to keep the customers happy and satisfied. The continued relationship between the customers and the organization gives strength to the organization amidst intense competition. Apart from customer relationships, an organization must also develop associations with employees, suppliers, intermediaries, competitors, government and public in general. These associations require the marketers to understand how stakeholders affect them and how the organization affects these stakeholders. The organization must also keep on adding value to these relationships by revisiting the needs and expectations of different stakeholders from time to time.

Societal Marketing

The concept of marketing has a limited focus in terms of the transaction that takes place between the firm and the customer. It emphasizes on the realization of organizational objectives through taking care of what customers want and offering the desirable products and services according to customers' specifications. The concept of marketing gives unlimited freedom to what customers' desire. In accordance with the marketing concept, the marketer should go by customers wants. However, products or services such as hard drugs, tobacco, alcohol etc., if demanded by customers are not socially justified as they can harmfully affect the individual, his family and the society. Being customer centric, the business may be unaware of the damage it may be causing to the society.

The societal marketing concept overcomes the limitation of marketing concept as it asserts that the practice of marketing should be harmonious with the interests of the society. The societal marketing concept combines the concept of marketing with social welfare in the sense that the realization of organizational objectives through the understanding and satisfaction of customers' wants should be done within the broader framework of long term wellbeing of consumer and society. The societal marketing concept takes care that the society does not have to pay costs for the benefits of the individual consumers. Organizations have to strike a balance between the customers' desires and society's welfare. Whereas the marketing concept is a self-absorbed approach, the societal marketing concept represents a holistic approach towards the way of doing business.

The changing business landscape and the dynamic environmental forces have urged organizations of all types to imbibe marketing in their objectives and policies. The philosophy of marketing embraces not only organizations but also people, ideas, events, places, social causes and so on. In the era of changing and challenging times, organizations have experienced that they cannot sustain with the earlier approaches to marketplace namely production, product or selling orientation. The competent concept of marketing has been extended as the societal marketing concept which integrates organizational and social goals in order to achieve customer happiness and societal wellbeing simultaneously.

Marketing Research

Marketing Research is the systematic gathering, recording and analyzing of data about problems connected with the market place, i.e., problems relating to products, price, promotion and distribution of the 4 Ps of the marketing mix. Marketing Research is said to be "moving away from simple surveys to action-oriented, decision oriented, and problem-solving research".

Marketing Research is defined as the scientific and controlled process of gathering of non-routine marketing information helping management to solve marketing problems. Marketing Research is concerned with all those factors which have a direct impact upon the marketing of products and services.

It concentrates on the study of product planning and development, pricing policies, effectiveness of personal selling, advertisement and sales promotion (three wings of marketing communication), distribution structure, marketing strategies, market competition and the entire area of buyer behaviour and attitude in the market place.

Marketing Research is directly interested in offering sound alternative solutions to all marketing problems relating to exchange of goods and services from product to consumer. Beginning and end of marketing management is marketing research. Marketing Research covers the following:

- Market research,
- Sales research,
- Product research,
- Advertising and promotion research,

- Research on sales methods and policies,

- Distribution research including dealers research.

Market Research

Market Research is only one branch of marketing information system. Market Research is the systematic and intelligent investigation or study of the "who, what, where, when, why and How of actual and potential buyers". Market Research deals with customer demand i.e., behaviour and attitudes of consumers. Market Research is primarily concerned with investigation, analysis and measurement of market demand. Market Research covers the following items of study:

- Size of market,

- Geographic location of customers,

- Demographic description of customers,

- Market Segmentation on the basis of age, sex, income, education, standard or living etc.,

- Analysis of market demand,

- Sales analysis by customers,

- Consumer needs, wants, habits and behavior,

- Dealer wants and preferences,

- Degree of competition and the market end.

Elements of Marketing Research

There are three elements of marketing research:

- Intensive Study: Systematic and intensive study of a marketing problem.

- Scientific Approach: Scientific method and objectivity in the solution of a marketing problem.

- Decision Tool: Marketing Research is a tool for decision-making and control in the marketing of goods.

Importance of Marketing Research

- The wide communication gap between the marketer (producer) and consumer due to existence of numerous middlemen creates single large importance of marketing research to fill up this gap.

- Emergence of buyer's market and increasing competition demanded continuous need of marketing research to ensure maximum consumer satisfaction and repeat purchases and to lay down appropriate marketing strategies to meet competition.

- Marketing research assumes unique importance when the customer becomes the center of the marketing universe. Realistic information of consumer demand—tastes, preferences, fashions etc. can ensure quick way to profit making.

- Marketing information and research helps a marketer to manage efficiently all challenges and problems created by environmental changes because only change is permanent and change means progress.

- Marketing research helps management to bring about prompt adjustments and innovations in product in the event of technology advancement.

Types of Marketing Research

Types of marketing research are the four strategic areas of marketing mix:

- Product,
- Price,
- Promotion,
  - Personal Selling,
  - Advertising,
  - Publicity,
  - Sales promotion,
  - Public relations.
- Distribution.

Objectives of Marketing Research

- Marketing research is used in the formulation of all marketing plans, policies, programmes and procedures.

- It is employed for control and evaluation of these plans, policies etc., when they are brought into practice.

- It is used in reducing and minimizing all marketing costs, particularly, selling, advertising, promotion and distribution costs.

Problems Formulation

Marketing problems demanding best solution through marketing research can be classified under three major heads:

- Problems relating to the product itself—Product includes branding, packaging and labeling and services.

- Problems relating to consumer markets.

- Problems relating to each phase of the entire marketing process.

Problems Formulation/Conflicts Resolution

A marketing manager through marketing research can bring about the sale of right product (brand and package) through right channels to right customers at right places and at right prices by evolving right plans, policies and programmers with the help of right personnel.

The main objective of marketing research is to enable manufacturers to make good acceptable and saleable and to see that they reach the market more easily, quickly, cheaply and profitably without sacrificing consumer interest.

Utility of Marketing Research for Business

There are six faithful service: Men at the disposal of market researchers.

1.	What?	What is our Product?	Product Research.
2.	Who?	Who are the buyers?	Consumer Research.
3.	Why?	Why do they buy?	Motivation Research.
4.	How?	How do they buy?	Research in buying habits.
5.	When?	When do they buy?	Channels of.
6.	Where?	Where do they buy?	Distribution.

Planning the Research Project

Techniques of Organizing Marketing Research

Marketing Research requires the application of the systems approach to the task of collecting, organizing, analyzing and interpreting desired marketing information. This means that each step in the research process must be carefully planned, effectively co-ordinated with all other related steps so that all the steps are properly integrated and executed as specified at the proper time and in the desired sequence. Basic characteristics of the marketing research process are given below:

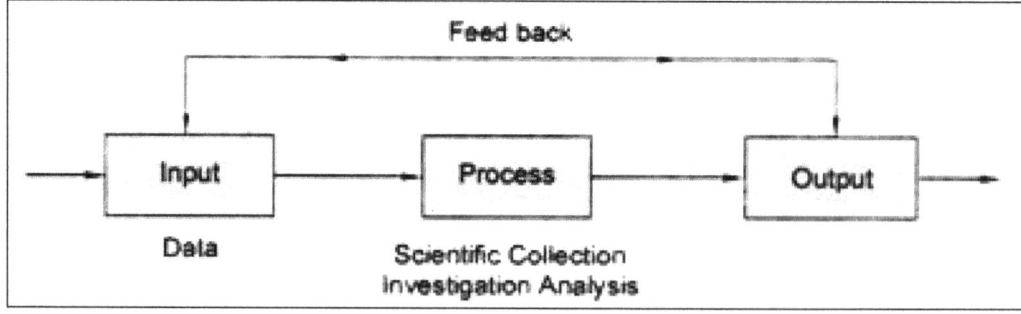

Marketing Research is directly concerned with all three operations, input, process and output. Input is usually data, i.e., facts and figures and values, often quantified. The collected data is processed by researchers. In data processing, we have the operations of editing, classification and analysis, and output is the result of processing. It is in the forms of information. Information is critical to successful marketing operations as intelligence is to warfare. Information must be timely, up-to-date, accurate, relevant, reliable, sufficient and economical for use in the marketing research.

Steps and Methodology in Marketing Research

A distinction is drawn between Market Research, and Marketing Research. Market Research relates to the market profile, market conditions, demand gap-present and projected (for new projects) and all that. Marketing Research relates to the specific aspects of the Marketing-Mix management of a particular marketing organization. However, for the purpose of discussions, we may treat Market Research and Marketing Research as synonymous. Professional market researchers usually adopt the following sequential steps for Marketing Research:

- Setting the purpose or objective of the proposal Marketing Research.

- Determining the information needed and the source from which it could be collected, i.e., Data Collection—data may be classified into primary and secondary data.

- Obtaining the relevant facts—for this several methods such as observation, experiments and survey methods may be used.

- Analysis and interpreting the facts with reference to the problem.

- Preparing the reports incorporating the findings and presenting the inferences or recommendations. Limitations of Marketing Research.

Marketing Research, however efficiently carried out, can seldom provide answers to all marketing problems and can be no substitute to executive judgment in the decision making process. Marketing Research findings may suffer from limitations mainly due to following three factors:

- Market: Market sometimes being in a state of flux, market size growing or contracting at a very high rate.

- Technique: Selection of sample, quality of questionnaires, choice of techniques, quality of interviewing, statistical errors in analysis of data etc.

- Decision Making: Decision based on erroneous interpretation of marketing research data.

An effective marketing research team should consist of both management graduates and sales personnel who have firsthand information about the market. This team should not only interact regularly with the sales force of the company but should pay frequent field visits in order to obtain a better feel of the market. For an entirely new project, this team should include some external marketing consultants.

Marketing Research is Essentially a Staff Function

Consequently, it is very difficult to establish accountability, in this area and provide a basis for strict financial evaluation of results vis-a-vis costs. The problem is further aggravated by the fact that substantial part of expenses are "spending on future" or investments.

Why is Market Research so Valuable?

Without research, it's impossible to understand your users. Sure, you might have a general idea of who they are and what they need, but you have to dig deep if you want to win their loyalty. Here's why research matters:

- Obsessing over your users is the only way to win: If you don't care deeply about improving user experience, you'll lose potential customers to someone who does.

- Analytics give you the 'what,' but research gives the 'why.': Big data, user analytics, and dashboards can tell you what people do at scale, but only research can tell you what they're thinking and why they do what they do. For example, analytics can tell you that customers leave when they reach your pricing page, but only research can explain why.

- Research beats assumptions, trends, and so-called best practices: Have you ever watched your colleagues rally behind a terrible decision? Bad ideas are often the result of guesswork, emotional reasoning, death by best practices, and defaulting to the Highest Paid Person's Opinion (HiPPO). By listening to your users and focusing on their customer experience, you're less likely to get pulled in the wrong direction.

- Research keeps you from planning in a vacuum: Your team might be amazing, but you and your colleagues simply can't experience your product the way your customers do. Customers might use your product in a way that surprises you, and features that seem obvious to you might confuse them. Over planning and refusing to test your assumptions is a waste of time, money, and effort because you will likely need to make changes once your untested plan gets put into practice.

Marketing Control

Marketing control is a crucial part of the marketing job. It is the tool for ensuring that the marketing programmes and activities of the firm always get directed towards the marketing objectives of the firm. Marketing control provides the means of testing whether the desired goals and results are actually being achieved or not. It is an ongoing monitoring of the marketing activity in all its aspects.

Inherent in the process is the assumption that the desired results are known beforehand. And knowledge of the desired results will advance, involves planning. In this sense, planning and control are closely interrelated. In fact, "Planning -Happening -Evaluating – Controlling" are the four interrelated phases of the marketing job.

Whenever we want to do anything, we have certain objectives before us and we plan our efforts beforehand to achieve those objectives. Throughout the causes of activity, we observe the progress of work to compare the actual results or standards. If the difference between the actual result and the desired result is too much, then certain steps are to be taken to lesson this difference.

All measures by which an effort is made to bring the actual result and the desired results together are known as control. Thus, the main aim of control is to see that actual results are as close to the desired standards as possible. In management, the term control has been defined by different authors in different ways.

According to Koontz and O'Donnell it is "the measurement and correction of the performance of subordinates". Phelps and Westing define control as an "exercise, directing, guiding or restraining power over people or other events." Philip Kotler defines control as "the process of taking steps to bring actual results and desire results closer together."

In simple words, control of marketing operations may be defined as the managerial function of monitoring and feedback of actual marketing performance and its measurement and solution against the preplanned performance standards with a view to identify deviations, correct the deviations and provide inputs for plan reformulation. Control involves the following:

- Observation of activity by the management actual results.

- Some of the actual results which are not according to the desired standards are not acceptable to the management.

- The management has certain devices by which the difference between die actual results and the standards desired can be controlled.

Scope of Marketing Control

Marketing control involves gathering information on marketing performance and comparing the achieved performance against planned or budgeted performance, using predetermined standards and yardsticks. It provides feedback; it regulates; and it exercises a restraining influence or a redirecting influence.

It ensures that the marketing activity does not derail or go off the track; it acts as a radar system for marketing, recording and signaling the ups and downs and deviations in the marketing performance; it also provides the required clues for the timely correction of deviations. In a dynamic environment, marketing programmes cannot be implemented effectively without continuous controlling and corrective adjustments. Marketing control takes care of this requirement. It paves the way for the maximization of profitability and the maximization of productivity of all the marketing activities.

Annual Plan Control

It refers to the steps taken during the year to check on going performance against marketing plan and to apply corrective measures when necessary. The heart of annual plan control is the establishment of a system of management by objectives, which consists of four elements. First, the annual plan must establish a clear set of marketing goods for each responsibility center in the firm.

Second, provision must be made for periodic performance measurement against the goals to spot any serious performance gap. Third, performance gap should be subjects to casual analysis to determine when they have accused i.e., whether the environment has changed the goals were set to high, or the implement of the plan are not doing this job. Fourth, management must take corrective measures to close the gap between goods and performance.

The model of control is applied to every level of the organization. Managers use five performance tools to check the progress in reaching the goals in the annual plan, viz., sales analysis, market share analysis, marketing expenses to sale ratio's, financial analysis and corrective measures.

Profitability Control

Besides annual plan control companies carry a periodic research to determine to actual profitability of their different products, territories, customer groups, trade channels and other marketing variables. This task requires an ability to assign marketing and other costs to specific marketing entities and activities.

Marketing profitability analysis is a tool for helping the marketing executives to determining whether any current marketing activities should be eliminated, added or altered in scale. The starting point for marketing profitability analysis is the company's profit and loss statement.

The marketing executive's interest would be developing analogous profit statements by functional marketing break-downs such as products, customers or territories. To do this the natural 'expense' decisions such as salaries, rent, supplies would have to be reclassified into 'functional' expense designation.

Efficiency Control

Efficiency control is the task of increasing the efficiency such marketing activities as personal selling, advertising, sales promotion and distribution. Marketing managers regularly watch certain key ratios that indicate how efficiently these functions are being performed and they also implement studies to find ways to improve performance.

Strategic Control

Strategic control is the task of marketing to ensure that the company's marketing objectives, strategies and systems are optimally adapted to the current and forecasted marketing environment. In this connection the use of two tools is worth mentioning i.e., marketing effectiveness rating review and marketing audit.

Importance of Marketing Control

- Matching of Marketing Efforts with Environmental Changes: Regular monitoring of performance and other environmental changes helps the company in updating its marketing effort in time with environmental changes. It becomes all the more important in the context of rapid changes in technological, social and political fields and in consumer's preferences and public policy postures.

- Deletion of Deviation in Performance: A marketing control system helps the management in identifying deviations from the planned programme. It finds out the fault and lacuna in performance and takes corrective action at the proper time.

- Identifying Responsibility for Failure: An appraisal of performance helps the management in identifying the responsibility for weak performances. The person responsible for performance below specific standards gets an opportunity for self-assessment and others are relieved of an inefficiency and ineffectiveness.

- Organizational Complexity: The vertical marketing system has more or less come to stay as a phenomenon of modern marketing. The size of the organization and its growth makes control more complex and yet essential. The span of control enlarges with the size of the enterprises and creates of problem of control. Therefore, a realistic, effective and yet simple marketing control system as a prerequisite of effective marketing management.

- Assisting Plan Reformation: The feedback provided by the marketing control system helps in reappraising performance standards, marketing policies and programmes. Such reappraisal helps in the realistic reformulation of the marketing plan.

Main Characteristics of an Effective Control System

- Control should be Objective: Appraisal of the performance of a subordinate should not be a matter of subjective determination. In other words, controls should be definite and objective. Employees will respond favorably to objective standards and impartial appraisal of their work performance.

- Control System should give Immediate Feed Back: Feedback is the process of adjusting future actions based upon information about past information. An essential requirement of an ideal control system is immediate feedback of information about deviations in performance.

- It should be Flexible: The control mechanism should be flexible in the sense that it should respond favorably to the conditions. In consequence of unforeseen circumstances, when plans are changed, control should reflect corresponding changes to remain operative under the new conditions. The basic idea is that control should remain workable under dynamic business conditions including the failure of the control system itself.

- Organizational Suitability: Control is exercised through managerial positions, and as such it should be according to the organizational structure. Each managerial position should be provided with adequate authority to exercise self-control and take corrective action.

- Control should be Economical: A control system should be economical in the sense that the cost of its installation and maintenance should be justified by its benefits; simply stated control must be with in its cost. Thus, a small company can hardly afford the extensive system of control practiced by large companies.

- It should be Simple to Understand: It is essential that those who administer the control should understand it. Control specialists very often recommended sophisticated and advanced techniques of control on the pretext of providing their expertise, and tend to overlook the question of there being understood by the marketing executives of the company.

- Control System should Suggest Corrective Action: An important characteristic of the effective control system is that it should indicate deviations and suggest corrective actions promptly and in time. Merely recording of deviations and errors and fixing responsibility for their occurrence is not sufficient, if it is not followed by suitable actions to prevent recurrence.

Process for Designing a Control System

Marketing control provides the means of testing whether the desired goals and results are actually being achieved or not. It is an ongoing monitoring of the marketing activity in all aspects. Marketing control involves gathering information on marketing performance and comparing the achieved performance against the planned or budgeted performance using predetermined standards and yardsticks.

In a dynamic environment, the marketing programs cannot be implemented effectively without continuous monitoring, controlling and corrective adjustments. Marketing control is an integral part of management control.

Marketing Control System

In designing a control system, the following steps are involved:

- Starting with the predetermined objectives.

- Setting clear measures of performance.

- Defining the levels at which different controls are to be active.

- Developing an effective monitoring system to provide the feedback to the different levels.

- Choosing the tools and techniques of control.

- Observing, analysing, interpreting and evaluating the variance.

- Developing a mechanism that can correct existing activity so as to achieve the predetermined norm / objective.

The control system design must ensure that major variance are automatically distinguished and highlighted. It must also be capable of correctly interpreting the variance; the true meaning of the variance should be brought out by the control process. Further, the control process should facilitate the focusing of attention on exceptions.

While using marketing information for marketing control, it is however essential that control data, planning data and general purpose statistics are properly distinguished from one another out of the various marketing information outputs. Only then marketing information can be used as an effective control tool.

Top Six Techniques of Marketing Control

There are several tools and techniques with which marketing control is exercised by a business firm. The important ones among them are briefly discussed:

Marketing Audit

Marketing audit is a continuous, systematic and objective study of the total marketing efficiency of the firm. Marketing audit is concerned with the long-term business interests and challenges of the firm rather than the short-term achievements. Marketing audit seeks to review even basic assumptions of strategy. For the major part, marketing audit is qualitative and strategic.

Marketing Cost Analysis

Marketing cost analysis helps in reducing the marketing costs; identify costs of performing specific marketing functions/activities, throws up alternative ways of performing these functions/activities and provides an evaluation of relative cost benefits of various alternatives to improve the market.

It helps drop unprofitable customers, products, channels and markets and enables the firm to identify and concentrate on relatively high profitable customer's product and markets; appraise the true cost and true value of each marketing service provided by the firm, such as delivery, pre-sale service, credit facilities, etc.

Credit Control

Business firms are often forced to extend credit to increase sales. As a part of credit control, it must be ensured that customers and the channel do not exploit the credit policy of the firm. Credit has two dimensions – (i) the interest on the money involved in credit transaction and (ii) the risk of bad debts. Bad debts must be seen and understood as an important part of the cost of credit. Credit rating ensures that the creditworthiness of the client or dealer, as the case may be, is assessed objectively before the firm proceeds with the risk of extending credit facility to a buyer.

Market Share Analysis

Market share analysis can be utilized for evaluating the market / business performance of a firm; for setting targets for the firm and for developing long term sales forecasts for the firm. Market share has to be measured on rational grounds. Comparisons may be made with the most efficient firms in the industry, or the industry leader, or a group of growing firms. Comparisons can also be made against industry average performance. The general economic conditions which have a bearing on the industry's performance have to be given due weightage.

Budgetary Control

Budgetary control essentially involves preparation of control statements at specified intervals of time, showing the budgeted figures, the achieved figures and the variance. Review and remedial action is the other part of a budgetary control. In marketing, sales volume, sales expenses and profits are the main aspects to be controlled through the budgetary control device.

Ratio Analysis

As far as marketing is concerned, ratio analysis seeks to measure the effectiveness and profitability of the various marketing functions and activities by the use of certain ratios. Ratio analysis focuses attention on relative figures. Return on Investment (ROI), Return on the Net Worth (RONW), Inventory to Turnover Ratio is examples. Proper integration of marketing and financial control tools is essential for meaningful and effective marketing control.

Annual Plan Control: Tools to Monitor Plan Performance

The aim of this control is to ensure that the organization achieves its targeted sales, profits and other goals for the said annual period. The basis of annual-plan control is managerial objectives – that is to say, specific goals, such as – sales and profitability that are established on a monthly or quarterly basis. Organizations use five tools to monitor plan performance. These are:

- Sales analysis.
- Market share analysis.

- Marketing expense to sales analysis.

- Financial analysis.

- Market based scorecard analysis.

Sales Analysis

This involves measuring the actual sales in comparison to the set targets or goals. The Two specific tools used in the sales analysis are:

- Sales variance analysis.

- Micro sales analysis.

Sales Variance Analysis

Sales variance analysis measures the relative contribution of different factors to a gap in sales performance.

Micro Sales Analysis

The sales of specific products, territories, sales persons etc., who have failed to perform up to the expected set target level.

Market Share Analysis

Organizations need to know how they are performing in relation to their competitors. This can be done in three ways:

- Overall Market Share: It is the organization's sales expressed as a percentage of the total market sales.

- Served Market Share: It is the organization's sales expressed as a percentage of the total sales to its served market. The server market comprises of all buyers who are willing and able to buy its products. The server market share is always larger than the overall market share.

- Relative Market Share: It can be expressed as a market share in relation to the biggest competitor. If the relative market share is over 100%, it means that the organization is a market leader.

Another useful way to analyze the market share, is in terms of four components,

Overall Market Share = Customer Penetration × Customer Loyalty × Customer Selectivity
× Price Selectivity

Customer penetration is the percentage of all customers who buy from the organization. Customer Loyalty is the purchases from the organization by its customers, expressed as a percentage of their total purchases from other suppliers of the same products. Customer Selectivity is the size of the average customer purchase from the organization, expressed as the size of the average customer purchase from an average organization.

Price Selectivity is the average price charged by the organization, expressed as a percentage of the average price charged by all the organizations. A reduction in the overall market share means that the organization is not performing well on any of the above four parameters.

Market-Expense-to-Sales Ratio

It is necessary to monitor that an organization is not overspending to achieve its sales targets. For this the marketing expense to sales ratio must be monitored. There are several components of this ratio like expense-to-sales ratio, sales force-to-sales ratio, and advertising-to- sales ratio, sales administration-to-sales ratio and marketing research-to-sales ratio.

Financial Analysis

The expense-to-sales ratio should be analyzed in the overall financial framework to determine how and where the organization is making its money; which simply means, look into the areas which are profitable. Financial analysis can be used by the Management to identify those factors that affect the organization's rate of return on its net worth. The main factors that affect the organization's rate of return on the net worth and their calculations are as follows:

- Profit Margin = Net Profits/Net Sales.

- Asset Turnover = Net Sales/ Total Assets.

- Return on Assets = Net Profit/Total Assets.

- Financial Leverage = Total Assets/ Net Worth.

- Rate of return on net worth = Net Profits/ Net Worth.

Basically the rate of return on the net worth is a product of the organization's return on its assets and the financial leverage. To increase the rate of return on the net worth, the organization must increase either of these two factors:

- Return on assets.

- The financial leverage.

For this the organization will be required to analyses the composition of its assets and see if the asset management can be improved. Return on assets can be improved by improving the profit margin. For improving the profit margin, the organization must increase profits by increasing the sales or by cutting the costs in some way.

Similarly return on assets can also be improved by improving the asset turnover ratio. This can be done by increasing the sales or reducing the assets (e.g., inventory, receivables etc.) that are held at a given level of sales.

Market Based Score Card Analysis

The measures that we have studied so far are mostly financial in nature. However, financial factors are not the only indicators of the Organization's health. The organization can also look at other different measures like the Market based Score Card. The Market Based Score Card is made up of two kinds of scorecards:

- Customer performance score card.

- Stakeholder performance Score card.

The Customer Performance Score Card will look at various measures such as:

- New customers.

- Dissatisfied customers.

- Lost customers.

- Target market awareness.

- Relative product quality.

- Relative service quality.

- Target market preference.

The Organization should set a benchmark or target figures, for each of these parameters, and monitor them, to ensure that they are as desired. The stakeholder score card will look at monitoring the stakeholders of the organization like:

- Employees,

- Suppliers,

- Banks,

- Distributors,

- Retailers,

- Stockholders,

- Shareholders.

Their opinion should be monitored from time to time and dissatisfaction should be registered and taken care of.

Five Essential Determinants

Marketing is an integrated effort of various attributes linked with the corporate objective of the organization. The environment which encompasses the marketing activity is volatile and keeps changing in reference to the business policy of the competing firms, fashion, legal interventions and innovations.

Thus, in the modern era, most of the companies put growing efforts on organizing their marketing avenues in response to significant changes in the market. In this process, it is essential to know the consumer orientation at the very beginning. The research and development wing of the company need to attend on the new ideas and engineer them to manufacture the products desired by the consumers. Some of the essential determinants in the process are:

- Consumer feedback.

- Product improvement.

- Distribution and purchase.

- Marketing set-up.

- Zero defects.

In a marketing organization, there should be a continuous flow of information from the consumers which encourages the learning process for the manufacture to improve the product. The ideas generated through the feedback of consumers need to be evaluated in order to accelerate the product improvement process. However, the company should develop a proper match with the supply and distribution system to ensure the availability of the products to the consumers.

Two Important Activities Marketing Control

> "Marketing is a learning game. You make a decision. You watch the results. You learn from the results. Then you make better decisions". "Those who learned from their mistakes are the best marketers".

Lots of things can go wrong in a Marketing Plan. Segmenting may be wrong, targeting could be unclear, differentiation may be insignificant, positioning may not be specific and marketing mix aspects may need change, therefore to ensure that these elements are on the correct track sound marketing evaluation and control systems are necessary. To achieve them are two important controlling activities:

Evaluate and Interpret Current Results

In a tremendously competitive environment a company needs to monitor, evaluate and interpret its performance over a shortest the possible period of time and to that end it's best to do so on a monthly basis. Monthly accounts are a virtual standard everywhere in this information age. Three different sets of information that can be produced are:

The Financial Scorecard

A company's financial statements are the best documents to develop a financial scorecard. Budgets can be compared with actual achievements on a monthly basis with current month, previous month and month of the previous year. It will also show variances in elements of the cost of sales and overheads as well as return on sales.

Budgeted gross profits may not be achieved and the reason found would be an increase in cost of fuel against budget. This when observed through the financial scorecard can be corrected or reduced by either cutting down on usage, shifting to alternative fuel or other suitable means. Alternatively if packing material cost has gone up it may be mundane to find alternative suppliers or enter into long-term contracts. The actions that can be taken are limitless but it is possible to do so only if the information is available to evaluate and interpret an organization's performance.

The Marketing Scorecard

The marketing scorecard is based on market related performance and can be done quarterly and annually. Most of this information is available inside the company. Total market growth for a particular category will indicate whether the market for the category is growing. This will help in evaluating strategic choice and deciding on marketing strategy. Some may not want to continue to serve shrinking markets and may wish to diversify or sell it to a competitor.

Accurate information of whether there is growth in a brand within the total market can be ascertained. Many successful brands may record a higher growth surpassing even the market growth and its competition, which would mean that it is not only keeping abreast with the overall market growth but also gaining shares from competition.

Brand market share is an indication of the success of the brand. One business may be content with a small share of a large market whilst another would be pursuing a large share of a small market. All this depends on the individual marketing objective and corporate strategy. For example, the corporate strategy of a SBU will be to get 30% market share for a specific brand, this will be a marketing objective for the marketing planner who will initiate their own marketing strategy and tactics towards achieving that objective.

Customer retention is an important aspect today. The world is focused on retaining existing customers rather than gaining new customers, purely due to -the cost of acquiring new customers. The marketing scorecard will give this information as a percentage of the customers retained during the month, quarter or year. This will help the business to take corrective action in keeping with its objectives.

New customers in the case of FMCG are a little difficult to ascertain but it's easier in the case of non-FMCG and the service industry. Ultimately the effort will be to provide superior value to customers and delight them.

Dissatisfied customers can be obtained through customer complaints, but the danger lies in cases where customers who would not want to complain but resort to the most detrimental action to the business, migrate to competition.

Relative product quality cannot be obtained through the internal information process. A qualitative research has to be carried out to ascertain this. A consumer panel is the most suitable method where a comparative study of the product's quality can be carried out amongst them and rated accordingly. Depending on this the business can make adjustments to provide desirable optimum quality.

Relative service quality to trade can be ascertained in the case of FMCG in comparison with competition on aspects such as deliveries, sales visits, logistics, and payment and credit facilities. In the case of the service industry as there is direct access to the final customer whilst delivering the service it is possible to ascertain relative service quality in comparison to the competition.

A relative new product sale in the case where a new product is launched or even an improved product is re-launched is vital and available in relation to competitive products. This can be conducted through marketing research and audit programmes. Separate marketing researchers may not be necessary as the company's sales personnel can obtain this information. Usually, a launch or a re-launch is supported by a promotional plan, and a big bang to create awareness and trial. At this stage the competitors are very likely to react.

The Stakeholder Scorecard

Purpose of a business is to create profitable customers. The destiny of a business is to deliver a reasonable profit to its shareholders. To do this the business has around it strategic partners who are stakeholders. They are:

- Employees – Internal stakeholders.

- Suppliers – Connected stakeholders.

- Marketing Intermediaries – Connected stakeholders.

- Community – External stakeholders.

They are the four pillars of the business, which is owned by shareholders. These stakeholders help create value and it is they who deliver value not only to the customer but to the shareholder too. They are a vital part of the business and their participation and commitment is indispensable. Hence, they have to be delighted as much as the customers outside. Recognizing their importance, Professor Robert Kaplan of the Harvard University called it the balanced scorecard.

The balanced scorecard tracks the level of satisfaction so that in the event there is any unpleasantness the management must initiate action to overcome them. The purpose of the stakeholder scorecard or balanced scorecard is to ascertain, initiate, create and implement a win-win situation in the relations and contentment of the internal partners and those external to it.

Marketing Audit

The dictionary meaning of Audit is a formal examination or settlement of accounts. This itself connotes that audit is one that is carried out after an event, could be soon after or much later. The financial accounts of a company are audited at the end of a financial year. Marketing audit is similar and is carried out after the launch of a marketing programme. A marketing audit concerns marketing activity and focuses on marketing issues. Professor Philip Kotler defines a marketing audit as follows:

> "A marketing audit is a comprehensive, systematic, independent and periodic examination of a company's or business unit's marketing environment, objectives, strategies and activities with a view to determining problem areas and opportunities and recommending a plan of action to improve the company's marketing performance".

He also developed a marketing audit instrument, which examined seven marketing components:

- Macro environment,

- Task environment,

- Marketing strategy,

- Marketing organization,

- Marketing systems,

- Marketing productivity,

- Marketing functions.

A marketing audit of the above components will ensure proper control in the implementation of the Marketing Plan.

Macro-Environment

The Macro-environment is an external force that can bring about several changes to a business; these changes may provide opportunities or threats.

- Demographic: A set of influences that has a significant impact on the Marketing Plan. A business that targeted the middle and low income families which included adults, children, sports persons, pregnant and lactating mothers for a nutrition supplement changed strategy and focused on children when they found in their marketing audit that the core consumers were school going and smaller children.

- Economic: Inflationary conditions may bring about requests for credit and delayed payments by the trade. Consequently they can affect the cash flow of a business and create other financial implications. Business has to change direction to meet this crisis. Perhaps giving upfront discounts for cash sales may be an idea or better still a free issue of product. A free issue is given at cost but valued at the price to trade.

- Natural Environment: From time to time the laws about the natural environment and pollution keep changing as needed by the society. A business with social responsibility must comply and respond to such demands and thus internal changes may be necessary to meet them.

- Technological: Production process has undergone several changes; the typewriter is almost a thing of the past. The telex is almost forgotten. Packaging has gone through drastic change pursuing better and cost effective solutions.

- Political and Legal: Changes in law and regulation can result in opportunities or disaster. Lower excise duty of Beer would result in price cuts and promote consumption.

- Social and Cultural: Lifestyles and current trends influence people. In some countries people do not cook in their homes and eat out. This is an opportunity to the restaurant industry and fast food.

All the elements above are external and not controllable by the company. The need to identify them and interpret them correctly is important.

Operational Environment

The task environment is also external to the business but it is an environment with which the business works.

- Markets: There may be changes in the market place such as the markets the business plans to serve; market segments that have been identified may confront change. A marketing audit will enlighten the business on the real ground conditions so that where necessary corrective action can be taken. Customer profile and buying behaviour, their attitudes to the business and its product portfolio, company's pricing strategy and distribution are important to analyse to ensure the plan is in the right direction and are delighting customers.

- Competitors: They can change their strategies that may affect the consumer off take or slow down distribution of the products. They may invest more on promotional activities and threaten the progress of the previously planned marketing programme. Marketing audit will provide all the necessary information about competitors' actions and strategies.

- Collaborators: Ascertain how distributors and dealers respond to 'push' tactics of a business, margins and merchandising. Stocking patterns of one's own as well as competitive products, frequency of visits required, and average stock holding are important information that can be achieved through a marketing audit.

Suppliers help keep a continuous supply to ensure uninterrupted production. Hence it is necessary to see whether the right supply chain is in place. If this isn't the Strategic Marketing Plan will fail.

Facilitators such as – logistics providers, marketing research and marketing communications agencies are very important stakeholders of the company.

General public — is there a public relations plan of the business, is it necessary? If so, which groups should be influenced to gain support for the business?

Marketing Process

The business should find out whether the marketing process, which it planned, is correct and whether it is bringing results or does it need adjustment. The following key areas need to be considered:

- Business Mission: The clarity and comprehension of the business mission is important to both internal people and those outside. Is the mission market driven and aimed to serve markets or erroneously product oriented without any focus on the markets it plans to serve? The audit must address this.

- Goals and Objectives: They must be clearly stated, must be SMART and appropriate and be achievable.

- Strategy and Tactics: The Business Must Evaluate STDP – segmenting, targeting, differentiating and positioning, as they have to be done correctly. The elements of the marketing mix must be planned appropriately and be effective. The resource allocations need to be looked at to ensure it is adequate to accomplish the marketing objectives and strategies.

Once the marketing process audit is carried out the business is in a position if found necessary to make changes or modifications. This too can be undertaken on a quarterly basis or short term to ensure it is reaching its destiny.

Marketing Organization

To implement and control the marketing plan the right marketing organization is necessary. The following aspects need to be audited to ensure that the right organization in place:

The Organization Structure

Marketing is a team game, which involves several key players and their support staff. An experienced leader, empowered to make decisions and lead his or her team to victory, must head the team. Often it would be Director Marketing or General Manager Marketing reporting to the Managing Director or CEO.

Some companies may outsource Marketing Research; they will have Category Managers or Brand Managers to take care of product categories or brands respectively. Sales and Distribution Director or General Manager Sales will head the sales and distribution division reporting to the Managing Director or CEO. The National Sales Manager, Provincial Sales Mangers and District Sales Managers will lead the Sales Force made up of Sales Representatives and other sales personnel. The structure of the marketing organization should be established according to the needs of the organization and not as an emulation of another or competitive organization.

Today, some companies are outsourcing Brand Management whilst some of the smaller ones hand over the entire distribution to external distribution companies. There is no scientific formula for setting up an organization structure but it must be one that will be market driven responding to market needs and wants and also result oriented. Marketing audit must ascertain this important aspect as to whether the marketing organization is properly structured.

Functional Efficiency

How does the Marketing Department perform is the next area of concern. The inter-relations of the Brand Managers, Field Sales Management and Sales Administration are vital and must be of the highest professional levels.

Interface Efficiency

Often marketing people have problems with finance, production and the logistics divisions purely due to lack of proper direction. Delayed reimbursements of expenses by the finance people, rejection of market returns and damages by the production people, short deliveries and stock outs by the logisticians are the main causes for disharmony. These aspects must be subject to audit and systems put in place to avoid recurrence. Inter-departmental harmony is an essential prerequisite to a good marketing organization. A marketing audit on the organization is the starting point to build up a strong well-knit organization internally and it is only then they can as a team face the challenges of the external environment.

Marketing Systems

This audit concerns systems, information, planning, control and new product development or product improvement.

Marketing Information System

The importance of information has been observed in the 12 'P' MODEL where the planning process commenced with the first P – Marketing Probe that is geared to provide vital information. Therefore, the purpose of the audit is to ascertain whether the information system is appropriate, and substantial to determine key issues make the right assumptions. If the marketing information isn't right all decisions can be wrong. Information provides knowledge and knowledge helps to evaluate a situation and take suitable action to make things work.

Marketing Planning System

A business may have all the right information, the statistics, interpretation and so forth, but the light at the end of the tunnel is in the right planning system which will enable to create the right plan. The right plan is invaluable to any business. No business must venture without a proper plan. Instead of having several plans a business can have a single Marketing Plan to cover a period of 3 years updated annually or when the necessity arises, and it should incorporate both the strategic and tactical elements instead of doing a separate Strategic Plan and an Annual Plan.

Marketing Control System

There are two elements to the marketing system, the planning aspect and the implementation aspect, if neither has the right controls it can be in jeopardy. This is why there is an important control systems evaluation and audit to ensure that progress will be in the correct direction.

NPD and Product Improvement System

A true innovation would be one that would proclaim to the world "take a pill a day and you don't have to eat" or "this drink can make you 15 years younger". Innovation in this sense is not very easy. Naturally, a business would rather be concerned about a brand or value proposition's improvement rather than innovation.

Perhaps creating a sub-category and becoming the first in it may be a prudent option. The Japanese theory of Kaizen which is about continuous improvement must be the goal of any marketing professional. Certainly not tinkering or doing unnecessary changes which would neither benefit the market nor organization.

In essence, improvements must be to provide superior value to present and potential markets. A filling station introduced this concept where all cars that lined up for fuel got a free windscreen wash at no cost. The marketing audit must be directed to identify what more the company or the product can provide to customers, to delight them — the benchmark of any business. A marketing system audit provides a business an opportunity to identify how best and what more can be offered to delight present and potential markets.

Marketing Productivity

Marketing is about producing results, generating revenue, making profits and a marketing productivity audit is focused in that direction.

- Profitability Analysis: The ultimate goal in marketing is profitable sales volume, not just sales turnover, or the large numbers the businesses sold and even the satisfied customers by doing so. All this is in vain if they weren't profitable. Hence, constant appraisal should be made to see whether the business is getting there, profitably. A sale is about turnover and volume focus whilst marketing is profit driven.

- Cost Effectiveness: To achieve the former all other inputs must be cost effective. But it does not mean that one must cut the promotional budget as many do to be cost effective. The marketing productivity audit must be carried out to ascertain where costs can be trimmed. A company in FMCG even after getting a substantial market share kept sampling the same customers over and over again, the purpose of sampling is to induce trial not to encourage repeat purchase, and marketing communications does that. Profitability and cost effectiveness are two key features in a marketing productivity audit. One cannot achieve profitability without being cost effective.

Marketing Functions

The marketing audit should be concerned with the elements of the marketing mix. The vehicle that delivers superior value to win and sustain customers is the marketing mix. The business must ascertain whether it is correct, the functions audit does that.

- Product: Whether it is a bank account or a cake of soap they are both value propositions that customers want. Marketing aids in creating form utility or producing goods and services. R&D unit can create them but it is marketing that adds the finesse by telling them what markets would want. Marketing must communicate as to what type, size, color and design they should be produced.

- Price: Unless goods and services are at the right price one will not buy them. If BMW cuts its price by 50% the BMW customers will never buy them again. If coke increased its price by the same margin their customers might consider shifting to Pepsi. Goods and services have a price tag with which they are associated. Price must be right, not cheap; cheap is not the only criterion for purchase, its value. Hence price must be evaluated within those parameters, above all VALUE, which is the measure of worth of a value proposition.

- Distribution: Often referred to as PLACE in the 4/7 P theories, is an important element in the marketing mix. Its fundamental purpose is to bring the customer and the offering together and facilitate an exchange. Width and depth of distribution are other considerations or is about reaching all outlets where target customers are likely to visit and getting sufficient stock cover till the next date of delivery. The Area Sales Managers, in addition to the tasks they would handle on the field, could carry out the marketing function audit in the form of a field audit Businesses could also outsource this service through undergraduates awaiting exam results or on their break after some familiarization.

- Promotion: There is a joke of one scientist who produced a permanent hair dye but kept it under his pillow and slept. It neither helped his hair nor that of any other's. Marketing Communications as it is referred to today is the engine to create awareness, image and initiate target markets to trial in case of new products and re-purchase in case of existing products. It is achieved through several means. What is required through the audit is to know whether all these methods such as – TV, Radio and Press communications, POPM, Personnel Selling etc., does the job or is superfluous just like the sampling campaign. Those in service marketing can audit on the following:

- People,
- Process,
- Physical evidence,
- Customer care.

The purpose of any plan is to do something effectively and the purpose of the audit is to be the watchdog and see whether it is actually being done.

Control of Marketing Plan

Ideally, the system should be specific enough that when it triggers the indication that some kind of a problem exists, the particular area of the problem is identified. The problem should be automatically formulated, and the control system should indicate not only that a problem exists but also what kind of a problem it is. It could indicate, for example, that the advertising medium is unsatisfactory. If this happens, the decision model should then proceed to evaluate all possible alternatives of media. Thus the control system would identify that a problem exists and formulate the problem in the sense of indicating in what area of the marketing plan there is a deficiency, while the decision model would specify the alternative solutions and evaluate them in terms of maximum short-term profits.

This assumes away the practical problem of time lag – the brand manager must be notified in sufficient time to make the change in the plan and to execute it, a fact which was incorporated into the MIS. In this way a new marketing plan would be ready for execution. This highly idealized version of control was implicit in the MIS. The brand manager currently does not have the luxury of such a system. He has a control system which warns him about some of his problems, but he finds out about these problems in other ways, too. Further, his control system is general; it may operate, for example, in terms of market share. Any of the three variables—advertising, price, or sales—could be the "problem." The system is not specific enough.

Finally, his decision models will not test all alternatives. These three aspects of his decision process—becoming aware of problems, formulating the problem, and deciding upon the alternatives to be tested—are now largely intuitive. Thus a large intuitive gap exists between the brand manager knowing he has some kind of a problem and the utilization of a decision model. Fortunately control is receiving increasing attention, both because the problem is becoming greater and the techniques for dealing with it have improved. The problem is more urgent, for one reason, because the marketing environment has become more dynamic, especially with the increased flow of new product developing out of the expanded research expenditures. Thus a market requires more careful and regular monitoring. Also, as companies have grown, they have more people to control or evaluate. Because the brand manager supervises so few people, however, he is almost entirely concerned with evaluating his plan and obtaining diagnostic insights rather than with controlling people. For this reason we have said nothing about controlling people here.

When such a problem exists, it can obviously arise either because the plan was incorrect in the sense that it did not "fit" that uncontrollable environment or because the plan was correct but improperly executed. To incorporate the evaluation of the execution into the system greatly complicates it. Finally, the power of adequate control has probably become better recognized. New control techniques are helping to define the practical problem of control more clearly. These techniques have developed out of quality control and servomechanism or feedback theory generally. Control, which involves a considerable and rapid flow of data, raises some sophisticated statistical questions. We can expect more attention to the control problem in marketing.

Designing a Marketing Control System

The broad pattern of steps in management control detailed above applies to marketing control as well. The control design must ensure that major variances are automatically distinguished and highlighted. It must also be capable of correctly interpreting the variances; the true meaning of the variances should be brought out by the control process. And the control information should lead to action. The control reports should be brief, lucid and pertinent.

There must also be a mechanism in the control design that translates the control information on variances into corrective courses of action. And, the control process should facilitate the focusing of attention on exceptions. The whole process should be oriented-to the present and the future rather than to the past. While control may involve appraisal of past performance, its main burden is current action and future course of action.

Fast Feedback is Essential for Marketing Control

In the nature of things, any deviation between the plan and the actual can be identified only after the event has occurred. As such, the interval between noticing the deviation and taking corrective action becomes very crucial the control process. If the intervals are long, control becomes a fraction. Once planning IS completed and c implementation is underway, the feedback should start flowing fast.

In other words, the essence of control is speedy feedback and speedy action that adjusts the operations to the prefixed norms. It is through feedback that control is achieved, and feedback and action have to be viewed as two sides of the same coin, the two components of a unified job, viz. control. Feedback is essential for timely understanding of the actual performance against the norms/targets. Action is essential for modifying the direction and level of performance so that it falls in line with the predetermined norms.

Marketing Control Monitors the Key Result Areas of Marketing

Marketing control as we shall see uses a variety of techniques. But whatever be the technique used, marketing control basically has a single purpose, viz. monitoring the key result areas in marketing management, some of the key result areas that are monitored by various marketing controls are:

- Sales volume,
- Market share,
- Market standing,
- Marketing costs,

- Profits,
- Productivity in each marketing activity.

Tools and Techniques of Marketing Control

There are several tools and techniques with which marketing control is exercised by a business firm. The important ones among them are listed below:

- Marketing audit,
- Marketing cost analysis,
- Credit control,
- Market share analysis,
- Budgetary control,
- Ratio analysis,
- Contribution margin analysis,
- Marketing information inputs and warning signals,
- MBO.

Marketing Audit Marketing audit is a continuous, systematic and objective study of the total marketing efficiency of the firm, It critically evaluates the marketing policies and marketing activities of the firm, and measures the external and direction of its growth Marketing audit is concerned with the long-term business interests and challenges of the firm rather than short-term achievements.

No firm can ever take the stand that everything is fine with its marketing. It is essential for the firm to assess whether the marketing policies, programmes, systems and methods established in the past are now valid and would be effective for the future. Marketing audit ensures such assessment.

Wide Ranging Scope of Marketing Audit

The strength of marketing audit lies in the fact that while other control techniques aim at a piece-meal evaluation of various marketing functions, marketing audit aim at a total evaluation of the entire marketing system and process. It leads to specific plans for improving the marketing efficiency of the firm. It also measures the evaluates the effectiveness of all other marketing control techniques employed by a firm. In this sense, marketing audit can be described as a control of controls.

The Importance of Marketing Cost Analysis

The marketing chief of any firm has to give maximum attention to marketing cost control and if he has to effectively control the marketing costs, he has to comprehend the components of the marketing costs and the methods available for their control. He must have an effective system to track them down. He must also analyse them systematically.

For, without systematic analysis of the marketing costs, it will not be possible to control these costs, and without such cost control, marketing control is meaningless. Today, in most firms, marketing cost analysis has become a prominent marketing control technique. Benefits Flowing from Marketing Cost Analysis a variety of benefits are derived by the firm from a careful and systematic marketing cost analysis.

It helps improve the competitive position of products of the firm in the market. If costs are reduced, prices can be kept competitive. It helps drop unprofitable customers, products, channels and markets and enables the firm identify and concentrate on relatively profitable products, customers, channels and markets. The firm may even take a decision to carry on with the unprofitable customers, products and markets.

But with marketing cost analysis, the decision is a conscious one, to support the long-term interests of the firm. Helps appraise the true cost and true value of each marketing service provided by the 'firm -such as delivery, presale and after-sale service, credit facilities, etc. It helps set responsibility for individual executives in the controlling of costs and ensures cost related performance.

Marketing Mix

Marketing mix of a firm comprises of a complex set of elements. Different firms create different marketing mix for each of their product. Let us classify the the set of marketing tools, used by the firms to pursue its marketing objectives in the target market, into four broad groups called the four Ps of marketing – product, price, place, and promotion.

Each of the elements of marketing mix further have a combination of sub-elements, for example, promotion mix, product mix, and so on. Moreover, while certain elements can be changed frequently in the short run, others can be modified only in the long run. For example, while marketer frequently changes the price of the product, it rarely does so in case of its distribution channel. Diagrammatically, marketing mix can be represented as a hub with the four elements joined with it.

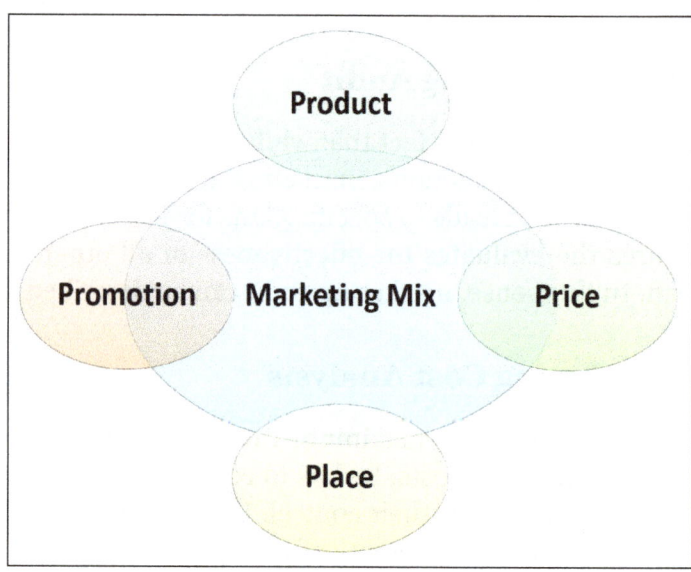

"The marketing mix is the set of controllable, tactical marketing tools that the firm blends to the product and the response it wants in the target market. The marketing mix consists of everything the firm can do to influence the demand for its product." - Gary Armstrong and Philip Kotler.

According to William Stanton, "Marketing mix is the term that is used to describe the combination of the four inputs that constitute the core of a company's marketing system: the product, the price structure, the promotion activities and the distribution system." Hence, marketing mix is a combination of four important elements - product, price, promotion and place.

Features of Marketing Mix

The features of marketing mix are as follows:

- Combination of four elements or variables: The marketing mix is a combination of four variables or elements, i.e., product, price, promotion, and place. For different areas like, services marketing, additional variables include, people, processes, physical evidence.

- Dynamic concept: The environment is volatile. The tastes and preferences of people changes overtime. New products and newer product features are being developed and introduced in the market. Marketing mix is a dynamic concept as each of the elements has to be changed with changes in the product and environment.

- Equally importance of variables: A systems approach is required while creating a marketing mix keeping in mind the fact that each of the variables or elements is important and all of them are interrelated and interdependent.

- Applies to business as well as non-business organization: Marketing mix is essential whether you are selling goods, services or idea; whether it's a business organization or non-business organization, as it ensures success in all types of ventures.

- Achievement of objectives: Marketing mix ensures achievement of marketing objectives of the organization and hence is instrumental in fulfilling broad organizational goals.

- Inter-related or co-related: The elements of marketing mix are interrelated and interdependent and hence, success depends on perfect blending of all the elements together.

- Customer oriented concept: The first step in designing marketing mix is to understand the needs and preferences of the customers. Each of the element of marketing mix is then designed keeping in mind those needs and preferences. The idea is to make the product successful by maximizing customer satisfaction.

Importance of Marketing Mix

A perfectly blended marketing mix ensures greater chances of success for the product since it provides the following benefits:

- Synergy: If the four elements of the marketing mix are blended well it will lead to positive synergy, i.e., the whole is greater than the sum of its parts.

- Creates brand loyalty and value: The marketing mix envisages meeting the needs and preferences of the customers. This ensures customer satisfaction as they get value for their money and leads to brand loyalty among them. In that process it also enhances the worth of the goods, services, and of the business.

- Serves as a link: While designing the marketing mix, the marketer will determine the needs and preferences of the customers. Once, it is designed and the product launched, it gives an indication to the customer about the marketer's offering and positioning of the product. The customers derive satisfaction when the marketing mix matches with their needs. Hence, the marketing mix can be considered as a link between the firm and its customers.

- Proper integration: Marketing mix works only when the four variables are integrated with each other to create a unique positioning in the minds of the customers. Hence, designing of marketing mix requires brainstorming and special abilities.

- Guides decision: The decisions regarding one of the element of the marketing mix is guided by the decisions taken for other elements since, all the elements are interrelated and interdependent.

- Customer satisfaction, brand loyalty, and higher sales volume: The outcome of well-designed marketing mix is overall customer satisfaction; creation of brand loyalty; and finally, greater sales volume and market share.

Elements of Marketing Mix

Developing the correct marketing mix for your product or service starts with understanding the Ps of Marketing.

4 P's of Marketing Mix

- Product: Product is a good (such as music players, shoes etc.) or service (such as hotels, airlines, etc.) that is offered as a solution to satisfy the needs of your customer. When developing the product, you need to consider its life cycle and plan for different challenges that may arise during the stages of it. Once the product reaches its final stage (sales decline phase), it's time to reinvent the item to win the demand of the customers again.

- Price: The next element of the marketing mix is the price your customer is willing to pay for your product. This helps determine the profit you will be able to generate. When setting a price for your product, consider how much you have spent on producing it, the price ranges of your competitors, and the perceived product value.

- Place: This is about the distribution center of the product and the methods used in distributing it to the customer. Wherever this is, it should be easily accessible to the customer. For example, if you have a physical store, it should be located in a place that can be easily discovered by the customer. If you own a website to market your product, make sure it is easily navigable.

- Promotion: Promotion refers to the methods a business uses to gain the attention of the customers to their product. These include sales promotions, customer service, public relations, advertising etc. When creating your promotion strategy, consider the tactics used by your competitors, the channels that are most effective in reaching your customers, and whether they match the perceived value of your product.

7 P's of Marketing Mix

7 Ps of marketing mix is an extended, modified version of the 4 Ps of marketing. This model is widely used in the service industry. It adds 3 more elements to the 4 Ps.

- People: This refers to the people – both your customers and employees – who are directly related to the product or service. While you need to study your target market to understand whether they are in need of the type of product you are offering, you need to hire the right people who are capable of giving their best to build it.

- Process: Systems and processes play an important role in building and delivering a quality service to your customer. Make sure that you process is free of bottlenecks and blockers in order to reduce the unnecessary expenses associated with executing the service. You can use process maps to map process steps and analyze them to identify where you need to make improvements.

- Physical Evidence: Physical evidence refers to what the customers see when consuming your product or service. This could include your branding, packaging, the physical environment where you are selling your product etc. Make sure that all physical aspects associated with your product or service adheres to its values.

Marketing Management

Marketing management is the process of decision making, planning, and controlling the marketing aspects of a company in terms of the marketing concept, somewhere within the marketing system. Before proceeding to examine some of the details of this process, comments on two aspects will be helpful background. The marketing concept is simple in principle but often very difficult, if not impossible, to fully implement. Adam Smith's comment cited above is most consistent with it. The concept is that a company can more effectively serve its own objectives if it will integrate the various aspects of its marketing activities explicitly so as to meet the preferences of its customers. To one unfamiliar with company practice the need for implementing the concept and the capacity to do it would seem to be so obvious as not to merit discussion.

This process of marketing management takes place "somewhere" within the marketing system. Having seen the marketing system portrayed, you know that "somewhere" can be within any of the many, many companies—manufacturing, wholesaling and retailing—that make it up. Marketing management is practiced in every one of them. Assume, to simplify, that we are concerned only with the manufacturing level in a direct sense because the manager we are considering occupies a marketing management position there. Marketing management involves:

- The setting of marketing goals and objectives,

- Developing the marketing plan,

- Organizing the marketing function,

- Putting the marketing plan into action,

- Controlling the marketing programme.

Marketing Management is both a science as well as an art. Those responsible for marketing should have good understanding of the various concepts and practices in marketing, communication, and analytical skills and ability to maintain effective relationship with customers, which will enable them to plan and execute marketing plans.

Continuous practice in the areas of personal selling, sales promotion, advertising, etc. would enable them to become artists. Scientific and artistic aspects of marketing would influence each other, leading to a new generation of marketing managers.

- Analyzing Market Opportunities: Marketing management collects and analyses information related to consumer's needs, wants and demands, competitor's marketing strategies, changing market trends and preferences. This helps to identify market opportunities.

- Determination of Target Market: Marketing management helps to identify the target market that the organization wishes to offer its product.

- Planning and Decision Making: Marketing management helps to prepare future course of action. Planning relates to product introduction, diversification. Decision making regarding pricing, selection of promotional mix, selection of distribution channel is taken by the marketing management.

- Creation of Customer: Consumers determine the future of the market. Therefore providing the best product to the consumer according to their preference is the important task of marketing. Marketing management helps in creation of new customers and retention of current customers.

- Helps in Increasing Profit: Marketing caters to the varied and unlimited needs of consumers. Marketing management helps to increase profit and sales volume. This is achieved by expansion of market and increasing customers.

- Improvement in Quality of Life: Marketing management aims at providing innovative product and services to the customers. Marketers continuously strive to incorporate new technology and mechanism in their product to provide more satisfaction to customers than before. This improves quality of life and makes life of consumers easier than before.

- Employment Opportunities: Marketing process is a combination of different activities like research work to assess the marketing environment, product planning and development, promotion, distribution of product to customers and after sales service. Marketing process requires researcher, production engineer, different distribution intermediaries, sales personnel also creates employment opportunities in advertisement section. Thus marketing management opened up different employment avenues thus creating employment opportunities.

References

- Marketing-features-top-11-important-features-of-marketing-explained, marketing-32290: yourarticlelibrary.com, Retrieved 10, August 2020

- Marketing-research-meaning-elements-areas-and-objectives, marketing-research, marketing-30000: yourarticlelibrary.com, Retrieved 04, March 2020

- Market-research: hotjar.com, Retrieved 09, May 2020

- Marketing-control, marketing-management-20955: businessmanagementideas.com, Retrieved 02, January 2020

- Elements-of-marketing-mix, diagrams: creately.com, Retrieved 16, June 2020

- What-is-marketing-management, marketing-management: economicsdiscussion.net, Retrieved 18, February 2020

Sub-Disciplines of Marketing

Marketing is a broad term which encompasses many smaller niches of marketing. Business marketing, social marketing, service marketing, rural marketing, green marketing, relationship marketing and international marketing are some sub-disciplines of marketing which are thoroughly discussed in this chapter.

Business Marketing

The business market consisting of commercial enterprises, institutions, and government as buyers; also known as B2B; constitutes the largest market in terms of the volume and the value of business generated. This market can be for goods or services, local or international, concentrated or diversified, and for consumption or for resale. Thus, the challenges are many as well as diversified.

Business marketing focuses over the buying behavior of all such organizations; commercial, institutes, or government; that buy goods or services for use in the production of other goods and services or for resale or renting or supplying at a profit.

The factors that distinguish consumer marketing (B2C) from business marketing (B2B) are chiefly in terms of the intended use of the product and intended customers- their buying and consumption behavior. Unlike consumer products, sometimes the products are differentiated as per individual customer and sometimes the identical products are to be marketed through different approaches.

Nature of Business Marketing and its Implications

Business and consumer marketing draw many points of similarities and differences. A common body of marketing practices and theory applies to both consumer and business marketing, but these markets differ in terms of their demand structure and nature, buyer behavior, environmental influences, and market strategy and emphasis.

Market Structure and Demand

The key characteristics of the business market in respect of its structure and demand patterns are quite different from the consumer market. The business or organizational marketer deals with fewer but large buyers who are the producers of the consumer goods.

It is because of the smaller customer base and the importance and power of the large customers, the suppliers-customer relationship is very close and the seller is expected to customize the product offering on one-on-one basis for this niche market. The market is usually geographically concentrated; majorly according to the availability of natural resources, capital, infrastructure, technology, and above all market demand concentration.

The demand of industrial goods is a derived demand, i.e., it is ultimately based upon the demand of consumer goods. It implies that the demand patterns need to be carefully monitored as it keeps fluctuating as per the consumer goods demand fluctuations. Another implication of the derived demand is that the marketer can develop derivative marketing programs to stimulate the ultimate consumer demand. In fact, by being sensitive to the consumer market, the business marketer can identify both the impending challenges and opportunities in real time.

Nature of the Buying Unit and Buying Behavior

A business purchase is a complex process and therefore it involves more decision participants who are trained purchasing agents, with clear understanding of organizational policies, resources, strategies and constraints. Many a times purchase committees, also called buying center, are constituted with technical and management experts.

The buying decision is taken through a long professional process of deliberations, suggestions, offers and influences. There are multiple buying influences with members of the buying center playing different roles in the purchase decision as initiators, users, influencers, deciders, approvers, buyers and gatekeepers.

The consumer and business buying behavior and buying process show significant differences. The decision making unit, i.e., the buying center consists of the individual and groups who participate in the purchase decision and play different roles to influence the purchase decision as discussed earlier. The marketing (4 Ps) and other environmental stimuli (economic, technology, political, cultural etc.) have an impact over the buying center's behavior. The deliberations of the buying center with an impact of the stimuli lead to the buying response in terms of product or service choice, supplier choice, order quantities, as well as the terms of delivery payment, service etc.

Another significant feature of the business buying is that the buyer often demands the complete packaged solution from the single supplier i.e., instead of buying and assembling individual components, the buyer would always prefer the purchase of a complete system along with continues assistance and services of the technical experts for smooth functioning of the production process.

Types of Decisions and Marketing Strategy

The buying decisions are very complex as the purchase decision involves large sum of money as well as complex technical, managerial, and economic considerations. The focus is over relationship marketing and personal selling in order to have a close and enduring buyer- seller relationship. Role of advertising is limited and distinguished. Advertising is mostly through trade journals or direct mail so as to reach the specific buyers.

The product strategy focuses significantly over the service components along with the customization of the product as per technical specifications of the buyer. Price negotiations are an important part of the business buying and are based on the formulation of the product package. Often these negotiations are a long process involving diplomatic influences.

Direct distribution of the products along with the installation is the marketing strategy in respect of the physical distribution. However, the business representatives and industrial distributors or brokers may also be the intermediaries for cracking the deal.

The Decision Process

The buying process is more formalized in terms of detailed product specifications, formal approvals, careful market search for suppliers, and written purchase orders. In order to capture the business order, the marketer works closely with the customer at all stages of the buying process in terms of matching the buyer's problem with his product solution, supporting the sales operations and providing long run support services. Understanding the key participants in the buying center and their relative importance, influences, and their motivations is also very important for the marketer.

A Relationship Emphasis

Relationships in business market are often close and enduring. A sales agreement signals not the end but the beginning of a relationship. Beyond negotiating and establishing a relationship, the marketer is to continuously center its focus over nurturing and sustaining this relationship as the loss of even a single buyer can be immense.

Supply Chain Management

The business marketer is usually a valued partner in a customers' supply chain as the rewards are substantial. A successful business marketer demonstrates the ability to meet the precise quality, quantity, delivery, service and information needs and becomes the partner in information sharing, joint planning, shared technology, synchronized production and delivery scheduling, and hence shared benefits.

Classification of Goods and Services for Business Marketing

The following figure depicts the classification of business goods and services so as to understand their distinguishable characteristics and the important marketing implications for each class and category. Understanding of these implications can be useful for a practicing marketer in this field.

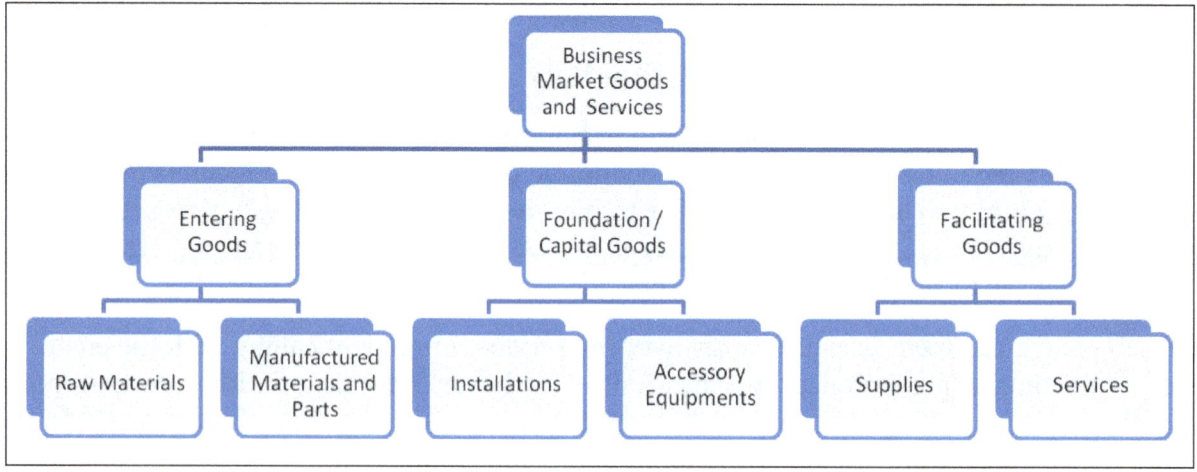

Entering Goods

This category of goods get entered or absorbed in the manufactured goods completely and become a part of the finished product after losing or retaining their identity. They are of the following two types:

- Raw Materials: The raw materials are both the farm and the natural products. The farm products are cotton, wheat, cereals, oils, fruits and vegetables, livestock etc., while the natural products are crude petroleum, ores, mines and minerals, fisheries, etc. The market of farm products is highly competitive with very large number of suppliers who provide similar goods at a very low margin and the differentiation is possible in terms of grading, assembly, storage, transportation, and selling services. As against farm products, fewer but large sellers, bulk supply, low unit value, long term supply contracts, and huge capital investment for processing are some of the features of natural industrial products.

- Manufactured Materials and Parts: The manufactured materials and parts are the one that have undergone some processing or manufacturing. They are again of two different categories depending upon their fabrication components materials and components parts. The component materials; such as cotton yarn, cement, wires, iron rods and pig iron, semi-processed food etc.; need further processing and their product quality form the quality of the finished product. Thus, their price, standard, and quality are very important for the buyer. The components parts are the finished products for one industry and do not need further fabrication. These products like tires, small motors, generators, cooling kits are outsourced by the manufacturers to be fitted in their product and thus, they become a part of the ultimate finished product. A long term relationship, close integrated operations, price and service considerations are very important in these marketing transactions as the interruption in the supply of one can hinder the complete supply chain.

Foundation or Capital Goods

The foundation goods are the capital assets meant to be used or worn out during the production processes. These goods do not form part of the finished output in any form but the manufacturing of the finished goods is not possible without the usage of such goods, and hence the name foundation goods. The cost of such capital items- machinery, installations, tools and equipment etc. - is assigned to the cost of production as the depreciation cost. These goods are further categorized as installation and accessory equipment:

- Installations: Buildings, machinery, lifts and elevators, generators, mainframe computers etc. are the installations that are purchased for long term use in the production processes and the cost of which is appropriated over the period of their useful life. Such goods are purchased directly from the producer after a long negotiation period and fine tuning as per the individual manufacturer's needs. Due to the nature of the deal, personal selling and willingness to meet the technical specifications is a must in such transactions.

- Accessory Equipment: These are the portable factory and office equipment meant for general administrative usage. These include hand tools, small motors, light equipment, plumbing and electrical equipment, desktop computers etc. This equipment has a shorter life span, less cost, and is for general use as against installations. Given these characteristics, the equipment' market is dispersed and varied with larger number of buyers and sellers. Also, the selling procedure and negotiations are not as complex as installations. Major focus in these transactions is over service, quality, branding, and price.

Facilitating Goods

The facilitating goods, as the name suggests are the goods and services meant for facilitating the production processes and developing and managing the finished products. Depending upon whether these are goods or services, they are categorized as supplies and business services respectively:

- Supplies: The supplies include maintenance and repair supplies (housekeeping materials, nails, paints, varnishes, chemicals etc.) and operating supplies (petrol, electricity, lubricants, stationery, oils, paper rims, etc.). The consumption of these goods can be estimated fairly on time basis without many technicalities and thus, these are purchased as straight rebuy through approved list of vendors.

- Business Services: The business services are that of business advisory consultants like accountants, legal advisors, engineers, media consultants, management consultants as well as the maintenance and repair services of plumbers, electricians, housekeeping staff, transporters, and upkeep staff. The services of advisory consultants are usually procured on contract or outsourcing basis where the goodwill and brand/ reputation are of utmost importance. For the repair and maintenance services either a department may be maintained by the organization or they may be purchased through contract.

Types of Business Buying

The business buying situations are varied depending upon the time constraints, the complexity of the problem at hand, the number of the people or influences involved, and the newness of the buying situation. Based upon these considerations the buying situations and types are broadly categorized as the following:

- Straight Rebuy: The straight rebuy refers to the routine purchases without any modifications for smooth functioning of the organizational operations. The task is handled by the purchase department and the items of purchase include the office supplies, the raw materials of production department, the purchases meant for maintenance and upkeep etc. The suppliers for such purchases are chosen from the approved lists and the focus is over timely delivery and quality products and services. The existing or "in" suppliers try to maintain relationship through automatic reordering system, whereas, the "out" suppliers try to offer a modified solution or exploit the dissatisfaction to get an entry.

- Modified Rebuy: This is a business buying situation in which the buyer wants to modify the product specifications, price, terms, delivery requirements, or the supplier. The modified buying decision is influenced by the deliberations of more decision participants than the routine straight rebuys. Such purchase influence the marketing strategy for both the "in" and "out" suppliers as the former observes a threat of losing a relationship while the latter an opportunity in gaining a business account.

- New Task: The new task buying situation is the one in which the product or service is to be purchased for the first time. The purchases of some capital asset like machinery or building, technology, operating systems, land and property etc. are the examples of such new task purchases. Usually these purchases involve greatest opportunities and challenges for the marketer as huge capital investments are the part of such deals. Because of the sensitivity of their nature and the risk involvement there is larger number of buying participants. On the supplier's side, the enormity of the opportunity calls for greater marketing efforts in terms of information supply, long bargain processes, service fulfillments, product modifications etc.

The Business Buying Process

The business buying process, just like consumer buying process is a sequential process involving many stages. These stages are more profound in case of a new task situation as compared to the modified or straight rebuy where some of the steps may be bypassed or compressed. The key stages have been explained as follows:

- Problem Recognition: An internal or external stimulus; like machinery breakdown, launch of new variety by the competitor, change in customers' taste, decision to launch a new product or a new variety of existing product, offer of better quality or price by the new supplier etc.; brings to fore the need to make purchases.

- General Need Description: The buyer assimilates the characteristics (durability, reliability, price, physical features etc.) and the quantity of the materials to be purchased. The task of the marketer at this stage is to match the buyer's needs with his product and service solutions. This stage is more objective for standard items purchase.

- Product Specifications: For complex, engineered, and non-routine items; a team of experts may take up the task of listing down technical specifications and doing product- value- analysis (PVA). A value analysis helps in working out the key technical and engineering details and the same is used by the marketer to frame the product specifications as per buyer's needs and to secure the business. Thus differentiation and positioning is achieved through PVA.

- Supplier Search: A list of qualified suppliers is prepared through the review of trade journals, internet, trade directories, auction or exchange sites etc. Now-a-days, e-procurement, i.e., online purchasing through websites is also becoming very popular as it not only saves cost and time but also forges direct relationship. B2B portals are also increasingly becoming very popular as they make available the e-hubs organized both industry wise (plastic, cement, iron ore, telecommunications, paper industry etc.) and functionality wise (logistics management, media, consultants, energy management, water conservers etc.).

- Proposal Solicitation: The proposal by an individual qualified supplier is solicited at this stage. For straight rebuy, this proposal may not be required at all, for modified rebuy it may be required in terms of catalogues but for complex engineering items purchased for the first time it may call for research, presentations, demonstrations, and technical documentations. Thus the marketer must be skilled in making oral and technical presentations so as to inspire confidence of the buyer and beat out the competition.

- Supplier Selection: On the basis of the presentations and negotiations, the technical aids and advices, competitive forces, ethical behavior, and the marketing strategy of the supplier in terms of price, service and product quality; the buying center identifies the most suitable supplier. The buying center may make this judgment intuitively but for all the reasons of reference, record and above all accuracy; a customer-value-assessment (CVA) may be taken up to compare the supply proposals over weighted scales of above stated attributes and hence making a logical comparisons of their score rating.

- Order-routine Specifications: Once the supplier is short listed final order is negotiated in the form of the order-routine that specifies the listed items, their technical specifications, the expected time of delivery, the return policies and warranties etc. Beyond the listing and understanding of these specifications, the industrial marketer may try to take leverage by introducing various methods of logistical arrangements (stockless purchase plans, continuous replenishment program, vendor managed inventory etc.) that reduce the cost of inventory and also save upon the time of inventory management routine jobs.

- Performance Review: This is a post purchase behavior that may lead the buyer to continue and extend the relationship or modify or drop the arrangements depending upon his need fulfillment and satisfaction. He may use a number of rating methods to periodically take up this kind of preview.

Business and Consumer Markets

One of the most common mistakes people make, when it comes to commercial transactions is thinking that business markets (B2B) are the same as consumer markets (B2C). This is quite an unfortunate mistake as the two, though similar in concept, are very different. One fact you should always remember about business markets is that it is a business to a business transaction where one company buys products from another business for resell or to facilitate the production of other goods.

The most important thing that you ought to remember about business markets is that it is a business to business type of transaction. It involves companies transacting with each other not for their consumption but in some cases to facilitate production, in other cases to supply the products to other firms or directly to resell the purchases to the consumers.

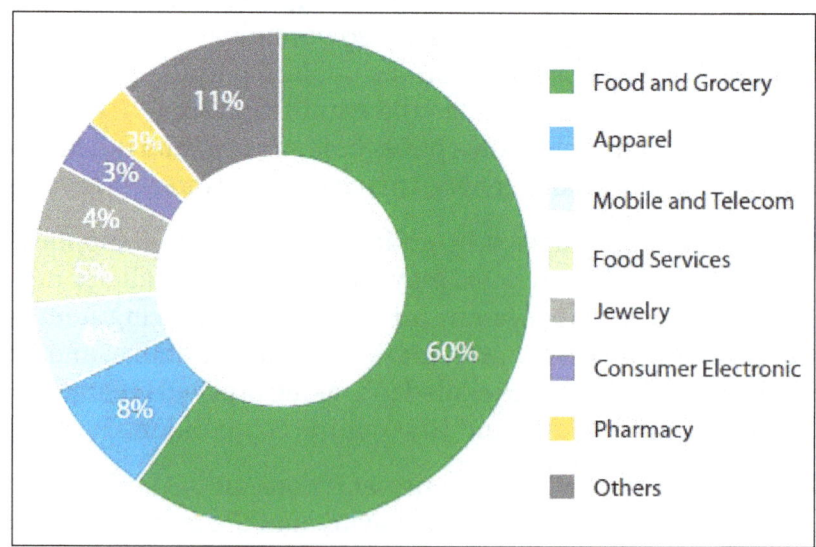

The procurement of the two markets also presents a significant distinction. For B2B markets, the purchasing process is quite complicated as the process is mostly influenced by a business'

executive and management depending on the type of purchase. Persons making purchasing often require authorization from these groups before making any purchasing decisions.

B2C markets, on the other hand, presents a very simplified procurement process because influences are not as complex as it is with B2Bs. The most common factors that affect consumers purchasing decisions include; reference groups, tastes and preferences, marketing campaigns and economic conditions. The payment structure for these two markets differs significantly. Large sums of money are involved in B2B markets as compared to B2C markets. This is because the former often involves large volumes of purchases unlike in B2C where purchases are only made as per the consumer's needs.

In this regard, B2B markets employ a more complex payment structure where a business makes an order and arranges for delivery through logistic procedures. After delivery, the seller then sends an invoice to the buyer business within which the buyer company can then make an official payment for goods delivered (based on the agreed terms of payment). In the consumer market, customers choose their product of interest and then pay for the product using cash, credit or checks.

Also, unlike in the consumer market where consumers buy products at the same price, in the business market buyers can negotiate for special terms depending on their volume of purchase, business relationship enjoyed with the selling business, etc.

Another distinction between these two market lies in how each market promotes their products and services. In the business market, products are sold to other companies, and thus the method of advertisement will slightly vary from that of the consumer market. Here, companies do not involve media advertisement to market their products and services. Instead, they use more formal channels like magazines, newspapers, and direct emails to concerned businesses.

Consumer markets as we now know targets the customers as the end user. Here, media advertisements are usually a large part of the promotions strategy that businesses use to market their products. Throughout the years, B2B markets have dependably been behind the operation of B2C markets. Be that as it May, as the years wore on and improvements on technological have been seen, it has been harvesting popularity in light of the increased development.

Companies in the B2B market today aimed at boosting their shareholder value in these markets. So, while their promotion techniques are not as aggressive as with B2C markets, branding of products and services in this particular market is always top-notch. Moreover, businesses operating in a B2B market often work purposely towards building up the business and giving it a strong position in the industry.

Difference between Business Markets and Consumer Markets due to the Nature of Purchases

- Organizational consumers purchase capital equipment, raw materials, semi-finished goods, and other products for use in further production or operations or for resale to others, whereas final consumers usually acquire the finished items for personal, family, or household use.

- Organizational consumers are likely to require exact product specifications. Final consumers more often buy on the basis of description, style, and color.

- Organizational consumers often use multiple-buying responsibility, in which two or more employees formally participate in complex or expensive purchase decisions. Final consumers employ it less frequently and less formally.

Difference between Business Markets and Consumer Markets on the Basis of Demand

- Derived demand occurs for organizational consumers because the quantity of items they purchase is often based on the anticipated demand of their final consumers for specific finished goods and services; therefore, organizational consumers are less sensitive to price changes. As long as final consumers are willing to pay higher prices, organizational consumers will not object to price increases.

- Demand is volatile due to the accelerator principle, whereby final consumer demand affects many levels of organizational consumers.

- There are fewer organizational consumers than final consumers.

- Business market consumers tend to be geographically concentrated.

- Buying specialists are often used.

- Distribution channels are shorter.

Differences of Business Markets and Consumer Markets based on a Global Perspective

- As with final consumers, there are many distinctions among organizational consumers around the world and sellers must understand and respond to them.

- Companies doing business in foreign markets must know how to deal with organizational consumers in those markets.

- Nations' cultures have a large impact on the way their organizational consumers negotiate and reach decisions.

Social Marketing

Social marketing is marketing designed to create social change, not to directly benefit a brand. Using traditional marketing techniques, it raises awareness of a given problem or cause, and aims to convince an audience to change their behaviors.

So, instead of selling a product, social marketing "sells" a behavior or lifestyle that benefits society, in order to create the desired change. This benefit to the public good is always the primary focus. And instead of showing how a product is better than competing products, social marketing "competes" against undesirable thoughts, behaviors, or actions. Social marketing is commonly used for causes like.

Health and safety, including:

- Anti-smoking,

- Anti-drug,

- Promoting exercise and healthy eating,

- Safe driving,

- Railroad station safety.

Environmental causes, including:

- Anti-deforestation,

- Anti-littering,

- Endangered species awareness.

Social activism, including:

- Illuminating struggles that people of color, people with disabilities, etc. face, then inspiring people to fight against mechanisms that create inequality,

- Anti-bullying,

- Fighting gender stereotypes.

Who initiates these social marketing campaigns? Nonprofit organizations and charities run the majority of social marketing campaigns. Government organizations, highway safety coalitions, and emergency services (police, fire, and ambulance) run them as well. But social marketing is not out of the question if you're a commercial business. Commercial brands will sometimes run social marketing campaigns for causes they are passionate about.

The Importance of Social Marketing

Why is social marketing so important? Well, think about "traditional" ads for products or services. You aren't convinced to check out a product or service through an ad alone. But how does a well-designed ad capture your attention? It either takes a super creative angle you didn't expect, or makes you laugh, cry, or think. Not every ad convinces you to check out the product or service it promotes, but the best ones appeal to creativity or emotion to motivate people to do so. It's the same way with social marketing. People don't like being told what to do. They might not be convinced by news and typically presented PSAs about a certain social issue. Or, they might not be aware of the problem or its scope.

Some people might also find a socially beneficial behavior too difficult to perform, or might think they can't help solve an issue on their own. Alternatively, they might have trouble breaking a long-standing habit (i.e. someone trying to quit smoking, or someone who uses disposable water bottles regularly).

But well-executed social marketing captures attention, and spreads awareness about a social issue, through creativity and emotion. Most importantly, it presents a compelling, simple way to make the world better, and makes this beneficial behavior more desirable than any "competing" behavior.

Through these elements, social marketing is able to successfully "sell" a beneficial behavior. Social marketing is especially powerful when it involves a charitable donation element, because people want to make a difference in the world. They're very willing to give—it's just a matter of where.

Eight P's of Social Marketing

- There are an ample number of definitions, but in essence social marketing is about applying commercial marketing's '4Ps' – Product, Price, Place, Promotion – with a social twist. Marketing is about persuading people to buy a product. Social marketing is about convincing people to adopt a behavior or not consume socially undesirable product like cigarettes, gutka and oral tobacco. This would enhance their quality of life or that of the community.

- Population Services International, a leading social marketing organization, says their social marketing work: "engages private sector resources and uses private sector techniques to encourage healthy behavior and make markets work for the poor".

Product

The social marketing "product" is not essentially a physical contribution. A variety of products is, ranging from tangible, physical products (e.g., condoms), to services (e.g., medical exams), practices (e.g., breastfeeding, ORT or eating a heart-healthy diet) and lastly, more intangible thoughts (e.g., environmental protection). In order to have a feasible product, persons must first recognize that they have a sincere problem, and that the product proposing is a good solution for that problem. The role of investigation here is to determine the consumers' opinions of the problem and the product, and to govern how significant they feel it is to take action alongside the problem.

Price

"Price" refers to what the consumer must do in order to obtain the social marketing products. This cost may be monetary, or it may instead require the consumer to give up intangibles, such as time or efforts, or to risk embarrassment and disapproval. If the costs outweigh the benefits for an individual, the perceived value of the offerings will be low and it will be unlikely to be adopted.

However, if the benefits are perceived as greater than their costs, chances of trial and adoption of the products is much greater.

In setting the price, particularly for a physical product, such as contraceptives there are many issues to consider. If the product is priced too low, or provided free of charge, the consumer may perceive it as being low in quality. On the other hand, if the price is too high, some will not be able to afford it. Social marketers must balance these considerations, and often end up charging at least nominal fee to increase perception of quality and to confer a sense of "dignity" to the transactions. These perceptions of costs and benefits can be determined through research, and used in positioning the products.

Place

"Place" describes the way that the product reaches the consumer. For a tangible product, this refers to the distribution system--including the warehouse, trucks, sales force, retail outlets where it is sold, or places where it is given out for free. For an intangible product, place is less clear-cut, but refers to decisions about the channels through which consumers are reached with information or training. This may include doctors' offices, shopping malls, mass media vehicles or in-home demonstrations. Another element of place is deciding how to ensure accessibility of the offering and quality of the service delivery. By determining the activities and habits of the target audience, as well as their experience and satisfaction with the existing delivery system, researchers can pinpoint the most ideal means of distribution for the offering.

Promotion

Finally, the last "P" is "promotion" because of its visibility, this element is often mistakenly thought of as comprising the whole of social marketing. Promotion consists of the integrated use of advertising, public relations, promotions, media advocacy, personal selling and entertainment vehicles. The focus is on creating and sustaining demand for the product. Public service announcements or paid ads are one way, but there are other methods such as coupons, media events, editorials, "Tupperware"-style parties or in-store displays. Research is crucial to determine the most effective and efficient vehicles to reach the target audience and increase demand. The primary research findings themselves can also be used to gain publicity for the program at media events and in news stories.

Additional Social Marketing P's

Publics

Social markets often have many different audiences that their program has to address in order to be successful. "Public" refers to both the external and the internal groups involved in the program. External publics include the target audience, secondary audience, policymakers and gatekeepers, while the internal publics are those who are involved in some way either approval or implementation of the program.

Partnership

Social and health issues are often so complex that one agency can't make a dent by itself. You need to team up with the organizations in the community to really be effective. You need to figure out which organization have similar goals to yours- not necessarily the same goals and identify ways you can work together.

Policy

Social marketing program can do well in motivating individual behavior change, but that is difficult to sustain unless the environment they're in supports that change for the long run. Often, policy change is needed, and media advocacy programs can be an effective complement5 to a social marketing program.

Purse String

Most organizations that develop socials marketing programs operate through funds provided by sources such as foundations, governmental grants or donations. This adds another dimension to the strategy development namely, where will you get the money to create your program?

Societal Marketing

The societal marketing concept began in 1972. The concept is meant to make marketing morally, socially and ethically responsible. Philip Kotler wrote about what consumerism means to marketers. He identified four categories which included deficient products, pleasing products, salutary products, and desirable products. Kotler felt there was no reason for deficient products and they should no longer be on the market, Pleasing and salutary products needed to revamped until they were considered desirable products. The societal marketing concept was an offshoot to the marketing concept wherein an organization's belief rest upon the premise of returning the favor to the society by committing to produce better quality products targeted towards society welfare.

A promotional process whereby a business first assesses the interests of targeted consumers and then aims to deliver products more effectively and efficiently than its competition so that it benefits their customer's and society's overall welfare. The societal marketing approach tends to balance the pursuit of business profits with consumer desires and society's best interest.

Features of Social Marketing

The features of social marketing are:

- The advertisement campaign does not necessarily show a product.
- It is not meant for furthering profit.
- It reflects upon a social idea.
- It may use de marketing to reduce consumption of a product that is socially undesirable.
- It is often done by Government Departments or Not for Profit organizations.
- It themes and messages are of purely social concerns and social ills.
- It does not relate to the product of the company.
- It often uses an emotional appeal that is shocking, scary, heart-breaking, unusual and informative.

- It uses marketing for developing social consciousness through its advertisements.

- It aims at quality of life, health, environment and a reduction in social ills.

Societal Marketing Strategies

Marketing managers within distinct commercial organizations might perceive some social issues as more pertinent than others. The pertinence of a given social issue is calculated by the company's products, promotional efforts, and pricing and distribution policies and is driven by the company's vision and philosophy of social responsibility. For instance, a company need to be aware about preserving the environment and enhancing the quality of life and are related to the issues that engulf conservation of natural resources, minimizing environmental pollution, protecting endangered species, and control of land use. The 3 Rs of environment protection are: Reduce, Reuse, and Recycle. Most of the companies realize that consumers are inclined towards the green products and hence will pay more for it. In this regard we can illustrate the success story of Toyota with their hybrid cars. Many consumer durable companies are using this strategy for increasing customer interest in their brands. Green marketing has become a significant strategy for contemporary marketers.

Ethics in Marketing

Kotler and Roberto lay strong prominence on the vitality of ethics in social marketing. Whenever marketing behavior change, it is essential to recognize the need for responsibility and accountability to the people in the target audience. Although in the end, the results of the program are the final measure of success, the means to that end are just as important. People should never be coerced into a behavior, even though it may be "for their own good." Programs may also have negative repercussions and unintended consequences, which might be detrimental in the long run. Programs which offer incentives for behavior change may encourage materialistic values and a disinclination towards anything that does not offer any extrinsic reward. Ethical criteria must be duly taken into account from the very inception in selecting the target audience, research design and determining an optimum social marketing mix, and ought to be used while evaluating, throughout a program to ensure that it "does no harm." Every element of the program must sound ethical.

For a marketing manager to take an ethical decision, knowledge of the subject matter should be there. He should have an assessment of risk, and experience to understand the risk involved in a decision affecting all the stakeholders.

Service Marketing

Services play an important role in one's life. They affect and ease one's life. One cannot imagine life without services. With the changing lifestyle and consumption patterns, services are emerging as a significant sector of the economy. The contribution of services to the growth of the economies worldwide has been well established. In both developed and developing countries, the significance and proportion of services in the GDP of the country is on a constant rise.

Service marketing is a specialized field of marketing that deals with the marketing of services. The debate between services being different from products led to the emergence of a separate field of marketing for services. Service marketing gained due recognition during late 20th century. Service marketing is a widely researched and studied discipline today. This stream of marketing is extremely significant and equally challenging for the marketers.

Services: Concept and Characteristics

Concept of Services

According to American Marketing Association, services are defined as "activities, benefits, or satisfactions that are offered for sale, or provided in connection with the sale of goods". Here, services are classified as pure services or services combined with the goods to maximize the value for the customers.

Kotler defines services as separately identifiable; essentially activities that provide want satisfaction. The definition postulates services as those activities which are distinguished from goods and which satisfy the wants of the customers. Berry defined service as 'acts, deeds and performances'. This definition implies services are the activities or deeds as performed by a doctor, lawyer, technician etc.

Characteristics of Services

Like physical goods, services possess an identity of their own which is marketed and sold. Services differ from goods in a number of ways. Following are the distinctive characteristics that define services.

Intangibility

Unlike physical products, services cannot be seen, touched and felt. Services are intangible in nature. Intangibility is the most distinguishing feature of a service. When a consumer buys a good such as car or a book, it can be seen, touched and felt but when a consumer consults a lawyer to fight a case or consults a doctor in case of illness, this guidance given by the lawyer or doctor cannot be touched or seen. A physical good can be possessed by a consumer but not a service. A consumer can purchase a medicine and possess it but he cannot possess a doctor's service. A consumer derives experience after consuming a service. Services provide an experience to the user of the service and it is this experience which the consumer uses to evaluate the service consumed. Also, each time a service is consumed; it results into a different experience. No two service experiences can ne similar.

This basic characteristic of services makes it challenging for a marketer to market services, marketers have to use tangibles and imagery to promote services. The intangibility aspect also makes it difficult for the consumers who are neither able to touch nor able to comprehend it mentally. Often consumers make use of tangible cues to evaluate services. For instance, the service provided by a restaurant is assessed through the ambience, hygiene, décor, courteous staff and efficient services.

Inseparability

Goods are tangible and can be taken away from their point of production. For example, a consumer purchases a burger and takes it away. However, in case of services, production and consumption cannot be separated. For example, as a teacher is teaching in the class, the students are consuming the knowledge imparted simultaneously; the knowledge given by the teacher cannot be taken later. Services cannot be separated from their production systems.

Service consumption is possible only when an interaction takes place between a consumer and the production system providing service. While in case of a good, these are generally produced in a batch and then transported to the marketplace for selling. However, in case of services, it is either the consumer who goes to the service production system like going to the parlor to get a haircut or the service production system going to the consumer like a home tutor coming to the student. A service is produced where and when the consumer needs it. Services are produced when the consumer and the service provider come together and this communication results in unique service being created.

Variability

The above two features of services: intangibility and inseparability makes services variable in nature. Goods are produced in bulk and goods of the same lot are identical. The production of goods results in a number of similar physical entities. For example, shirts of the same lot and same size will be exactly similar to each other. Services, on the other hand, cannot be identical. For example, two visits in a parlour or two lunches in a restaurant cannot be exactly same.

Services cannot be standardized on account of factors such as the inability to define the standards for measurement of intangible services. Also, services are created when the customer and service provider interact. The human element in the interaction lends variability to the services. Unlike products, services cannot be guaranteed with cent percent quality. As production and consumption of services takes place simultaneously, improvement of quality post production is not feasible. Further, the production of goods is a planned sequential process but the interaction in case of services cannot be pre-fixed; it takes shape depending upon the mood and feelings of the persons involved and situational circumstances.

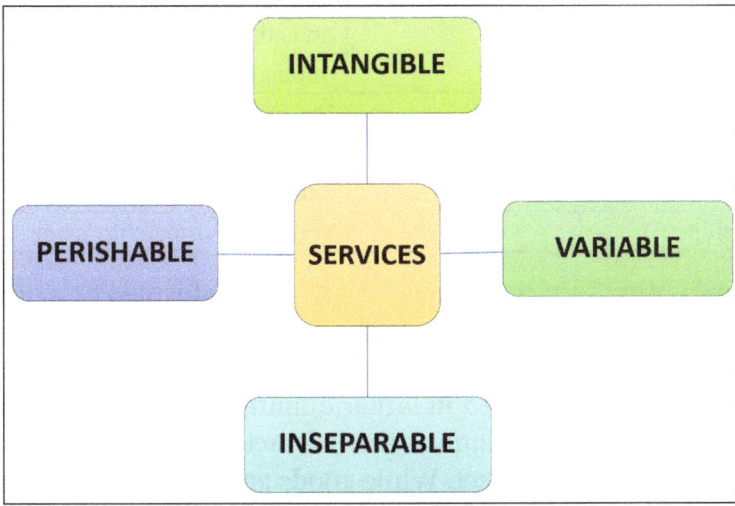

Figure: Characteristics of Services.

Perishability

Storage of goods is possible as there is a time lag between production and consumption. However, in case of services, production and consumption are concurrent and thus services cannot be stored. The supply of goods can be adjusted in accordance with the demand conditions. Goods stocked in abundance can be utilized to meet the demand during peak seasons and in case of short demand, goods can be stored back. But in case of services, demand fluctuations cannot be met. For example, during lunch hours, the capacity of a restaurant cannot be increased. Similarly, if the number of customers on a particular day in a restaurant falls short, the loss is unavoidable.

Differentiating between Goods and Services

Marketing initially was associated with tangible entities: goods. First agriculture and then industries took the center-stage in the development of economies across the globe. Services have gained recognition at a later stage. However, services have now surpassed both agriculture and industrial sectors. Services have become an indispensable part of living.

Product is a comprehensive term and includes anything that can satisfy customer needs and wants. A product may be a good, a service or a combination of good and service. Product is a combination of tangible and intangible features that a company provides to its customers. A product includes good, service, experience, person, place, event, organization, information and ideas. There exists a continuum along which goods and services can be depicted.

Pure good and pure service lies at the extremes of the continuum with several combinations in between. In the real world, it is difficult to find a pure good or pure service. It is not feasible to categorize a product as a pure good or service. Marketers often combine goods and services for satisfaction of customer wants. Companies producing pure goods and services to increase the value of the offer while service companies add tangible features to be able to market and sell services. However, for goods and services differ from each other on account of several features. The distinction between a good and service enables to comprehend the two concepts effectively. Following are the important differences between goods and services:

Goods	Services
A physical entity.	An activity or process.
Tangible.	Intangible.
Identical.	Unique.
Time lag between production and consumption.	Simultaneous production and consumption.
Can be stored.	Cannot be stored.
Transfer of ownership.	Transfer of ownership is not possible.

While good is a physical entity, service is an activity that is performed or a process that is executed such as the act of washing clothes by the washerman. Goods, being a physical commodity can be seen, felt and touched while services are essentially intangible in nature and therefore cannot be seen, felt or touched. Goods are produced in larger quantities and thus are homogeneous. On the other hand, each service provided is unique as the interaction between the consumer and the service provider varies in time as well as effect. While goods are produced and later consumed, in case of services production and consumption are simultaneous. Goods require storage as consumption of goods is not instant but services cannot be stored as these are consumed instantly as produced. Finally, goods are tangible and therefore their ownership can be transferred but services being intangible entities cannot be transferred.

Green Marketing

Green marketing is the marketing of environmentally friendly products and services. It is becoming more popular as more people become concerned with environmental issues and decide that they want to spend their money in a way that is kinder to the planet.

Green marketing can involve a number of different things, such as creating an eco-friendly product, using eco-friendly packaging, adopting sustainable business practices, or focusing marketing efforts on messages that communicate a product's green benefits.

This type of marketing can be more expensive, but it can also be profitable due to the increasing demand. For example, products made locally in North America tend to be more expensive than those made overseas using cheap labor, but they have a much smaller carbon footprint because they don't have to fly across the globe to get here. For some consumers and business owners, the environmental benefit outweighs the price difference.

Lohas

Consumers who prefer to purchase green products even though they might be more expensive fall into the 'LOHAS' category. LOHAS stands for Lifestyles of Health and Sustainability.

> "LOHAS describes an integrated, rapidly growing market for goods and services that appeal to consumers whose sense of environmental and social responsibility influences their purchase decisions."

These consumers are active supporters of environmental health and are the heaviest purchasers of green and socially responsible products. They also have the power to influence other consumers.

Green Marketing Methods

Beyond making an environmentally friendly product, business owners can do other things as part of their green marketing efforts. The following can all be part of a green marketing strategy:

- Using eco-friendly paper and inks for print marketing materials.
- Skipping the printed materials altogether and option for electronic marketing.
- Having a recycling program and responsible waste disposal practices.
- Using eco-friendly product packaging.
- Using efficient packing and shipping methods.
- Using eco-friendly power sources.

- Taking steps to offset environmental impact.

Greenwashing

Some marketers try to capitalize on the growing number of green consumers by simply taking a green marketing approach to products that might not otherwise be considered green. They try to position their products as a better choice for the environment when they're really not. An example of this is when a company uses the color green in their packaging, or the word green somewhere in their messaging, when there isn't anything particularly eco-friendly about their product, nor it's not more eco-friendly than competing products. Greenwashing is not only misleading, but it can also be damaging to a company's reputation.

Relationship Marketing

In this era of stiff competition, product innovation is definitely one of the key significant elements that the organizations need to depend upon to steer themselves ahead in the market. Along with the technical leadership the companies necessarily need to know how to reach out to the customer. Engaging the Customer, Understanding the Customer and building relationship has become the need of the day. According to Grooroos, Relationship Marketing (RM) is, "That marketing is a process that involves many parties or actors. The objective of each party has to be met and this is done by mutual exchange and fulfilling of promises – that makes trusts a significant element. It makes it evident in the definition that marketing is based on the network among all stakeholders—customers, suppliers, vendors and intermediaries, working together for common goals. It is thus possible to analyze the interactions and process of relationships in this system.

Relationship Marketing is also defined as "the ongoing process of engaging in cooperative and collaborative programmes with immediate and end-user customers in order to create and enhance mutual economic value at reduced cost." RM is a strategy designed to foster customer loyalty, interaction and long term engagement. This customer relationship definition emphasizes on CRM and customer retention than customer acquisition.

Relationships are the categorized as the most valuable things. A company maintains its relationships—with customers, employees, suppliers, distributors, dealers, and retailers. The company's relationship capital is the sum of the knowledge, experience, and trust a company has with its customers, employees, suppliers, and distribution partners. These relationships are often worth more than the physical assets of a company. Relationships determine the future value of the firm according to Kotler.

Traditional transaction marketing (TM) tended to ignore relationships and relationship building. The company was viewed as an independent agency always maneuvering to secure the best terms. The company was ready to switch from one supplier or distributor to another if there was an immediate advantage. The company assumed that it would normally keep its current customers, and it spent most of its energy to acquire new customers. The company neglected the interdependence among its main stakeholders and their roles in affecting the company's success.

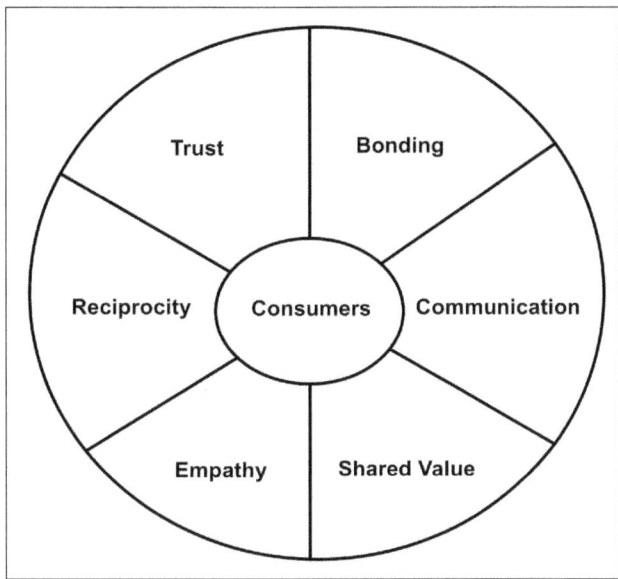

Relationship marketing (RM) marks a significant paradigm shift in marketing, a movement from thinking solely in terms of competition and conflict toward thinking in terms of mutual interdependence and cooperation. It acknowledges the significance of various parties—suppliers, employees, distributors, dealers, retailers—cooperating to deliver the best value to the target customers. Here are the main characteristics of relationship marketing:

- It focuses on partners and customers rather than on the company's products.

- It lays more significance on customer retention and growth than on customer acquisition.

- It relies on cross-functional teams rather than on departmental-level work.

- It relies more on listening and learning than on talking.

Four P's of Relationship Marketing

Product

- More products are customized to the customers' preferences.

- New products are developed and designed cooperatively with suppliers and distributors.

Price

- The company will set a price based on the relationship with the customer and the bundle of features and services ordered by the customer.

- In business-to-business marketing, there is more negotiation because products are often designed for each customer.

Distribution

- RM favors more direct marketing to the customer, thus reducing the role of middlemen.

- RM favors offering alternatives to customers to choose the way they want to order, pay for, receive, install, and even repair the product.

Communication

- RM favors more individual communication and dialogue with customers.

- RM favors more integrated marketing communications to deliver the same promise and image to the customer.

RM sets up extranets with large customers to facilitate information exchange, joint planning, ordering, and payments. Relationship Management forms part of the vision and business ethics that the company envisages to imbibe as its core value system. When an organization chooses to build its business blocks around relationship management, the organization is marrying its profit making goal with customer relationship to build a synergy by which all the divisions as well as the functions of the organization look at their function and business through the RM lens. This assists in creating a strong customer orientation and culture of customer sensitivity which is universal i.e. across the organization at all levels, branches and functions. In any organization several of its departments are involved with the external customers. Starting with Marketing, Sales, Distribution to After Sales Service, Quality as well as Finance Departments are involved with customers and their orientation towards the customer interaction is fashioned by the RM outlook of the organization.

CRM on the other hand can best be described as an enabler of RM in any organization. CRM involves process including software and hardware components that automates and helps manage customer engagement. While RM works at a strategy level, CRM assists in implementation of the Strategy. The success of CRM as a concept is widely seen due to the aggressive marketing of CRM solutions by the IT companies who have developed the CRM packages. With the help of CRM, Multi National Organizations are able to implement standardized process of Customer management on large scale across geographies and markets.

Dynamics of Relationship Marketing

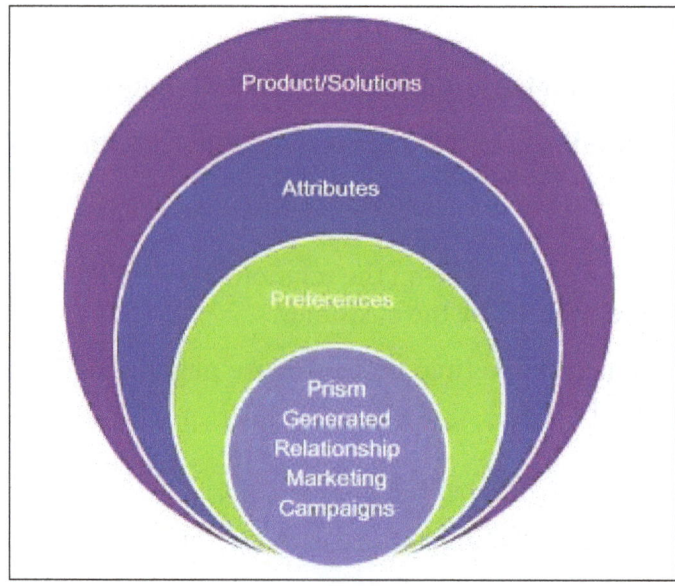

Relationship marketing is not just loyalty programs. It's about creating recipient centric communities that increase relationship values and business benefits.

Four R's of Relationship Marketing

RM comprises of 4 types of R's, i.e.:

- Reward: Customer purchase and sharing of information,
- Response: To generate high response and faith,
- Respect: Consumer privacy and respect,
- Relevant: Use of information for relevant communication offers.

The main objectives of RM is to share information with the loyal customers about upcoming products/ offers to generate higher response rate and building faith in the mind of customer by making him part of the company policies. Using the information of customers sparingly only for genuine benefit of both the firm and customer along with keeping the secrecy and respect for privacy of clients intact. Only relevant offers should be communicated to the customers and not flooding them with requests/ schemes, as it violates the privacy of the customers. This would amount to breach of trust among the customers.

Difference between Transactional and Relationship Marketing

Transactional marketing is basically most traditional form of marketing which is not different from selling. In this, emphasis is on selling already produced goods and not meeting customer expectations or understanding the need for their satisfaction. Acquiring new customers is the main objective of all marketing activities whereas in relationship marketing the focus is on building long term satisfying relationship with customers.

Table: Difference between Transactional Marketing and RM.

	Transacting marketing	Relationship marketing
Focus on	Obtaining new customers.	Customer retention
Orientation to	Service features	Customer benefits
Customer services	short	Long
Customer services	Little emphasis	High emphasis
Customer commitment	Limited	High
Customer contact	Limited	High
Quality	Primarily on operations concern.	The concern of all.

Thus retaining existing customer is a greater challenge. The focal point is consumer research in terms of their tastes and preferences and designing a product which fits those parameters. Marketing does not end with completion of sales transaction rather a long term contact with clients is established.

International Marketing

The International Marketing is the application of marketing principles to satisfy the varied needs and wants of different people residing across the national borders. Simply, the International Marketing is to undertake the marketing activities in more than one nation. It is often called as Global Marketing, i.e. designing the marketing mix (viz. Product, price, place, promotion) worldwide and customizing it according to the preferences of different nation people.

The foremost decision that any company has to make is whether to go international or not, the company may not want to globalize because of its huge market share in the domestic market and do not want to learn the new laws and rules of the international market. But however, there are following reasons that attract the organization to be global:

- Increased economies of scale,

- High-profit opportunities in the international market than the domestic market,

- Huge market share,

- Elongated life of the product,

- Untapped international market.

How to Enter the International Market?

There are following ways through which companies can globalize:

- Exports: The easiest way to enter the market is through exports that can be indirect or direct. In Indirect Exports, the trading companies are involved that facilitates the buying and selling of goods and services abroad, on the behalf of the companies. Whereas in Direct exports, the company itself manages to sell the goods and services abroad, by opting one of the following ways:

  ○ By setting Domestic based Export Department, working as an independent entity.

  ○ Through Overseas sales branch, that carries out the promotional activities and facilitates sales and distribution.

- ◦ The sales representatives traveling abroad.

- ◦ The distributors or agents in abroad working exclusively on the behalf of the company.

- Global Web Strategy: Nowadays, companies need not go to the international trade shows to show their products, they can very well create the awareness among the customers world-wide through an electronic media i.e. internet. Through the company website, customers can read the detailed information, generally written in different languages, about the product and can order online.

- Licensing and Franchising: One of the ways to globalize is through licensing, wherein the domestic company issues the license to the foreign company to use the manufacturing process trademark, patent, name of the domestic company while facilitating the sales. In licensing, the domestic company has a less control over the licensee. But, in the case of franchising, the domestic company enjoys the higher control as it allows the franchise to function on its behalf, and in line with the terms and conditions of the domestic company. MC Donald's, Dominos are the examples of franchising.

- Joint Ventures: The companies can go international by joining hands with other country based companies with the intention to monetize their existing relationships with the local customers.

- Direct Investment: Ultimately, the firms can establish their own business facilities or own a part of the local company to facilitate the sale of goods and services. The companies go international with the objective to have increased sales along with the huge market share. But certain things such as political, social, technological, cultural situations should be kept in mind while designing the marketing principles since these are different for the different nations.

Marketing: Product and Brand Management

The development of a new product, pricing, profitability, demand, launch, marketing and any other related research falls under product management. A brand is a unique name, term, design or symbol that sets apart a business product from other similar products. The techniques that go into positive enhancement of the image and value of a particular brand over time are called brand management. This chapter provides a comprehensive summary of product and brand management.

Product

A new product can shape up the company's future. That product can be acquired from someone else or can be produced by the organization. Earlier, the production team used to design a product and the marketers were simply expected to sell what has already been produced. But, these days, marketers play a very important role in the new product development process, by identifying and evaluating various new product ideas and working with the research and development team of the organisation at every stage of the evolution of product. In a very narrow sense, a product is a set of tangible physical attributes assembled in an identifiable form. However, in marketing, the concept of a product is much wider.

A product can be more than a physical thing and it may be a service, a feeling, a pleasure, a reputation, or an experience. In reality, the consumer obtains a bundle of satisfaction as a result of buying a product. Thus, the organizations have to consider the product from the customer's perspective. For example, the cosmetic companies are combining chemicals to make beauty creams, vitamin manufacturers produce little pills, mobile makers produce mechanical devices that provide connectivity—but for a customer, a beauty cream becomes a hope to look young and beautiful, vitamins become a hope for a healthier life and mobiles become status symbols.

According to Philip Kotler and Kevin Keller:

> "A product is anything that can be offered to a market for attention, acquisition, use or consumption that might satisfy a need or want. It includes physical objects, services, persons, place, organizations or ideas."

According to William J. Stanton:

> "A product is a set of tangible and intangible attributes, including packaging, colour, price, manufacturer's prestige, retailer's prestige, and manufacturer's and retailer's services, which the buyer may accept as offering want-satisfaction."

Therefore, it should be clear that a product is not only a bundle of physical and chemical attributes, but also includes various intangible attributes that have the potential to satisfy the present and future customer's needs and wants, and is received in exchange for money or money's worth. In addition to the physical good itself, other elements include packaging, branding, labeling, manufacturer's prestige, wholesaler's and retailers' prestige, guarantee, warranty, installation, after sales services, etc., which add tremendous value to the product. For example, a customer buying a car buys it for the prestige value, aesthetic value, comfort, features, guarantee, and warranty and after sale service network.

Composition of Product

Before getting into the various details it is important for us to understand the basic composition of a product. Generally speaking, a product is like an onion, which has various layers. As the top layer is peeled, the next layer comes out. In the same manner, a product has five layers or levels. At each layer or level, marketers add more customer value by adding some more features or services to the product. The various product levels have been listed out in Figure.

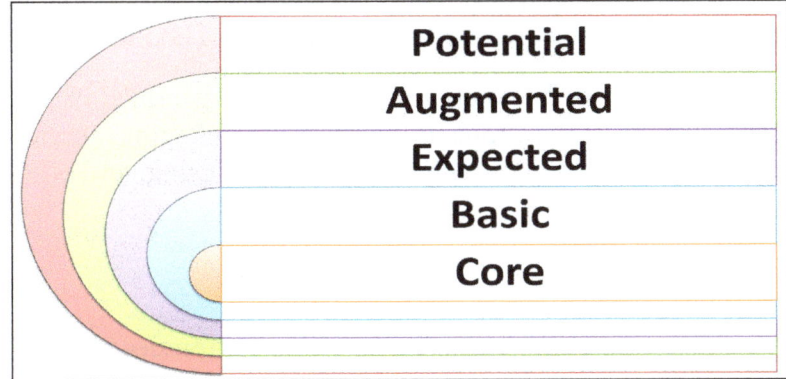

Figure: Composition of a product.

Level I-Core Product

The first level is the core product which provides the fundamental service or benefit which the customer is looking for. It is the genuine reason for which the product is purchased or the basic satisfaction a consumer wants from the purchase of that product. For example, a woman buying a lipstick is not buying simply lip colour or the physical and chemical attributes but is buying a hope or feeling of looking pretty. In other words, a product in its pure raw or natural form is called the core product, as in the case of tea leaves, which are freshly plucked from the tea gardens and after processing get converted into the core product.

Level II-Basic Product

At the second level, the marketer has to turn the core product into a basic product. Core product is generally in a very raw form, so marketers have to add a certain quality level, some more features, design the product's packaging, give it a label and a brand name to convert it to the basic level. For example, tea leaves plucked from the tea garden and processed simply in raw form is the core product, but when these leaves are graded, packed, labeled and are given a brand name, they get converted into the basic product.

Level III-Expected Product

At the third level, the marketer prepares an expected product, wherein another set of attributes and conditions are added to the product, to make it more valuable to the customer, for example the convenience of a product purchase and economical prices. As explained in the previous level, varieties of tea leaves are made available to the customer at convenient locations in the market with different levels of pricing, keeping the quality levels and the cost of packaging into account.

Level IV- Augmented Product

At the fourth level, the marketer prepares an augmented product that exceeds customer expectations. At this level, new improved features are added to the product, which are not being offered by any competitor. The tea producers launch various flavors of tea in the market, such as ginger tea, green tea, honey lemon tea, premium tea, etc. Thus, in today's scenario, competition essentially takes place at the product augmentation level because at this stage different features are added by marketers in their products to give their product a distinct identity than that of their competitors. This view has been supported by the renowned marketing author Theodore Levitt. According to him:

> "The new competition is not between what companies produce in factories, but between what they add to their factory output in the form of packaging, services, advertising, customer advice, financing, delivery arrangements, warehousing, and other things that people value."

Level V- Potential Product

At the fifth level stands the potential product. This is where companies try to add certain exclusive features in their product. They search for new, innovative and creative ways to satisfy customers and give their product a distinct identity from that of the competitor. Successful companies add benefits to their offering that not only satisfies the customer, but also surprises and delights them. Delighting is a matter of exceeding expectations. This is one of the reasons that banks provide their customers with e-banking or some other online services, so that they do not have to travel long distances to perform banking transactions. These are the added benefits which add tremendous value to the marketers' goods or services. Thus, a product can have all these levels, as it is introduced in the market.

Classification of Products

3 Main Types: Consumer Products, Industrial Products and Services

There are a number of useful ways of classifying products. One of the most basic ways was the different ways of making a journey. These included travelling in a car owned by the traveller, in a hired car, and by train, bus or plane. It was clear from this that the journey could be made by using purchased physical objects, i.e. the car, petrol and so on, or by purchasing the service offered by the car hire company or one of the organizations providing one of the alternative modes of transport.

This is an interesting example since although the use of a hire car or other transport provider involves purchasing a service; the use of the traveller's own car involves purchasing in addition to the essential physical objects at least two mandatory service products.

The first of these is vehicle insurance and the second is that offered by the Vehicle Licensing Authority which collects the Road Fund License Fee on behalf of the Government and issues the Road

Fund License or tax disc. In addition, the car user will usually require other services such as those offered by garages who supply and service cars, sell petrol and provide toilet facilities.

Thus while it would at first sight seem possible to separate products or product offerings into physical objects and services, in practice it is useful to see this as a continuum, with any specific product offering being either a service or a combination of a service and a physical object.

Another way in which products may be classified is by the type of customer. Some products such as heavy machinery, cooling towers, factories, ships and Lorries are with few exceptions purchased by industrial organizations. Such products can thus be classified as industrial products. Other products such as shoes, tea, visits to the cinema, and cans of soft drink and so on are typically purchased for use or consumption by individuals. These products are accordingly generally classified as consumer products.

Unlike industrial products which are only occasionally purchased by individuals, most consumer products are also purchased for use within organizations. Thus hotels need to buy essentially the same food and household products as are purchased for use in the home. The difference is the quantities in which these products are typically purchased. For instance, whereas toilet tissue might be purchased in packets of one to nine rolls for use in the home they could well be purchased by the 100 or 1000 rolls for a hotel or hotel chain.

Consumer Products

Consumer products are classified by how they meet the need for which they are purchased and by the way they are purchased rather than on the basis of the characteristics of the products themselves. The three main categories of consumer product are consumables, durables and services. Consumables are those products which are used up in the process of satisfying the need for which they were purchased. Thus a thirsty person who buys a bottle of Coca-Cola needs to drink the contents to benefit from that purchase. If it is a large bottle and only half is drunk the remainder may be saved for later or discarded.

Durables are purchased for the benefit they provide in themselves. Thus a bicycle purchased to take part in the London to Brighton cycle ride will, providing there are no mishaps, be essentially the same at the end of the journey as it was at the beginning or at any stage in between.

Providing it is looked after it could be used year after year for the same purpose. Over time it will suffer from use until eventually it will need to be overhauled or discarded and replaced. It may then be considered to have come to the end of its useful life. The third main category of consumer products is consumer services. These are essentially different from the other two categories. Consumable consumer products can be further divided into:

- Convenience goods,
- Specialty goods.

Convenience Goods

These represent the majority of frequently purchased consumer goods, bought with little effort or deliberation, e.g., newspapers, breakfast cereals, coffee, soap and cosmetics. These are all classic mass-market products which can be purchased from any supermarket or corner shop.

It is often useful to further differentiate products within this category using the following subcategories – staples, impulse, and emergency. Staples are those products which are usually bought as part of an everyday shopping-list. Impulse goods are those purchased on sight without being considered previously, e.g., special offers or the chocolates, sweets and magazines sold at supermarket checkouts.

Emergency goods are those consumable products for which buyers are likely to make a special visit to the shops when supplies run out or are low. Disposable nappies, milk, coffee, and cigarettes are all products likely to come within this category.

Specialty Goods

These are consumable products which can only be purchased from specialist retailers and which consumers select deliberately. Examples are prescription medicines, alcoholic beverages, and hobby consumables including DIY products such as paint, photographic processing chemicals and artist supplies. In a second category would be food products purchased for a special occasion or, as a gift, cosmetics and personal care products. Consumer durable products can be further divided into the following three categories:

- Shopping Goods: These are those products which are usually selected after 'shopping around' to compare price, quality, design or colour. Clothes, white goods (washing machines, refrigerators, etc.), brown goods (television, stereo systems, etc.), furniture, and motor vehicles are typical of products in this category. Buyers generally exhibit dissonance-reducing buying behaviour when purchasing this type of product.

- Specialty Goods: These are generally products which are only available from a limited number of outlets. Car spares, text books, foreign maps, specialist tools, lamp shades and musical instruments are examples of products in this category.

- Emergency Durable Goods: These are those products which buyers are likely to need without delay. Typical of this category would be replacement windscreens, exhausts and tyres.

Industrial Products

Industrial products, sometimes termed business products, are products bought by organizations manufacturing or supplying products or providing services. Unlike consumer goods, they are bought not for their own sake or for personal consumption, but in order to contribute to an organizational objective.

For the economist they are considered intermediate products or inputs, which mean that the demand for this type of product will ultimately depend upon that of the final market being served by the organization. This relationship is termed 'derived demand'. For this reason the markets for most types of industrial product are subject to greater fluctuations in demand and periodic cycles of activity than is usual for consumer products.

The major industrial product categories depend upon the relationship between the product and the purchasing organization. Thus, depending upon the user, a computer may be classified either as a capital equipment item or as an accessory. The importance of recognizing this difference will be seen in the detailed sections discussing these different categories.

Capital Plant and Equipment

This category includes those products which are required by an organization to carry out the objective for which it exists and which thereby increase the organization's revenue-generating capacity. Thus items of power station equipment such as boilers or turbine generator units come into this category for an electricity utility.

A power press, transfer or assembly line would be within this category for a vehicle manufacturer. Similarly an airliner such as an Airbus A300 would be a capital item for an airline since it would enable this organization to carry more passengers or freight and thus earn more revenue.

Accessories

These are also capital items but differ from plant and equipment in that accessories do not directly increase the capacity of the organization to carry out the objective for which it exists or by which it generates revenue. Thus investment by a vehicle manufacture in electricity generating plant may be cost-effective but since it does not increase the organization's capacity to manufacture vehicles it should be classed as an accessory. Likewise the airline purchasing a computer system to schedule passengers or a hanger in which to service their new Airbus A300s is investing in accessories not capital plant.

Recognizing the difference between capital plant and equipment and accessories is important to suppliers since organizations purchasing capital plant and equipment tend to be extremely knowledgeable regarding their requirements. These requirements will thus normally be specified very precisely and suppliers will be expected to comply with these specifications.

Accessories, in contrast, although often involving items of similar value to capital plant and equipment, are generally specified less rigorously and the specifications are more likely to be changed on the recommendation of the supplier. Clearly, by correctly classifying a product from the customer's point of view as either plant or equipment or as an accessory, a supplier can make an offer which is more likely to meet the customer's actual requirements.

Both of these product categories normally involve carefully prepared production plans, design investigations and trials, protracted supplier discussions and negotiations. Marketing such products involves direct links with prospective purchasers, specialist-to- specialist technical contacts, presale service, and often contractual relationships extending far beyond the installation and commissioning stage.

In marketing terms, equipment markets will be characterized by the number of competing manufacturers who deal directly with their major corporate customers and specialist stockholding dealers who serve the market at large.

Materials and Components

These represent the physical inputs to the production and delivery of the final product. This category includes raw materials, processed materials and components. Raw materials are often bought direct from domestic or overseas suppliers on long-term contracts. Processed materials such as chemical formulations, cloth or sheet steel are sourced either directly or through intermediaries as finished materials which are then used to manufacture the product being produced for instance detergents, vehicle components or clothing.

Contractual arrangements may be preferred by customers when justified by the volumes involved to ensure continuity of supply and quality standards. Promotional elements are unlikely to feature heavily in the marketing of materials, as standard grading systems may limit competition to differences in price, technical support and distribution arrangements.

Components vary from standard items such as nuts, bolts and other fasteners, valves, pumps and switches, to more specialist customised items such as fabrications and subassemblies. While standard items may be bought in by volume-contract arrangements, or multiple-sourced distributors, key components and customised parts may be subject to individual contracts.

Such subcontractor relationships increasingly involve close collaboration between customer and supplier. Following practices pioneered in Japan, increasingly this collaboration can include implementing JIT (just-in-time) systems, quality vetting programmes and single sourcing agreements. Unlike materials and components which form part of the product produced by the organization, supplies are those products which are used within the production process.

These include the materials used in production such as lubricants, abrasives and cleaning materials, office sundries such as paperclips and note pads, and a whole miscellany of other items needed for various functions within the organization such as the food supplied in the canteen and the refills needed to stock the vending machines. Generally these are standard, easily substituted, products purchased through intermediaries who often compete as much on the basis of the service provided as on price.

Services

Very few 'products' are purely 100 per cent service or 100 per cent tangible product. Usually they involve a mix of the two. Kotler suggests there are four categories of products:

- A pure service,
- A major service with accompanying minor goods and services,
- A tangible good with accompanying service,
- A pure tangible product.

Sometimes customer services are sub-classified as service products and product services. Service products are those directly offered to individuals such as hairdressing, healthcare, transportation, education and insurance, a pure service or major service component. Product services are those associated with a physical object such as car repairs, property repairs and plumbing services, each of these involving tangible goods.

Industrial and business service products can vary from those above where there is a legal requirement, such as accountants and civil aviation inspectors, to those providing peripheral services such as cleaners and the catering contractors who provide canteen services.

Some industrial service companies provide an essentially financial benefit, as, for instance, the contract car leasing companies who are often the legal owners of the cars provided by employers to their employees. Such companies have developed the service offered so that for their customer organizations it is significantly cheaper to lease these cars than it would be to own them.

However, Kotler's categories can apply and be used to enhance the benefit offered. For instance, servicing of key equipment and installations such as photocopiers or computers is often integral to the supply contract for the equipment. Pure services can be exemplified by technological developments which have created new industrial markets for advisory services in specialist fields such as expert-systems software development.

Like vehicle leasing, haulage and distribution services are likely to involve contract arrangements. Other specialist business services such as market research, advertising or management consultancy are likely to be selected and managed by the relevant functional managers. It is possible to put products and services on this model to produce a continuum of tangibility.

While it is generally accepted that the marketing of services involves fully appreciating those characteristics which are fundamental to this type of product, and often involves some element of a tangible product, it is useful to otherwise consider services as simply a specific product category. The key aspect of services is that they are intangible. There are three other distinctive features that must be considered:

- Inseparability: The fact that the production of a service takes place at the same time as its delivery.

- Perishability: Services cannot be stored or kept in a warehouse. Time is part of services and once that time has not been used then the service opportunity has gone.

- Variability: Because each delivery is unique there is no standardization of output. The product and delivery depend on the two parties involved at the time of delivery.

Services have to be considered in great detail when it comes to marketing. They are part of the total product offered to customers and can be a vital ingredient to gain advantage over competition.

Product Management

Product management is a way to organize the planning, production, marketing and other tasks related to the creation and distribution of a product. It involves the coordination of teams, data, processes, business systems and more. In reality, product management can be a complicated matter. There are a lot of moving parts in the creation of any product, regardless of its size. Without a methodology and proper tools to manage the many elements that must be tracked throughout the life cycle of the product, the risk of failure is greatly increased.

To understand product management and its challenges requires a deeper dive than a two sentence definition. There are, for example, complementary disciplines that can be part of product management, such as product development and product marketing. Their objective is to maximize sales revenues, market share and profit margins.

What is the Objective of Product Management?

The main objective of product management is the development of a new product or products. This product should be better than what is currently available, or at least be able to differentiate itself as unique, in order to be of value for the customer.

What determines whether the product is profitable and successful is the customer's reaction. While product management can vary in its function and the roles related to it, according to the size of the company, there is always a product manager to make certain that the objectives of the product are met. This can be a person or a group of people in the organization.

Product management doesn't only add to meet the objectives of the product and organization; it can also choose to remove something from the process, which is called an elimination decision. This includes a detailed report on the impact that this elimination will have on the whole business.

Product Mix

Product mix, also known as product assortment or product portfolio, refers to the complete set of products and/or services offered by a firm. A product mix consists of product lines, which are associated items that consumers tend to use together or think of as similar products or services.

Dimensions of a Product Mix

Width

Width, also known as breadth, refers to the number of product lines offered by a company. For example, Kellogg's product lines consist of: Ready-to-eat cereal, pastries and breakfast snacks, crackers and cookies and frozen/Organic/Natural goods.

Length

Length refers to the total number of products in a firm's product mix. For example, consider a car company with two car product lines (3-series and 5-series). Within each product line series are three types of cars. In this example, the product length of the company would be 6.

Depth

Depth refers to the number of variations within a product line. For example, continuing with the car company example above, a 3-series product line may offer several variations such as coupe, sedan, truck, and convertible. In such a case, the depth of the 3-series product line would be 4.

Consistency

Consistency refers to how closely related product lines are to each other. It is in reference to their use, production, and distribution channels. The consistency of a product mix is advantageous for firms attempting to position themselves as a niche producer or distributor. In addition, consistency aids with ensuring a firm's brand image is synonymous with the product or service itself.

Illustration of a Product Mix

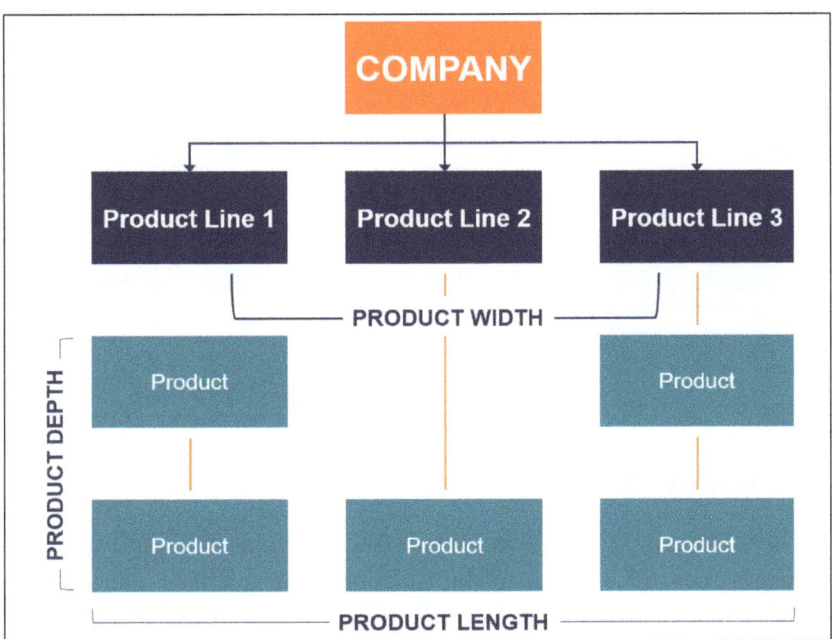

In the illustration above, the product mix shows a:

- Width of 3,
- Length of 5,
- Product line 1 depth of 2,
- Product line 2 depth of 1,
- Product line 3 depth of 2.

The mix is considered consistent if the products in all the product lines are similar.

Example of a Product Mix

Let us take a look at a simple product mix example of Coca-Cola. For simplicity, assume that

Coca-Cola oversees two product lines: soft drinks and juice (Minute Maid). Products classified as soft drinks are Coca-Cola, Fanta, Sprite, Diet Coke, Coke Zero, and products classified as Minute Maid juice are Guava, Orange, Mango, and Mixed Fruit.

The product (mix) consistency of Coca-Cola would be high, as all products within the product line fall under beverage. In addition, production and distribution channels remain similar for each product. The product mix of Coca-Cola in the simplified example would be illustrated as follows:

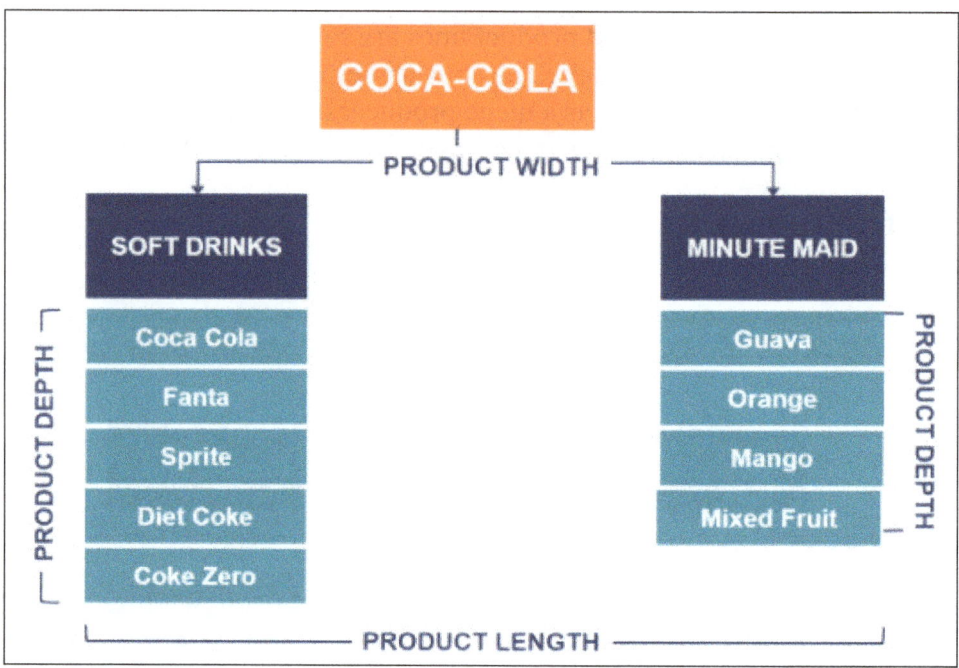

Importance of a Product Mix

The product mix of a firm is crucial to understand as it exerts a profound impact on a firm's brand image. Maintaining high product width and depth diversifies a firm's product risk and reduces dependence on one product or product line. With that being said, unnecessary or non-value adding product width diversification can hurt a brand's image. For example, if Apple were to expand its product line to include refrigerators, it would likely have a negative impact on their brand image with consumers. In regard to a firm expanding its product mix:

- Expanding the width can provide a company with the ability to satisfy the needs or demands of different consumers and diversify risk.

- Expanding the depth can provide the ability to readdress and better fulfill current consumers.

New Product Development

Developing new products is a must for all the organizations these days. All those who fail to develop new products are generally at a high risk of closure, because of changing customer's needs and wants, new technological innovations, shortened product life cycles, and increased competition from domestic as well as foreign competitors. Despite that fact, conceptualizing a new product is not an easy task as it involves tremendous efforts, time and money. Generally a very small percentage of products are truly innovative and new to the world, while a majority of the products are the modified or improved versions of the existing products. Some of the categories of the new products have been explained as under:

Reasons for Failure of New Products

When a new product is introduced in the market, the probability of its success is always limited. Utmost care is needed in developing new products because there are hundreds of examples of products which have failed in the market due to one or the other reason. Some of the important reasons are depicted in figure given as under:

Suggestions for New Improved Successful Products

Given all these challenges, it becomes very difficult for all the organizations to come up with new improved successful products. In order to be successful in the market it is important for them to follow certain guidelines, such as:

- To carefully define and assess the target market, enquire about the consumer's product requirements and benefits which they want.

- In the light of consumer information it becomes equally important to define the product concept clearly prior to its development.

- It is important to design a unique superior product giving high product advantage to the firm.

- Technological sophistication, efficient execution of policy at all the stages and market attractiveness plays a significant role.

- New-product development is most effective when there is teamwork among R&D, engineering, manufacturing, purchasing, marketing, and finance departments. All the departments should work in a coordinated manner looking at the various perspectives carefully.

So, it can be safely concluded that developing a new product calls for an integrated effort on the part of the management.

New Product Development Process

It is really difficult to come up with a new product idea, but it is equally important to first have something to sell – a product, a service or an idea and that 'something' must be developed carefully. There are certain stages through which every company has to go before arriving at the final product. Figure nicely depicts the stages to be followed.

As shown in the figure, the development of a new product proceeds through a series of seven stages that are listed below. During each stage, management must decide carefully whether to move on to the next stage, abandon the product, or seek additional information. While it is not necessary for all the companies to follow the step- by- step approach, but still it is always recommended, as this approach helps them in minimizing the risk of product failure at a later stage.

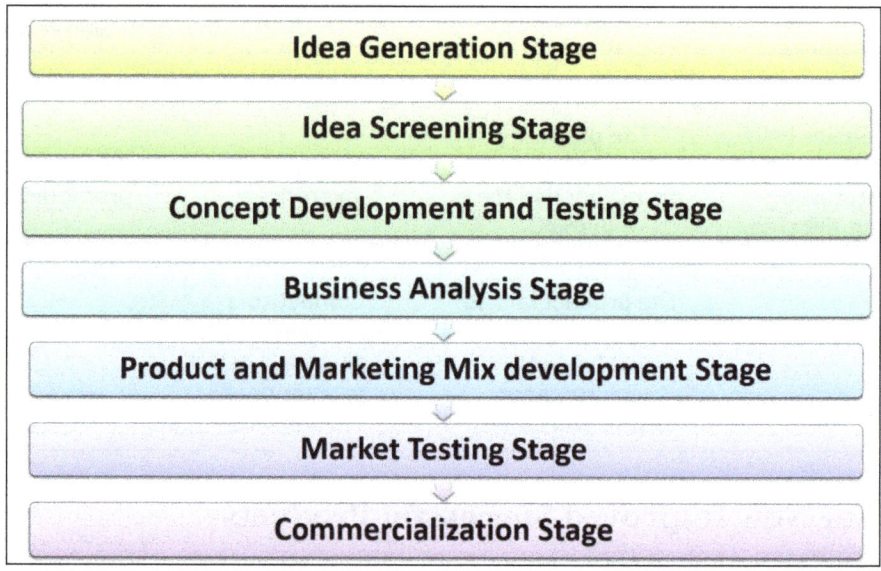

Step – 1: Idea Generation Stage

The first stage in the new product development process is to generate various ideas which can be later evaluated as potential product options. At this stage the focus is on inviting as many ideas as possible and from whatever source within or outside the organization, so that the manufacturer should not repent at a later stage that some ideas were not explored. Customer's needs and wants are the logical places to start in the search for new product ideas. Ideas can be generated by organizing focus group interviews with consumers, middlemen, feedback from sales personnel, employees' suggestions, and acquiring knowledge about competitor's product strategies through various sources.

Step – 2: Idea Screening Stage

At this stage the ideas generated at stage one are critically evaluated by the senior management in order to select the most attractive option. While selecting the ideas, the opinion of people at various levels is sought so that the chances of committing an error can be reduced to the minimum. At the screening stage, the company must avoid two types of errors – a drop error, which occurs when the company dismisses an otherwise good idea, or a go- error, which occurs when the company permits a poor idea to move into the development and commercialization stage. The purpose of screening is to analyze the ideas carefully and avoid committing both the types of errors.

Step – 3: Concept Developments and Testing Stage

At this stage, few selected ideas are discussed at length with customers, distributors and the company employees by showing them a detailed concept note or a storyboard displaying drawings of product ideas, so that their suggestions can be incorporated while designing an excellent product. During discussions with everyone, an effort is made to elicit their response in terms of their likes and dislike of the concept, the various features to be included in the product, their level of interest in purchasing the product and the likely price they would like to pay for the product.

Step – 4: Business Analysis Stage

At this stage, when marketers are left with one or two options, lots of efforts are made by them to check out the commercial viability of those product ideas because no organization would like to move to the next stage with a loss-making proposition. Even though the idea still remains on paper, an effort is made by marketers to estimate the tentative market size or the expected market demand of the product, calculations are made regarding the estimated cost of manufacturing the product and the resultant sales and profit figures are calculated. It is at this stage that the ideas are discussed with the purchase and production department personnel. So that it should be convenient for them to arrange for the necessary raw materials, machinery and infrastructure to ensure a smooth production process.

Step – 5: Products and Marketing Mix Development Stage

Ideas passing through business analysis enter into product and marketing mix development stage. At this stage, with the help of the research and development department of the organization, the basic design of the product is prepared and certain prototypes of the idea are developed. Lots of functional tests are performed on these prototypes under laboratory and field conditions to check their performance levels and safety standards. Decisions regarding the other three Ps, namely, Price, Place, and Promotion are also taken at this stage. Once the prototype is ready, a representative group of customers are invited to the company premises and are shown the real product. They are also encouraged to discuss the pricing strategy and give their comments on the sample advertisements. Customer's suggestions at this stage help the company to arrive at appropriate marketing-mix decisions and the product is finally ready to be launched in the market.

Step – 6: Market Testing Stage

Products surviving up to step six are ready to be tested as real products in the market. At times when the marketers are confident about the success of the product after the concept testing stage, they can skip this stage but generally when their stakes are higher, they go for market testing before finally going for commercialization of their product. At this stage, the product is finally packed, priced, promoted and introduced in a small geographical area. The response of the consumers is sought from the test marketing area and the required adjustments are made in the various marketing-mix elements. Once finally approved by the larger segment of target customers, the product is ready to move to the seventh stage, i.e. commercialization.

Step – 7: Commercialization Stage

This is a stage where the product is ready to be introduced to a wider market. Some firms introduce the product in phases to different parts of the market. This allows the company to plan the production in a more controlled way and to fine tune the marketing mix as the product is distributed to new areas. But before the product is distributed to new areas, certain important decisions are taken such as:

- When to Introduce the Product (Timing): Marketers have to decide about the right time to introduce the product in the market at a large scale, keeping the time factor into account, such as the seasonal nature of the products, festivities and the flow of disposable income with consumers.

- Where to Introduce the Product (Geographical Distribution): Marketers decide about the geographic dimensions of the market, i.e. whether to launch the new product in a single locality, a specific region, several regions, national market or at the international market?

- To Whom to Target the Product (Target Market Prospects): Within the markets, where the products have been introduced, the company must target its distribution and promotion policy to the best prospect group of customers.

- How to Introduce the Product in the Market (Introductory Marketing Strategy): Companies must develop a plan for introducing the new product in the market. Various marketing mix decisions are taken carefully to introduce the product in a big way in the markets. Sometimes attractive introductory offers are made to attract present and potential customers towards the new product, such as distribution of free sample, buy-back guarantee, etc.

Finally to conclude, it can be said that it is very important for marketers to follow all these stages carefully if they want to avoid costly mistakes at a future date.

Brands

While it seems an easy task to define 'product', the same cannot be said about a 'brand'. There are varying definitions of brands, some being narrow in scope and some encompassing a lot more in the periphery of what constitutes a brand.

One may understand a brand as just a promise that a firm makes to its customers. It tells customers what they can expect from the firm and how the firm's offering is different from its competitors. In more tangible terms, brands may be seen as just a name, logo or symbol – these in fact are just the visual manifestation of the concept of a brand. In other words, this is the surface of what a brand is, and digging deeper, one can understand the many more nuances that brands carry.

The American Marketing Association (AMA) defines brand as 'a brand is a name, term, sign, symbol, or design, or a combination of them, intended to identify the goods and services of one seller or group of sellers and to differentiate them from those of competition.'

This definition encompasses a number of aspects of a brand. However, packaging, distinctive colour, sound, smell or design are also features that are seen as part of what a brand means. It would not be incorrect to say that brands actually reside in consumers' minds – it is their perception of the above mentioned features that imparts meaning to a brand. Brands are made up of consumers' associations and experiences. They cannot be defined as a purely tangible concept. Evolved brands are more than mere utility giving objects – they become an important part of users' lives and consumers form deep rooted relationships with preferred brands. Brands are known to provide comfort to users, who sometimes imbue them with human like qualities.

Therefore brands serve to satisfy needs of consumers at many different levels – unlike products that are seen as undifferentiated functional objects. Of course a sound product lies at the heart of a good brand. However, brands may differentiate themselves on a non-product basis too. This is the case when apart from the product, the firm is able to excel in aspects like service accompanying the brand, distribution and logistics system, innovating advertising and marketing campaigns or simply creative packaging.

What All can be Branded?

Traditionally, only tangible consumer products were branded. However, with the growth of service sector and advent of competition, even services started to be branded. Service marketers wanted to woo customers to their businesses and branding was a smart way to create distinction amongst players in the same service industry. In fact, branding is even more important in the services sector, with the lack of a tangible product to distinguish between firms – it is the firm's way of providing the service, its staff, its values and culture that creates a distinct identity for a service firm.

The growing realization of usefulness and understanding of branding as a concept means that now, almost everything is branded. Right from consumer products like soaps, detergents or snacks or commodities like flour, pulses, oil, water to restaurants, hotels, grocery chains, medicines and even gold jewelry, everything is sold under a brand name. In fact, places are branded too campaigns like Incredible India or Malaysia. Truly Asia have worked wonders to promote tourism to these countries. People can be branded too the idea is to create certain kinds of associations with a person and make them popular – celebrities and politicians take advantage of such person-branding. So essentially, anything and everything can be branded since what branding does is impart identity and recognition to the object being branded.

Brand Elements

Brands are identified by their brand elements – these are the visible aspects of the brand that sets it apart from others. They include:

- The brand name,

- The brand logo,

- Packaging and colour,

- Jingles and slogans,

- Celebrities & characters associated.

Each of these elements needs to be chosen carefully as they convey special meaning about the brand to customers. They are also to be evolved over time, as per requirement of the brand. Brand elements should be flexible in this sense. They also need to be adaptable to various products sold under the same brand name. Needless to say, brand elements need to be attractive to consumers – they must stay with the consumer to be recalled at the time of purchase choice. Simplicity is another virtue they should ideally have, as it would help memorization and recall. Most brand elements are also protected by trademarks and copyrights so as to prevent any encroachment by competition.

The brand name is one of the most important decisions the brand manager needs to take. It is what remains with the brand throughout its life. Most names are chosen to convey special qualities of the brand, like Ray-Ban. They may be chosen to represent names of the founder or the firm, for instance Levi's Strauss. Names impart strong symbolic meaning to brands, for example, Surf or Tide as detergent brand names conjure images of white water washing up on a beach. In fact, brands create stories around how the brand name came into being and that becomes part of the brand's lore.

The brand's logo and packaging is a shortcut to recognition. In countries like India, where a large section of the population cannot read or write, it is these elements that help them form a connection with the brand. Logos can create feelings for the brand and also help convey its essence – for instance, the Fedex logo has an arrow cleverly built into the name, which reminds customers about its fast and reliable courier services. It is not just the name, but also the way it is written that creates meaning – a bold, solid font creates a sense of consistency, a fancy cursive font may invoke feelings of delicateness and beauty.

Colour has special connotations too – yellow evokes clarity, white stands for purity, red for energy, blue for dependability and so on. Packaging of the brand, aside from being utility oriented (that is, helping consume and store the product) also creates a distinction for the product through its shape and size. For instance, inverted shampoo bottles or hourglass shaped soft drink bottles help instant recognition, apart from ease of handling and consumption.

Jingles and slogans breathe life into the brand. Slogans are short, sometimes persuasive or provocative phrases that also help convey what the brand stands for. Slogans can be changed periodically, to reflect a brand's current philosophy, or the way they are presented through advertising and marketing can be changed to incorporate new meaning to the same slogan. Some slogans have been so memorable that they have survived in people's minds for many years together. Jingles too help create memorability- usually rhyming and attached to a piece of music, they can be stuck in consumers' minds where they can't help but hum a jingle and inadvertently, become advertisers for the brand. Characters are also an important brand element   they provide animate form to the idea of a brand.

Characters like the Amul girl demonstrate that using characters can be a hugely successful marketing strategy – of course the catch is to remain relevant and connect with consumers, which the

Amul girl has managed admirably over the years. The Marlboro Man and Ronald McDonald create feelings of ruggedness and fun for Marlboro cigarettes and McDonald's respectively. Celebrity endorsements also add appeal to a brand and they are chosen for their favourable qualities in the hope of transferring them on to the brand. Celebrity endorsements can create instant likeability and popularity for the brand. However, there is always the risk of a celebrity falling in public eye, and tarnishing the brand image in the process too. Therefore brand elements together represent what the brand stands for, and combined with a strong product/service offering, make for a successful brand.

Importance of Brands

Advantages of Brands to Firms

Brands are immensely valuable assets for firms. Studies have consistently shown that brands play an important role in financial performance of a firm. Successful brands can be used to steer the firm into profits and high earnings for years together. It is brands that help create the intangible asset of goodwill in firms' balance sheets. Brands are purchased and sold too, resulting in major earnings and market share improvements.

Brands allow firms to charge higher prices for their offerings, vis-à-vis non-branded ones. This is due to the advantage of distinction that brands provide to the underlying offering. While a number of products may compete on similar features, performance, price, design, distribution channels and associated service, it is the brand perception that may ultimately tilt the customer in favour of a particular offering. It is not possible to pinpoint the reasons for higher prices of brands – the complete experience of owning and using a particular brand and the prestige that comes along are justification enough. Brands such as Apple have proven this with almost all its products.

The competitive advantage that brands offer is really hard to imitate, and that secures successful brands from competition. Nonetheless, firms protect their brands legally through copyrights and patents. Brands represent the firm's promise to its consumers – what they can expect from the firm in terms of product and service, and in this sense, they help communicate to buyers a consistent image of what the firm stands for. They are an important tool for influencing consumer behavior.

Advantages of Brands to Consumers

For customers, brands first of all perform the function of identifying the seller. As mentioned earlier, in this regard, they stand as a pact between the buyer and seller – a pact of said quality, price and features. With brand identification there comes a whole host of associations consumers have with the brand – its overall image, price fairness, quality, durability, user-friendliness and so on. These associations are invoked anytime consumers see a brand's visible elements – its logo, symbol, name or distinctive colour. This is what brand managers ideally desire too – once consumers have a range of positive associations with the brand, it starts to become more than just the offering it represents.

Basically, when consumers buy trusted brands, they buy peace of mind – their expectations have been set by what the brand chooses to communicate about itself and on purchase, a consumer is assured of all those benefits. In this way, brands also help reduce the time and money spent in searching for the right product for consumers. Brands reduce the risks associated with purchase of the product or service.

Consumers of branded products can even derive their sense of identity from the brand – to the society; they are what brands they consume. In fact, certain brands are preferred only for the image they convey of the consumer to the society.

Brand Management

Brand management is a function of marketing that makes use of strategies and techniques to analyse and plan how the brand is perceived in the market. It aims to increase the overall perceived value of the brand in the long run and build a loyal customer base through positive brand associations.

Importance of Brand Management

The main aim of brand management is to build, measure, and control brand equity – making a brand to have its own value which, when associated with the product, increases its overall value both monetarily and non-monetarily. In this era of extensive competition where different companies sell almost similar products, a brand is what makes a difference. It helps in positioning the offering in a unique way that provides the company with marketplace advantage and boosts the value of a product.

Creating a brand out of the product not only personifies it, but it also creates an experience which stays in the mind of the customers. They recall the experience whenever provided with certain triggers related to the product niche or product usage. Creating such an experience around the product not only helps in increasing its sales but it also helps in extending the product line in future.

The Intangibles of Brand Management

While the tangible elements of the brand management include the product and its price, packaging, shape, colour, etc., the intangible element that also plays a major part in selling it and building a long term experience are:

- Brand Equity: It's the value of the brand as a separate asset.

- Brand Image: It is an aggregate of beliefs, ideas, and impressions that a customer holds regarding the brand.

- Brand Positioning: Positioning is the unique space a brand occupies in the brains of the customers.

- Brand Associations: The images and symbols associated with a brand or a brand benefit.

- Other Brand Elements: Elements like brand personality, communication elements, etc.

Functions of Brand Management

Brand management forms a subset of marketing management. It deals with the overall brand development right from the birth of the brand until the time it ceases to exist. The functions of brand management include but are not limited to the following:

- Identifying the ideal target market, understanding what motivates them to choose one product over others and positioning the brand in the same domain.

- Developing an ideal brand message which resonates both with the needs of the target market and with the value proposition of the offering.

- Communicating the brand promise to the customers by making use of almost every possible touch point.

- Making efforts to build brand equity and measure it from time to time.

- Managing the brand architecture and making sure sub-brands structure and communication align with the master brand structure and communication policies.

- Building the brand identity and making sure that it aligns with the brand image in the market.

- Handling brand communication in the market.

- Anticipating and accommodating new brand identity needs.

Strategic Brand Management Process

Brand management aims at building brand equity and making it grow over time. The strategic brand management process revolves around this aim. This process involves planning, executing, and controlling marketing and branding strategies and activities to build, measure, and control brand equity. The strategic brand management process involves the following steps:

Identifying and Establishing Brand Positioning and Values

The first step of the brand management process involves the brand manager to identify an untapped yet beneficial position in the market which can be tapped to counter the existing competition and build a good brand image for the long run. This is usually done using mental maps and positioning maps. Once identified, the brand management team then works on building a core brand identity, brand associations, and brand essence.

Planning and Implementing Brand Marketing Programs

Once the positioning strategy is set, the next step involves the brand manager to actually plan and implement strategies to position the brand as planned. It further involves three steps:

- Choosing the brand elements brand name, logo, symbols, characters, packing, and tagline. These are usually the first things customers will come across before actually trying the product.

- Choosing the marketing activities and supporting marketing programs and the way the brand is integrated into them.

- Leveraging secondary associations like the country of origin, the channel of distribution, etc. These are usually other entities that have their own associations. They result in lending their own associations to add to the planned positioning.

Measuring and Interpreting Brand Performance

The next step involves designing and implementing a brand equity measurement system which helps the brand managers measure and manage brand profitability. A brand equity measurement system is a set of research procedure designed to provide timely, accurate and actionable information about the concerned brand to the brand managers so they can make best possible tactical and strategically decisions to benefit the brand in the short as well as the long run. Implementing this system requires marketers to complete these three steps:

- Conducting Brand Audits: A brand audit is a comprehensive examination of the brand's current position in the market with respect to its competitors. It involves assessing the strengths and weaknesses of the brands and providing suggestions on how to strengthen it.

- Designing Brand Tracking: Brand tracking involves the collection of brand-related information directly from the consumers on a routine basis over time, to measure the present health of a brand, both in terms of consumers' usage of it and what they think about it.

- Establishing a Brand Equity Management System: It is a set of organizational processes designed to improve how the brand equity concept is understood within the company. This framework identifies sources and outcomes of brand equity and permits tactical guidelines as to how to build, measure, and manage brand equity.

Diverse Strategies for Marketing

No two strategies of marketing are alike. Businesses often aim to outdo the other in marketing their products leading to an assortment of marketing strategies. This chapter's focus is on the diverse marketing strategies like promotional merchandises, sales promotions, advertisements, branding and publicity stunts employed by companies to promote their respective products and services.

Promotional Merchandise

Promotional merchandise, promotional items, promotional products, product media, promotional gifts, or advertising gifts, sometimes nicknamed swag, are articles of merchandise (often branded with a logo or slogan) used in marketing and communication programs. They are given away to promote a company, corporate image, brand, or event at trade shows, conferences, and as part of guerrilla marketing campaigns.

History

The first known promotional products in the United States are commemorative buttons dating back to the election of George Washington in 1789. During the early 19th century, there were some advertising calendars, rulers, and wooden specialties, but there was no organized industry for the creation and distribution of promotional items until later in the 19th century.

Jasper Meek, a printer in Coshocton, Ohio, is considered by many to be the originator of the industry when he convinced a local shoe store to supply book bags imprinted with the store name to local schools. Henry Beach, another Coshocton printer and a competitor of Meek, picked up on the idea, and soon the two men were selling and printing marble bags, buggy whips, card cases, fans, calendars, cloth caps, aprons, and even hats for horses.

In 1904, 12 manufacturers of promotional items got together to found the first trade association for the industry. That organization is now known as the Promotional Products Association International or PPAI, which currently has more than 10,000 global members. PPAI represents the promotional products industry of more than 22,000 distributors and approximately 4,800 manufacturers.

The UK and Ireland promotional merchandise industry formally emerged as corporate marketing became more sophisticated during the late 1950s. Before this companies may have provided occasional gifts, but there was no recognised promotional merchandise industry. The real explosion in the growth of the promotional merchandise industry took place in the 1970s. At this time an ever increasing number of corporate companies recognised the benefits gained from promoting their corporate identity, brand or product, with the use of gifts featuring their own logo. In the early years the range of products available were limited; however, in the early 1980s demand grew from distributors for a generic promotional product catalogue they could brand as their own and then leave with their corporate customers.

In later years these catalogues could be over-branded to reflect a distributor's corporate image and distributors could then give them to their end user customers as their own. In the early years promotional merchandise catalogues were very much sales tools and customers would buy the products offered on the pages.

In the 1990s new catalogue services emerged for distributors from various sources. In the nineties there was also the creation of 'Catalogue Groups' who offered a unique catalogue to a limited geographical group of promotional merchandise distributor companies. Membership of a Catalogue Group could also offer improved buying terms, a network of fellow distributor companies, & provide other support services. Examples of a Catalogue Group is Trade Only Spectrum Catalogue, Page Group and the Envoy Group, offering discounted products to a select group of distributors who have all been in the industry for over three years. Members of the Envoy Group have regional exclusivity as one of their perks providing some protection to the low barrier to entry of the market.

Up until the 1990s the industry had a peak season in which the majority of promotional products were sold. The season featured around Christmas & the giving of gifts. This changed significantly in the early 1990s as Christmas gifts became less appropriate in a multicultural Britain. Corporate companies were also becoming more inventive in their marketing and were now using promotional merchandise throughout the year to support the promotion of brands, products & events. In the early 21st century the role of a promotional merchandise catalogue started to change, as it could no longer fully represent the vast range of products in the market place. By 2007, catalogues were being mailed to targeted customer lists, rather than the blanket postal mailings that had taken place before. The catalogue had now become seen more as a 'business card' demonstrating the concept of what a company did, rather than a critical sales tool. In 2009 published results from research involving a representative group of distributor companies, which indicated the usage of hard copy catalogues was expected to fall up to 25% in 2010.

Distributor companies are experts in sourcing creative promotional products. Traditionally, to ensure that they had an effective manufacturer network, they kept themselves aware of the trade product ranges available from mailings received from manufacturers themselves and by attending trade exhibitions across the world, for example the Trade Only National Show in the UK, the Promotional Product Service Institute (PSI) show in Europe and the Promotional Products Association International (PPAI) Show in Las Vegas, NV.

In 2004, the way the trade sourced promotional products began to change with the launch an online trade sourcing service, which united distributors with manufacturers worldwide. This service is purely for vetted trade promotional merchandise distributor companies and is not available to corporate end user companies.

By 2008 almost every distributor had a website demonstrating a range of available promotional products. Very few offer the ability to order products online mainly due to the complexities surrounding the processes to brand the promotional products required.

Sourcing

In the USA, Canada, the UK and Ireland, companies and corporations mainly purchase their merchandise through promotional merchandise distributor companies. In the United States and Canada, these distributors are called "Promotional Consultants" or "promotional product distributors".

Promotional products by definition are custom printed with a logo, company name or message usually in specific PMS colors. Distributors help end-users gather artwork in the correct format, and in some cases also create artwork for end-users. Distributors then request the artwork from the manufacturers, printers or suppliers.

Many distributors operate on the internet and/or in person. Many suppliers wish not to invest in the staffing to service end-users' needs, which is the purpose of merchandise distributor companies.

Products and Uses

Swiss parking disk (early 1970s). Selected arrival time shows at the left window, departure at the right. Other side of disk is used for afternoon parking. Disk was a sales promotion for UBS bank.

Promotional merchandise is used globally to promote brands, products, and corporate identity. They are also used as giveaways at events, such as exhibitions and product launches. Promotional products can be used for non-profit organizations to promote their cause, as well as promote certain events that they hold, such as walks or any other event that raises money for a cause.

Almost anything can be branded with a company's name or logo and used for promotion. Common items include t-shirts, caps, keychains, posters, bumper stickers, pens, mugs, koozies, or mouse pads. The largest product category for promotional products is wearable items, which make up more than 30% of the total. Eco-friendly promotional products such as those created from recycled materials and renewable resources have been experiencing a significant surge in popularity.

Most promotional items are relatively small and inexpensive, but can range to higher-end items; for example celebrities at film festivals and award shows are often given expensive promotional items such as expensive perfumes, leather goods, and electronics items. Companies that provide expensive gifts for celebrity attendees often ask that the celebrities allow a photo to be taken of them with the gift item, which can be used by the company for promotional purposes. Other companies provide luxury gifts such as handbags or scarves to celebrity attendees in the hopes that the celebrities will wear these items in public, thus garnering publicity for the company's brand name and product.

Brand awareness is the most common use for promotional items. Other objectives that marketers use promotional items to facilitate include employee relations and events, tradeshow traffic-building, public relations, new customer generation, dealer and distributor programs, new product introductions, employee service awards, not-for-profit programs, internal incentive programs, safety education, customer referrals, and marketing research.

Promotional items are also used in politics to promote candidates and causes. Promotional items as a tool for non-commercial organizations, such as schools and charities are often used as a part of fund raising and awareness-raising campaigns. A prominent example was the livestrong wristband, used to promote cancer awareness and raise funds to support cancer survivorship programs and research.

Using promotional merchandise in Guerrilla Marketing involves branding in such a way as to create a specific visual effect, attracting more attention.

The giving of corporate gifts vary across international borders and cultures, with the type of product given often varying from country to country.

Promotional merchandise is rarely bought directly by corporate companies from the actual manufacturers of the promotional products. A manufacturer's expertise lies in the physical production of the products, but getting a product in front of potential customers is a completely different skill set and a complex process. Within the UK & Ireland promotional merchandise industry a comprehensive network of promotional merchandise distributor companies exist. A promotional merchandise distributor is defined as a company who "has a dedicated focus to the sale of promotional merchandise to end users". (An 'end user' is a corporate company or organisation that purchases promotional merchandise for their own use.) These distributor companies have the expertise to not only take the product to market, but are also to provide the expert support required. The unique aspect of promotional merchandise is that on most occasions the product is printed with the logo, or brand, of a corporate organisation. The actual manufacturers rarely have the set up to actually print the item. Promotional merchandise distributor companies are expert in artwork and printing processes. In addition to this the promotional merchandise distributors also provide full support in processing orders, artwork, proofing, progress chasing & delivery of promotional products from multiple manufacturing sources.

Trade Associations

In the UK, the industry has two main trade bodies, Promota (Promotional Merchandise Trade Association) founded in 1958, and the BPMA (British Promotional Merchandise Association) established in 1965. These trade associations represent the industry and provide services to both manufacturers & distributors of promotional merchandise. The BPMA provides a range of services including market research into the UK promotional merchandise industry. Since 2010 the BPMA has partnered with Trade Only, A UK company that organizes the primary UK Trade Show for the Promotional Product Industry, this takes place at the Ricoh Arena in Coventry usually the third week of January. The BPMA host an awards dinner and banquet on the middle night of the exhibition which is called the Trade Only National Show.

In the United States, PPAI (the Promotional Products Association International) is the not for profit association, offering the industry's largest tradeshow (The PPAI Expo), as well as training, online member resources, and legal advocacy. Another organization, the Advertising Specialty Institute, promotes itself as the largest media and marketing organization serving the advertising specialty industry.

In Europe, the existing EPPA will be replaced by a new organization setup by the key countries welcoming all other countries to join. The new umbrella organization will be called EPMO or PME (Product Media Europe).

Top Promotional Products Companies in the United States in 2013

According to the Advertising Specialty Institute's Counselor Magazine Awards, 2013's top 40 promotional product distributors are as follows:

2013 Rank	Distributors	2013 North American Sales
1	Staples Promo Products	$409.4 million
2	Proforma (Business)	$322.6 million
3	BDA	$286.4 million
4	Group II Communications/IMS	$257 million
5	4imprint	$256.5 million
6	Halo Branded Solutions	$186.2 million
7	Geiger	$184.8 million
8	National Pen Corp.	$153 million
9	Cintas	$145 million
10	AIA Corporation	$136 million
11	Branders.com	$131.1 million
12	Inner Workings	$114.1 million
13	WorkFlowOne	$100.6 million
14	American Solutions for Business	$99.5 million
15	Kaeser & Blair	$89.9 million
16	Tic Toc	$89.6 million
17	Banyan Incentives	$89.5 million
18	iPROMOTEu	$88.8 million
19	Summit Group	$88 million
20	EmbroidMe	$84.9 million
21	Jack Nadel International	$72.8 million

22	Myron	$71.3 million
23	Accolade Reaction Promotion Group	$70.7 million
24	MTM Recognition/Mid West Trophy	$69.1 million
25	G & G Outfitters	$66 million
26	The Vernon Company	$62.7 million
27	Brown & Bigelow	$60.8 million
28	Newton Manufacturing	$53.0 million
29	Boundless Network	$53 million
30	Artcraft Promotional Concepts	$52.8 million
31	Brand Alliance	$49.7 million
32	GMPC LLC	$44.2 million
33	Axis Promotions	$38.7 million
34	Safeguard Business Systems	$38.4 million
35	Touchstone	$35.8 million
36	Robertson Marketing Group	$34.2 million
37	Promo Shop	$34.1 million
38	CSE	$33.9 million
39	Positive Promotions	$33.7 million
40	Genumark Promotional Merchandise	$33.6 million

UK Market Statistics

According to research completed and published in 2008 the UK and Ireland promotional merchandise industry had an overall value of £850m. By mid 2009 the market had decreased to £712m as the UK's worst ever recession took grip. In July 2009 published research demonstrated that the top 10 promotional merchandise products were promotional pens, bags, clothing, plastic items, USB memory sticks, mugs, leather items, polyurethane conference folders, and umbrellas. The July research from a representation industry focus group also found that the current fastest growing product was hand sanitiser, which at the time coincided with the outbreak & growth of swine flu in the UK.

Australian and New Zealand Market Statistics

The Australasian Promotional Products Association (APPA) has conducted research to show the value of the promotional merchandise industry in Australia and New Zealand. According to APPA the industry has a turnover of AUD$1340m in Australia and NZ$144m in New Zealand APPA states the effectiveness of promotional merchandise is demonstrated by their research which shows that 52% of recipients of promotional merchandise say their impression of a company is more positive after receiving a promotional product, 76% recall the name advertised on the product, 55% keep the item for more than one year, nearly 50% of recipients use them daily and 52% of people do business with a company after receiving a promotional product. Other considerations and benefits of promotional merchandise include product definition, residual value marketing, accountability, "The Power of Purpose", product types, such as printing and artwork.

Promotional Items

Premium (Marketing)

Premiums are promotional items — toys, collectables, souvenirs and household products — that are linked to a product, and often require box tops, tokens or proofs of purchase to acquire. The consumer generally has to pay at least the shipping and handling costs to receive the premium. Premiums are sometimes referred to as prizes, although historically the word "prize" has been used to denote (as opposed to a premium) an item that is packaged with the product (or available from the retailer at the time of purchase) and requires no additional payment over the cost of the product.

Premiums predominantly fall into three categories, free premiums, self-liquidating premiums and in-or on-package premiums. Free premiums are sales promotions that involve the consumer purchasing a product in order to receive a free gift or reward. An example of this is the 'buy a coffee and receive a free muffin' campaign used by some coffee houses. Self-liquidating premiums are when a consumer is expected to pay a designated monetary value for a gift or item. New World's Little Shopper Campaign is an example of this: consumers were required to spend a minimum amount of money in order to receive a free collectible item. The in-or out-package premium is where small gifts are included with the package. The All Black collectors' cards found in Sanitarium Weet Bix boxes are a good example of this.

A successful premium campaign is beneficial to a company as it aids in establishing effective consumer relationships. A good campaign will:

- Strengthen early-stage consumer relationships.

- Encourage continued repeat business.

- Assist with targeting a specific audience or cohort of your target market.

- Create an emotional connection with your consumer by serving as a motivational driver to investigate further or purchase a product.

It's also important not to confuse premiums with other forms of sales promotions as there are a number of ways in which retailers can entice consumers.

History

Early Premiums

A merchant in Sudbury, New Hampshire, started giving out tokens made of copper when a customer made a purchase in 1793. The customer could then exchange the tokens for products in the store. This practice caught on and was used by many merchants throughout the 19th and 20th Century. Sweet Home laundry soap, a product of the B. A. Babbit Company, came with certificates that could be collected and redeemed for color lithographs. Beginning in 1872, the Grand Union Tea Company gave tickets to customers that could be exchanged for merchandise in the company catalog of Grand Union stores. The first trading stamps were introduced in 1891, the Blue Stamp Trading System, where stamps affixed to booklets could be redeemed for store products.

The Business of Premium Redemption

The Sperry and Hutchinson Company, started in 1896 in Jackson, Michigan, was the first third-party provider of trading stamps for various companies, including dry goods dealers, gas stations and later supermarkets. S&H Green Stamps, as the company was commonly called, opened its first redemption center in 1897. Customers could take their filled booklets of "green stamps" and redeem them for household products, kitchen items, and personal items. World War II put the trading stamps premium business on hold for a while, but when the G.I.s returned, the economy was robust, and the trading stamps business took off like a storm when numerous third-party companies created their own trading stamp programs to offer to supermarkets and other retailers. The bottom fell out of the trading stamp business in 1965, when supermarkets stopped issuing stamps altogether and started spending more money to advertise lower prices. Trading stamps have gone by the wayside of the modern retail marketing method of loyalty cards used widely in supermarkets where, instead of premiums, customers benefit from savings and convenience through coupon-free discounts.

Children's Premiums

Kellogg's Corn Flakes had the first cereal premium with The Funny Jungleland Moving Pictures Book. The book was originally available as a prize that was given to the customer in the store with the purchase two packages of the cereal. But in 1909, Kelloggs changed the book give-away to a premium mail-in offer for the cost of a dime. Over 2.5 million copies of the book were distributed in different editions over a period of 23 years.

At the beginning of the Second World War, radio was a big player in the promotion and distribution of premiums, usually toys that were closely related to the radio program. There were many radio shows that offered premiums to their listeners, but Captain Midnight was one of the best known. The early sponsor of Captain Midnight was Skelly Oil, and parents could get forms to mail-in for radio premiums at the gas stations. Later, Ovaltine became the sponsor of Captain Midnight, and it continued the premiums through advertising on the labels and foil tops of Ovaltine that could be collected to exchange for Captain Midnight premiums and offering membership to the "Secret Squadron".

Premiums Hit Home

Betty Crocker products, owned by General Mills, had one of the best-known premium programs when the company started inserting coupons in bags of flour in 1929 which consumers could collect and use to purchase Oneida flatware at a reduced price. In 1932, the popular coupon program was improved so that consumers could redeem coupons for an entire set of flatware — the pattern was called "Friendship". Beginning in 1937, the coupons were printed on the outside of the box with point values and could be redeemed through the Betty Crocker Catalog in exchange for cookbooks, kitchenwares, and home accessories, as the box tops stated, for 25 to 75 percent savings. To avoid confusion with cents-off coupons, the premium program was renamed "Betty Crocker Catalog Points" in 1992. General Mills retired the Betty Crocker Catalog in December 2006 and ended the premium program after 75 years. (Now that the premium program is no longer in effect, consumers can clip "Box Tops for Education" that are printed on Betty Crocker products to help schools pay for educational supplies.)

Premiums in the 21st Century

Premiums have come a long way since the 19th century and although they are rarely referred to as "premium campaigns", the concept itself is still very much relevant to today's marketing professionals. Let's look at New World's Little Shopper promotion implemented by Foodstaffs in 201. The promotion called for customers to spend a minimum of $40 in store, in order to receive one of 44 free mini grocery items. The grocery items were identical, miniature replicas of actual products found within the supermarket. The brands of the products in which were represented in the campaign had paid Foodstaffs to be included.

In taking this approach, Foodstaffs created an opportunity for its suppliers to also take advantage of brand encounters targeting consumers who may not have necessarily been aware of their products. The use of persuasive communication techniques, i.e, television and radio advertisements created positive attitude changes amongst shoppers who may not have necessarily been loyal to a particular supermarket, aiding the company to expand their consumer reach and market share. The Little Shopper promotion also created a buzz amongst the younger generations with reports of parents succumbing to the 'pester-powers' of their child's fear of missing out.

The return on investment for the Little Shoppers 'premiums' campaign was as much tangible as it was financial. It also left a lasting impression on consumers even after the campaign had closed. Media reported on countless social media posts and TradeMe listings from consumers attempting to buy or swap the collectables in order to complete their set. The promotion also led to creative spin-offs with consumers upcycling the miniature products for wearable art competitions, again expanding Foodstaffs consumer reach.

The Little Farmers of Kissanpur is another highly successful premium campaign run by the Indian Ketchup brand Kissan. The campaign placed 22nd on the 2015 WARC list of the world's 100 best marketing campaigns. The brands tagline 'made with real tomatoes' was brought to life inside the consumer's home. By redesigning the products packaging to be more effective and of use to the consumer, the company designed a new bottle top. The new bottle top included tomato seeds in which consumers were encourage to plant in order to grow their own Kissan tomato plant. In addition to providing the means to grow your own plant, Kissan followed up with a competition giving children who grew the best plants the opportunity to feature on the bottles. WARC reported that consumption of the brand grew to over 2.5 times the rate of the category.

Premiums in the Digital World

It's pretty safe to say that the rise in online consumer purchasing is showing no signs of slowing. Of the 23,000 shoppers surveyed across the world, 54% stated that they frequently buy products online and 34% agreed that their mobile phone will become their main purchasing tool. The digital disruption in this space is enabling consumers and transforming marketing practice. Marketing professionals are being forced to reconsider how their company and product information is presented to the digital world. The free download of an eBook is a common premium campaign, but companies like Flossie.com stepped it up a notch when they offered free credit in exchange for app downloads. The digital era has also opened the doors for the online gaming industry. It is no longer unusual to find offers to free game downloads or free game trials accompanying new gaming purchases.

The demonstrated versatility of the premium marketing concept over the years is a firm indicator that this is one marketing tool that is likely to be around for many more years to come.

Legality

Whilst the law in the United States and the United Kingdom governing premiums is relatively lax, it is comparatively stricter in several other countries. Belgium, Germany, and Scandinavia have strict consumer protection laws regulating the use of premiums. In Argentina, Austria, Norway, and Venezuela, the law governing premiums is so strict that they are effectively banned. In Japan, the value of a premium is restricted to being no more than 10% of the value of the product that is purchased in order to obtain it. In Finland, it is illegal to describe a premium as a free gift. In France, premiums may not be made conditional upon the purchase of a third product.

Prize (Marketing)

Prizes are promotional items—small toys, games, trading cards, collectables, and other small items of nominal value—found in packages of brand-name retail products (or available from the retailer at the time of purchase) that are included in the price of the product (at no extra cost) with the intent to boost sales. Collectable prizes produced (and sometimes numbered) in series are used extensively—as a loyalty marketing program—in food, drink, and other retail products to increase sales through repeat purchases from collectors. Prizes have been distributed through bread, candy, cereal, chips, crackers, laundry detergent, margarine, popcorn, and soft drinks. The types of prizes have included comics, fortunes, jokes, key rings, magic tricks, models (made of paper or plastic), pin-back buttons, plastic mini-spoons, puzzles, riddles, stickers, temporary tattoos, tazos, trade cards, trading cards, and small toys (made from injection molded plastic, paper, cardboard, tin litho, ceramics, or pot metal). Prizes are sometimes referred to as "in-pack" premiums, although historically the word "premium" has been used to denote (as opposed to a prize) an item that is not packaged with the product and requires a proof of purchase and/or a small additional payment to cover shipping and/or handling charges.

History

Smokers Become Collectors

Some of the earliest prizes were cigarette cards — trade cards advertising the product (not to be confused with trading cards) that were inserted into paper packs of cigarettes as stiffeners to protect the contents. Allen and Ginter in the U.S. in 1886, and British company W.D. & H.O. Wills in 1888, were the first tobacco companies to print advertisements and, a couple of years later, lithograph pictures on the cards with an encyclopedic variety of topics from nature to war to sports — subjects that appealed to men who smoked. By 1900, there were thousands of tobacco card sets manufactured by 300 different companies. Children would stand outside of stores to ask customers who bought cigarettes if they could have their card. Following the success of cigarette cards, trade cards were produced by manufacturers of other products and included in the product or handed to the customer by the store clerk at the time of purchase. Other inserts in tobacco included tin litho prizes, called tobacco tags (in plug tobacco), and tobacco silks (popular from 1910 to 1916) that could be collected to put in quilts were inserted in or attached to tobacco tins and sometimes catalogued as cigarette cards. World War II put an end to cigarette card production due to limited paper resources, and after the war cigarette cards never really made a comeback. After that collectors of prizes from retail products took to collecting tea cards in the UK and bubble gum cards in the US.

The Home Run of Prizes

The first baseball cards were trade cards featuring the Brooklyn Atlantics produced in 1868 by Peck and Snyder, a sporting goods company that manufactured baseball equipment. In 1869, Peck and Snyder trade cards featured the first professional team, the Red Stockings. Most of the baseball cards around the beginning of the 20th century came in candy and tobacco products produced by such companies as Breisch-Williams confectionery company of Oxford, Pennsylvania, American Caramel Company, the Imperial Tobacco Company of Canada, and Cabañas, a Cuban cigar manufacturer. In fact it is a baseball set, known as the T206 tobacco card set, issued from 1909 to 1911 in cigarette and loose tobacco packs through 16 different brands owned by the American Tobacco Company that is considered by collectors to be the most popular set of cigarette cards. A T206 Honus Wagner card sold on April 6, 2013 for $2.1 million in an online auction, the highest price paid for a card in a public sale. In 1933, Goudey Gum Company of Boston issued baseball cards with players biographies on the backs and was the first to put baseball cards in bubble gum. Bowman Gum of Philadelphia issued its first baseball cards in 1948 and became the biggest issuer of baseball cards from 1948 to 1952.

Topps in Cards

Topps Chewing Gum, Inc., now known as The Topps Company, Inc., started inserting trading cards into bubble gum packs in 1950 — with such topics as TV and film cowboy Hopalong Cassidy; "Bring 'em Back Alive" cards featuring Frank Buck on big game hunts in Africa; and All-American football cards. Topps introduced the topic of baseball in trading cards in 1951, and Sy Berger created the first modern baseball card, complete with playing record and statistics, produced by Topps in 1952. The 1952 Topps Mickey Mantle card is one of the most desirable baseball cards for collectors. Topps purchased the Bowman Gum company in 1956. Topps was the leader in the trading card industry from 1956 to 1980, not only in sports cards. Many of the top selling non-sports cards were produced by Topps, including Wacky Packages (1967, 1973–1977), Star Wars (beginning in 1977) and Garbage Pail Kids (beginning in 1985). Topps inserted baseball cards as prizes into packs of gum through 1981, when the gum became a thing of the past and the cards were sold without the gum.

Prize or Premium Coupon; or Both?

Bazooka Joe appeared on comics in Topps' Bazooka Bubble Gum beginning in 1953. There have been numerous kids (and adults) who have collected the Bazooka comics as prizes for over 50 years. Bazooka started issuing premium catalogs in 1956, and the comics prizes doubled as coupons that, when collected in certain quantities, could be exchanged for premiums, such as bikes, microphones, or plastic rings. Bazooka Bubble Gum has a successful loyalty marketing program, through the prizes (comics) and the premiums (mail-order merchandise). Over the years, Bazooka Bubble Gum has been shipped to over 100 different countries and it has been translated into over 50 different languages. Topps sells a half a billion pieces of Bazooka Bubble Gum a year.

"A Prize in Every Box"

The most famous use of prizes in the United States (and the word "prize" in this context) is Cracker Jack brand popcorn confection. Prizes have been inserted into every package of Cracker Jack continuously since 1912. A familiar jingle to people who watched television in the United States in the 1960s and '70s goes "Candy-coated popcorn, peanuts and a prize. That's what you get with Cracker Jack!" Cracker Jack sales are not what they used to be, with much more competition in the snack industry and less creative prizes. The most valuable prizes found in Cracker Jack are the baseball cards distributed in 1914 and 1915. Although most of the prizes recently are just printed paper, in 2004, a complete set of 1914 Cracker Jack baseball cards — including the highly sought after "Shoeless" Joe Jackson and Ty Cobb cards — was sold for a record $800,000.

Cereal Prizes

W.K. Kellogg was the first to introduce prizes in boxes of cereal beginning in 1906. The marketing strategy that he established has produced thousands of different cereal box prizes that have been distributed by the tens of billions. The first breakfast cereal prize was The Funny Jungleland Moving Pictures Book given to customers in the stores by merchants at the time of purchase of two packages of Kellogg's Corn Flakes. In 1909, Kellogg's changed the book give-away to a premium mail-in offer for the cost of a dime. By 1912, Kellogg's had distributed 2.5 million Jungleland books. The book underwent various edition changes and was last offered to consumers in 1937. In 1945, Kellogg inserted a prize in the form of a pin-back button into each box of Pep cereal. Pep pins have included U.S. Army squadrons as well as characters from newspaper comics. There were 5 series of comic characters and 18 different buttons in each set, with a total of 90 in the collection. Kellogg's 3D Baseball and Football Cards produced by Optigraphics were a big hit from 1970 to 1983 in packages of Kellogg's cereals, initially Corn Flakes and later other brands. Other manufacturers of major brands of cereal (including General Mills, Malt-O-Meal, Nabisco, Nestlé, Post Foods, and Quaker Oats) followed suit and inserted prizes into boxes of cereal to promote sales and brand loyalty.

Margarine Spreads Prizes in Europe

Oleomargarine was big business in Germany with hundreds of brands. Since 1920 margarine brands have put prizes in margarine, produced cards similar to tobacco cards of the time, and promoted albums for consumers to place their collections. Prizes made from metal and paper were also used from time to time. The Great Depression of 1929 slowed the previously unbridled development of prizes used in margarine. But after World War II, margarine prizes flourished with many series of printed cards and albums.

With the advent of injection molding came the plastic prizes. Cracker Jack had introduced plastic flats in its popcorn confection in the United States in 1948, and beginning in 1950, Fri-Homa, one of the leading German manufacturers of margarine owned by Fritz Homann, inserted prizes into its retail packages to promote brand loyalty. The first plastic margarine prizes were made by SIKU toy company owned by Homann's friend Richard Sieper. Many margarine brands followed suit. Most of the plastic prizes from German margarine were molded in a light cream color designed to make them look like tiny carved ivory figures — though made of polystyrene. These prizes are generically called "margarinefiguren" (EN: margarine figures), because they originated in oleo-margarine products, but they were also found in tobacco and other retail food products.

The era of margarine prizes ended in 1954 due to an agreement between German margarine producers to stop using in-pack prizes to promote their products. In the short period between 1950 and 1954, over 258 series (thousands of individual shapes) of plastic prizes were produced. The retail companies that used margarine figures as in-pack prizes included Ei-Fein Margarine, Fri-Homa Margarine, Voss Margarine, Wagner Margarine, Kothe Tobacco, and Mampe Liquor, as well as coffee, tea, oatmeal, and shoe cream. Other businesses and attractions that distributed these prizes with purchase were Markt-Apotheke Pharmacies, Siebenhaar and Braunschweig shoe stores, and Berlin and Magdeburg Zoos. For many post-war German children, margarine prizes were the only toys they possessed for years. More than casual collectibles among nostalgic adults today, these tiny plastic loyalty marketing tools are a noteworthy element in the cultural history of German-speaking countries.

Modern Prize Giant

Frito-Lay is a world icon in the field of in-package prizes. Besides being the current owner of Cracker Jack, the U.S. popcorn confection brand known for the "Prize Inside", Frito-Lay also regularly includes tazos and tattoos in packages of Lay's chips worldwide. In parts of Latin America, Frito-Lay has even introduced a brand called Cheetos Sorpresa (English: Surprise), which includes a licensed prize (from movies, television, and video games) in every 29–gram bag. Cheetos Sorpresa Era de Hielo (available in Mexico) included plastic ice molds with characters from the film Ice Age 3 in 45–gram bags. Game and television series Bakugan Battle Brawlers were featured on tazos in packages of Cheetos and Cheetos Sorpresa from India to Peru in 2009 and 2010.

Usefulness and Collectability

Winter's, a Peruvian brand of chocolates owned by Compañía Nacional de Chocolates de Perú S.A., has a confectionery product called Chocopunch that is a cream chocolate in small individual packages. A key promotional aspect of Chocopunch since 1997 has been, packaged with the product, colorful injection molded plastic cucharitas (mini spoons) — in the shapes of different characters from movies, television, and video games — that are collected as prizes. Chocopunch El Chavo came with two flavors (chocolate and vanilla) combined in one 17 gram container. Packaged with Chocopunch El Chavo were mini spoons in the shape of characters from the syndicated cartoon television series El Chavo del Ocho. The injection molded plastic mini spoons came in 12 different shapes and five different colors, with a total of 60 different items in the collection.

Technical Advances

Sticky Business

An important development in prizes is credited to American inventor R. Stanton (Stan) Avery. In 1935, Avery invented a machine to create self-adhesive labels. He started a company called Kum Klean Products to produce them. Self-adhesive labels with pre-printed designs on the front became commonly known as stickers. Today this company is known as the Avery Dennison Corporation and is a major supplier of self-adhesive stamps to the U.S. Postal Service. Stickers had their fads beginning in the late 1950s with bumper stickers through the 1960s and children's sticker trading albums of the 1980s. Prizes used in retail products, including breakfast cereal, bubble gum, and Cracker Jack, reflected these trends, and many thousands of examples of colorfully printed self-adhesive works of art have found their way as prizes into packages of retail food and household products.

Plastic Injection Molding

The invention of a screw injection molding machine by American inventor James Watson Hendry in 1946 changed the world of prizes forever. Thermoplastics could be used to produce toys and other plastic objects much more rapidly, and much more cheaply, because recycled plastic could be remolded using this process. In addition, injection molding for plastics required much less cool-down time for the toys, because the plastic is not completely melted before being injected into the molds. By 1948 the process was widely available, and injection-molded plastic prizes began to appear by the millions in boxes of Cracker Jack, breakfast cereal, and German margarine (1950-1954). Hendry also developed the first gas-assisted injection molding process in the 1970s, which permitted the production of complex, hollow prizes that cooled quickly. This greatly improved design flexibility as well as the strength and finish of manufactured parts while reducing production time, cost, weight and waste.

Lenticular Technology

Lenticular lens technology, a major development in printing with significant applications in consumer marketing, brought numerous prizes — sometimes called tilt cards, flickers, or wiggle pictures — including images illustrated to morph from one view to another, show motion, or show depth (3D). Victor Anderson, a leader in the commercial success of lenticular printing, co-founded the Vari-Vue company in New York, which by the 1950s had produced millions of lenticular products, and lenticulars had become a pop culture craze. Anderson created the first animated advertising button with the "I LIKE IKE" slogan for Eisenhower's campaign in 1951. In the 1950s, Vari-Vue produced lenticular prizes under the "Magic-Motion" brand that were inserted into packages of numerous consumer products, including Cracker Jack popcorn confection in the US, and Locatelli's popular Formaggino Mio cheese in Italy. Anderson related in a 1996 interview that he had made animated prizes for Cheerios, about 40 million of them, that were stuck to the side of the box, but so many of the prizes were being stolen before they even hit the shelves that Cheerios had to start inserting the prizes inside the boxes. Two Japan companies provided prizes around the world in the 1960s and 70s, Toppan, with their "Top Stereo" brand, and Dai-Nippon.

Photographic Lenticular Printing

Lenticulars from the 1940s and 50s had been developed from drawings or cartoon images. In the 1960s, Eastman Kodak Company in Tennessee developed "Xograph" technology for photographing and printing 3D lenticular images. The first mass-produced ink-printed "parallax panoramagram" (a black and white 3D photograph of a bust of Thomas Edison) was published in Look Magazine on February 25, 1964 and sold 8 million copies. Look Magazine followed up with the first color 3D lenticular photograph on April 7, 1964. Optigraphics Corporation of Grand Prairie, Texas was formed in 1970 and—under the guidance of Victor Anderson, the inventor of the modern lenticular production process who worked well into his 80's—produced Kellogg's 3D Baseball Cards from 1970 to 1983. Optigraphics produced the lenticular prizes for Cracker Jack in the 1980s,

7-Eleven Slurpee lenticular sports coins from 1983 to 1987, and in 1986 it produced the first set of 3D traditional baseball cards marketed as Sportflics, which ultimately led to the creation of Pinnacle Brands. In 1999 Performance Companies bought Optigraphics after Pinnacle Trading Card Company went bankrupt in 1998.

Prize Manufacturers

Cloudcrest

C. Carey Cloud, sometimes called "year-round Santa Claus", was best known as a designer and producer of hundreds of different prizes for Cracker Jack from the 1930s through the 1960s through his company Cloudcrest. It is estimated that he created, produced, and delivered to the Cracker Jack Company 700 million toys. At the same time he designed hundreds of premiums for companies such as Brach's Confections, Breck Candy Company, Bunny Bread, Carnival Candies, CoCo Wheats, Johnston Candies and Chocolates, New Orleans Confections Inc, Ovaltine, Pillsbury flour, Post Bran Flakes, Shotwell of Chicago, Thinshell Candies, and more.

Nosco Plastics

Nosco Plastics, Inc. (commonly called "NOSCO", the mark used on its molded products) was the plastics molding division of National Organ Supply Company created in 1934 to make plastic parts for electric organs and was located at 1701 Gaskell Avenue, Erie, Pennsylvania, 16503. Beginning in 1948 with the implementation of the newly developed screw injection molding process, NOSCO quickly became a major early producer of tiny plastic toys called "slum" (very cheap prizes that are bought in bulk, sometimes for as little as $1 a gross or less) sold to wholesalers as carnival merchandise, used by the millions as prizes in packages of Cracker Jack popcorn confection, and mail-order flats that were heavily advertised in American comic books as "100 Toy Soldiers for $1" by E. Joseph Cossman & Company. NOSCO also held a number of patents on plastic molded products including mechanical toys, storage containers, pallets, and medical syringes. From 1948 through 1960, The Cracker Jack Company at 4800 West 66th Street, Chicago, Illinois, the largest toy buyer in the world at the time, used many millions of NOSCO toys as prizes in their caramel coated popcorn confection. These include the "Animal Stand-ups" (CJ Archive #Z-1111) that were marketed by the Levin Brothers — as well as the "100 Cowboys and Indians" set of 12 different figures (CJ Archive #Z-1137) and "3 Ring Circus" set of 12 different figures (CJ Archive #Z-1154) marketed as mail order items by Cossman & Levine. Other sets made by NOSCO for Cracker Jack include Alphabet Animals set of 26 (Z-1179), People (Occupations) Stand-ups (Z-1124), Spacemen Stand-ups set of 10 (Z-1227), a set of 16 double-sided Stand-ups (Z-1144), and Zodiac Coins set of 12 disks (Z-1182).

R&L Plastics

Rosenhain and Lipmann Pty Ltd (commonly known as "R&L") was a plastics company in Melbourne Australia between 1954 and 1977. The company name is a fusion of the surnames of the founders Bruno Lipmann & Kurt Rosenhain. R&L designed and manufactured unique and innovative toys that became hugely popular both in Australia and in the United States., ultimately exporting them around the world. R&L started out making plastic hardware items. Its first product, a self-adhesive hook, was sold under an exclusive Australia license. Its hardware market was complimented by entry into the cereal box prize market with a flexible interconnecting plastic toy link "Flex-O-Link" in 1958. R&L's big breakthrough came with Stan Barton joining the firm as engineer, who conceived and developed the idea of miniature model kits, called snap-togethers — small plastic model kits that didn't need glue — issued in clear glassine bags, inside breakfast cereal boxes. They were used by companies such as Kellogg, Nabisco, Purina Grain Foods, and Sanitarium Health Food Company. Space Nits were found in retail packages of both Kellogg's cereals and Cracker Jack popcorn confection. During the company's 18-year run, over 70 different sets were released and it is estimated that about one billion R&L toys were delivered around the world. R & L's success was based upon unique toy designs and uncompromising engineering quality. However, the tide of success turned with the oil price shocks of the 1970s which sent the price of the raw material, plastic, up 300% in 5 years. Surprisingly too, the arrival of colour television saw cereal companies spend their marketing budgets on television advertising and not plastic inserts. Becoming unprofitable, R&L factory equipment and contents were sold off to a company in Mexico in 1977. This machinery was used to re-issue several series under the name "Tinykins". Although structurally the same, many colors varied and were brighter than the originals. The plastic and texture was also of a lesser quality. Tinykins flooded the market and are often mistaken for, or sold as, R&L originals.

Sales Promotion

Half Off Discount.

Sales promotion is one of the five aspects of the promotional mix. (The other 4 parts of the promotional mix are advertising, personal selling, direct marketing and publicity/public relations.) Media and non-media marketing communication are employed for a pre-determined, limited time to increase consumer demand, stimulate market demand or improve product availability. Examples include contests, coupons, freebies, loss leaders, point of purchase displays, premiums, prizes, product samples, and rebates.

Sales promotions can be directed at either the customer, sales staff, or distribution channel members (such as retailers). Sales promotions targeted at the consumer are called consumer sales promotions. Sales promotions targeted at retailers and wholesale are called trade sales promotions. Some sale promotions, particularly ones with unusual methods, are considered gimmicks by many.

Sales promotion includes several communications activities that attempt to provide added value or incentives to consumers, wholesalers, retailers, or other organizational customers to stimulate immediate sales. These efforts can attempt to stimulate product interest, trial, or purchase. Examples of devices used in sales promotion include coupons, samples, premiums, point-of-purchase (POP) displays, contests, rebates, and sweepstakes.

Sales promotion is implemented to attract new customers, to hold present customers, to counteract competition, and to take advantage of opportunities that are revealed by market research. It is made up of activities, both outside and inside activities, to enhance company sales. Outside sales promotion activities include advertising, publicity, public relations activities, and special sales events. Inside sales promotion activities include window displays, product and promotional material display and promotional programs such as premium awards and contests.

Sale promotions often come in the form of discounts. Discounts impact the way consumers think and behave when shopping. The type of savings and its location can affect the way consumers view a product and affect their purchase decision. The two most common discounts are price discounts ("on sale items") and bonus packs ("bulk items"). Price discounts are the reduction of an original sale by a certain percentage while bonus packs are deals in which the consumer receives more for the original price. Many companies present different forms of discounts in advertisements, hoping to convince consumers to buy their products.

Consumer Sales Promotion Types

Short term sales to achieve short term objectives:

- Price deal: A temporary reduction in the price, such as 50% off.

- Loyal Reward Program: Consumers collect points, miles, or credits for purchases and redeem them for rewards.

- Cents-off deal: Offers a brand at a lower price. Price reduction may be a percentage marked on the package.

- Price-pack/Bonus packs deal: The packaging offers a consumer a certain percentage more of the product for the same price (for example, 25 percent extra). This is another type of deal "in which customers are offered more of the product for the same price". For example, a sales company may offer their consumers a bonus pack in which they can receive two products for the price of one. In these scenarios, this bonus pack is framed as a gain because buyers believe that they are obtaining a free product. The purchase of a bonus pack, however, is not always beneficial for the consumer. Sometimes consumers will end up spending money on an item they would not normally buy had it not been in a bonus pack. As a result, items bought in a bonus pack are often wasted and is viewed as a "loss" for the consumer.

- Coupons: coupons have become a standard mechanism for sales promotions.

- Loss leader: the price of a popular product is temporarily reduced below cost in order to stimulate other profitable sales.

- Free-standing insert (FSI): A coupon booklet is inserted into the local newspaper for delivery.

- Checkout dispensers: On checkout the customer is given a coupon based on products purchased.

- Mobile couponing: Coupons are available on a mobile phone. Consumers show the offer on a mobile phone to a salesperson for redemption.

- Online interactive promotion game: Consumers play an interactive game associated with the promoted product.

- Rebates: Consumers are offered money back if the receipt and barcode are mailed to the producer.

- Contests/sweepstakes/games: The consumer is automatically entered into the event by purchasing the product.

- Point-of-sale displays:-

  o Aisle interrupter: A sign that juts into the aisle from the shelf.

  o Dangler: A sign that sways when a consumer walks by it.

  o Dump bin: A bin full of products dumped inside.

  o Bidding portals: Getting prospects.

  o Glorifier: A small stage that elevates a product above other products.

  o Wobbler: A sign that jiggles.

  o Lipstick Board: A board on which messages are written in crayon.

  o Necker: A coupon placed on the 'neck' of a bottle.

  o YES unit: "your extra salesperson" is a pull-out fact sheet.

  o Electroluminescent: Solar-powered, animated light in motion.

- Kids eat free specials: Offers a discount on the total dining bill by offering 1 free kids meal with each regular meal purchased.

- Sampling: Consumers get one sample for free, after their trial and then could decide whether to buy or not.

Online Deals Vs. In-Store Deals

There are different types of discounts available online versus in the stores. On-shelf couponing: Coupons are present at the shelf where the product is available. * On-line couponing: Coupons are available online. Consumers print them out and take them to the store.Although discounts can be found online and in stores, there is a different thought process when shopping in each location. For example, "online shoppers are more price-sensitive because of the readily available low search cost and direct price comparisons". Consumers can easily go to other websites and find better deals as opposed to physically going to various stores. In addition, buyers tend to refrain from purchasing bonus packs online because of the skepticism (of fraud and scams) that may come with the deal. Since "...bonus packs are more difficult than price discounts to process online, they are more difficult and effortful for the consumer to understand". For example, a buy-one-get-one-free deal on a website requires more work than the same bonus pack offered in a store. Online, consumers have to deal with payment processing, shipping and handling fees, and days waiting for the products' arrival, while in a store, the products are available without those additional steps and delays.

Trade Sales Promotion Techniques

- Trade allowances: short term incentive offered to induce a retailer to stock up on a product.

- Dealer loader: An incentive given to induce a retailer to purchase and display a product.

- Trade contest: A contest to reward retailers that sell the most product.

- Point-of-purchase displays: Used to create the urge of "impulse" buying and selling your product on the spot.

- Training programs: dealer employees are trained in selling the product.

- Push money: also known as "spiffs". An extra commission paid to retail employees to push products.

Trade discounts (also called functional discounts): These are payments to distribution channel members for performing some function.

Retail Mechanics

Retailers have a stock number of retail 'mechanics' that they regularly roll out or rotate for new marketing initiatives.

- Buy x get y free a.k.a. BOGOF for Buy One Get One Free.

- Three for two.

- Buy a quantity for a lower price.

- Get x% of discount on weekdays.

- Free gift with purchase.

Consumer Thought Process

Meaningful Savings: Gain or Loss

Many discounts are designed to give consumers the perception of saving money when buying products, but not all discounted prices are viewed as favorable to buyers. Therefore, before making a purchase, consumers may weigh their options as either a gain or a loss to avoid the risk of losing money on a purchase. A "gain" view on a purchase results in chance taking. For example, if there is a buy-one-get-one-half-off discount that seems profitable, a shopper will buy the product. On the other hand, a "loss" viewpoint results in consumer aversion to taking any chances. For instance, consumers will pass on a buy-three-get-one-half-off discount if they believe they are not benefitting from the deal. Specifically, consumers will consider their options because "...the sensation of loss is 2.5 times greater than the sensation of gain for the same value".

Impulse Buying

Impulse buying results from consumers' failure to weigh their options before buying a product. Impulse buying is "any purchase that a shopper makes that has not been planned... [and is] sudden and immediate". For example, if a consumer has no intention of buying a product before entering a store, but purchases an item without any forethought, that is impulse buying. Product manufactures want to promote and encourage this instant purchase impulse in consumers. Buyers can be very quick to make purchases without thinking about the consequences when a product is perceived to be a good deal. Therefore, sales companies "increasingly implement promotional campaigns that will be effective in triggering consumer impulse buying behavior" to increase sales and profit.

Comparing Prices

Many consumers read left-to-right, and therefore, compare prices in the same manner. For example, if the price of a product is $93 and the sales price is $79, people will initially compare the left digits first (9 and 7) and notice the two digit difference. However, because of this habitual behavior, "consumers may perceive the ($14) difference between $93 and $79 as greater than the ($14) difference between $89 and $75". As a result, consumers often mistakenly believe they are receiving a better deal with the first set of prices based on the left digits solely. Because of that common misconception, companies capitalize on this sales pricing strategy more often than not to increase sales.

Right Digit Effect

The right digit effect focuses on the right digits of prices when the left digits are the same. In other words, prices like $45 and $42 force consumers to pay more attention to the right digits (the 2 and 5) to determine the discount received. This effect also "implies that consumers will perceive larger discounts for prices with small right digit endings, than for large right digit endings. For example, in a $32-to-$31 price reduction, consumers will believe to have received a greater deal than a $39-to-$38 price reduction. As a result, companies may use discounts with smaller right digits to mislead consumers into thinking they are receiving a better deal and increasing profit. However, consumers also are deceived by the infamous 9-ending prices. "The right digit effect [also] relates to consumers' tendency to identify 9-ending prices as sale (rather than regular) prices or to associate them with a discount. For example, a regular price of $199 is mistakenly viewed as a sale or discount by consumers. Sales companies most commonly use this approach because the misinterpretation of consumers usually results in an increase of sales and profit.

Framing Effect

The Framing Effect is "the phenomenon that occurs when there is a change in an individual's preference between two or more alternatives caused by the way the problem is presented". In other words, the format in which something is presented will affect a person's viewpoint. This theory consists of three subcategories: risky choice framing, attribute framing and goal framing. Risky choice framing references back to the gain-or-loss thought processes of consumers. Consumers will take chances if the circumstance is profitable for them and avoid chance-taking if it is not. Attribute framing deals with one key phrase or feature of a price discount that is emphasized to inspire consumer shopping. For example, the terms "free" and "better" are used commonly to lure in shoppers to buy a product. Goal framing places pressure on buyers to act hastily or face the consequences of missing out on a definite price reduction. A "limited time only" deal, for example, attempts to motivate buyers to make a purchase quickly, or buy on impulse, before the time runs out.

Outside Forces

Although there are aspects that can determine a consumer's shopping behavior, there are many outside factors that can influence the shoppers' decision in making a purchase. For example, even though a product's price is discounted, the quality of that product may dissuade the consumer from buying the item. If the product has poor customer reviews or has a short "life span," shoppers will view that purchase as a loss and avoid taking a chance on it. A product can also be viewed negatively because of consumers' past experiences and expectations. For example, if the size of a product is misleading, buyers will not want to buy it. An item advertised as "huge," but is only one inch tall, will ward off consumers. Also, "the effects of personal characteristics, such as consumers' gender, subjective norms, and impulsivity" can also affect a consumer's purchase intentions. For example, a female will, generally, purchase a cosmetic product more often than a male. In addition, "some...shoppers may be unable to buy [a product]...because of financial constraints". Neither a discounted price nor a bonus pack has the ability to entice consumers if they cannot afford the product.

Political Issues

Sales promotions have traditionally been heavily regulated in many advanced industrial nations, with the notable exception of the United States. For example, the United Kingdom formerly operated under a resale price maintenance regime in which manufacturers could legally dictate the minimum resale price for virtually all goods; this practice was abolished in 1964.

Most European countries also have controls on the scheduling and permissible types of sales promotions, as they are regarded in those countries as bordering upon unfair business practices. Germany is notorious for having the most strict regulations. Famous examples include the car wash that was barred from giving free car washes to regular customers and a baker who could not give a free cloth bag to customers who bought more than 10 rolls.

Advertising

A Coca-Cola advertisement from the 1890s.

Advertising is a form of marketing communication used to promote or sell something, usually a business's product or service. Advertising by a government in favor of its own policies is often called propaganda.

In Latin, ad vertere means "to turn toward". The purpose of advertising may also be to reassure employees or shareholders that a company is viable or successful. Advertising messages are usually paid for by sponsors and viewed via various old media; including mass media such as newspapers, magazines, Television, Radio, outdoor advertising or direct mail; or new media such as blogs, websites or text messages.

Commercial ads seek to generate increased consumption of their products or services through "branding," which associates a product name or image with certain qualities in the minds of consumers. Non-commercial advertisers who spend money to advertise items other than a consumer product or service include political parties, interest groups, religious organizations and governmental agencies. Non-profit organizations may use free modes of persuasion, such as a public service announcement.

Modern advertising was created with the techniques introduced with tobacco advertising in the 1920s, most significantly with the campaigns of Edward Bernays, considered the founder of modern, "Madison Avenue" advertising.

In 2015, the world spent an estimate of US$592.43 billion on advertising. Internationally, the largest ("big four") advertising conglomerates are Interpublic, Omnicom, Publicis, and WPP.

History

Bronze plate for printing an advertisement for the Liu family needle shop at Jinan, Song dynasty China. It is considered the world's earliest identified printed advertising medium.

Egyptians used papyrus to make sales messages and wall posters. Commercial messages and political campaign displays have been found in the ruins of Pompeii and ancient Arabia. Lost and found advertising on papyrus was common in Ancient Greece and Ancient Rome. Wall or rock painting for commercial advertising is another manifestation of an ancient advertising form, which is present to this day in many parts of Asia, Africa, and South America. The tradition of wall painting can be traced back to Indian rock art paintings that date back to 4000 BC.

In ancient China, the earliest advertising known was oral, as recorded in the Classic of Poetry (11th to 7th centuries BC) of bamboo flutes played to sell candy. Advertisement usually takes in the form of calligraphic signboards and inked papers. A copper printing plate dated back to the Song dynasty used to print posters in the form of a square sheet of paper with a rabbit logo with "Jinan Liu's Fine Needle Shop" and "We buy high-quality steel rods and make fine-quality needles, to be ready for use at home in no time" written above and below is considered the world's earliest identified printed advertising medium.

In Europe, as the towns and cities of the Middle Ages began to grow, and the general populace was unable to read, instead of signs that read "cobbler", "miller", "tailor", or "blacksmith", images associated with their trade would be used such as a boot, a suit, a hat, a clock, a diamond, a horse shoe, a candle or even a bag of flour. Fruits and vegetables were sold in the city square from the backs of carts and wagons and their proprietors used street callers (town criers) to announce their whereabouts for the convenience of the customers. The first compilation of such advertisements was gathered in "Les Crieries de Paris", a thirteenth-century poem by Guillaume de la Villeneuve.

In the 18th century advertisements started to appear in weekly newspapers in England. These early print advertisements were used mainly to promote books and newspapers, which became increasingly affordable with advances in the printing press; and medicines, which were increasingly sought after as disease ravaged Europe. However, false advertising and so-called "quack" advertisements became a problem, which ushered in the regulation of advertising content.

19th Century

Thomas J. Barratt from London has been called "the father of modern advertising". Working for the Pears Soap company, Barratt created an effective advertising campaign for the company products, which involved the use of targeted slogans, images and phrases. One of his slogans, "Good morning. Have you used Pears' soap?" was famous in its day and into the 20th century.

Barratt introduced many of the crucial ideas that lie behind successful advertising and these were widely circulated in his day. He constantly stressed the importance of a strong and exclusive brand image for Pears and of emphasizing the product's availability through saturation campaigns. He also understood the importance of constantly reevaluating the market for changing tastes and mores, stating in 1907 that "tastes change, fashions change, and the advertiser has to change with them. An idea that was effective a generation ago would fall flat, stale, and unprofitable if presented to the public today. Not that the idea of today is always better than the older idea, but it is different – it hits the present taste."

As the economy expanded across the world during the 19th century, advertising grew alongside. In the United States, the success of this advertising format eventually led to the growth of mail-order advertising.

In June 1836, French newspaper La Presse was the first to include paid advertising in its pages, allowing it to lower its price, extend its readership and increase its profitability and the formula was soon copied by all titles. Around 1840, Volney B. Palmer established the roots of the modern day advertising agency in Philadelphia. In 1842 Palmer bought large amounts of space in various newspapers at a discounted rate then resold the space at higher rates to advertisers. The actual ad – the copy, layout, and artwork – was still prepared by the company wishing to advertise; in effect, Palmer was a space broker. The situation changed in the late 19th century when the advertising agency of N.W. Ayer & Son was founded. Ayer and Son offered to plan, create, and execute complete advertising campaigns for its customers. By 1900 the advertising agency had become the focal point of creative planning, and advertising was firmly established as a profession.

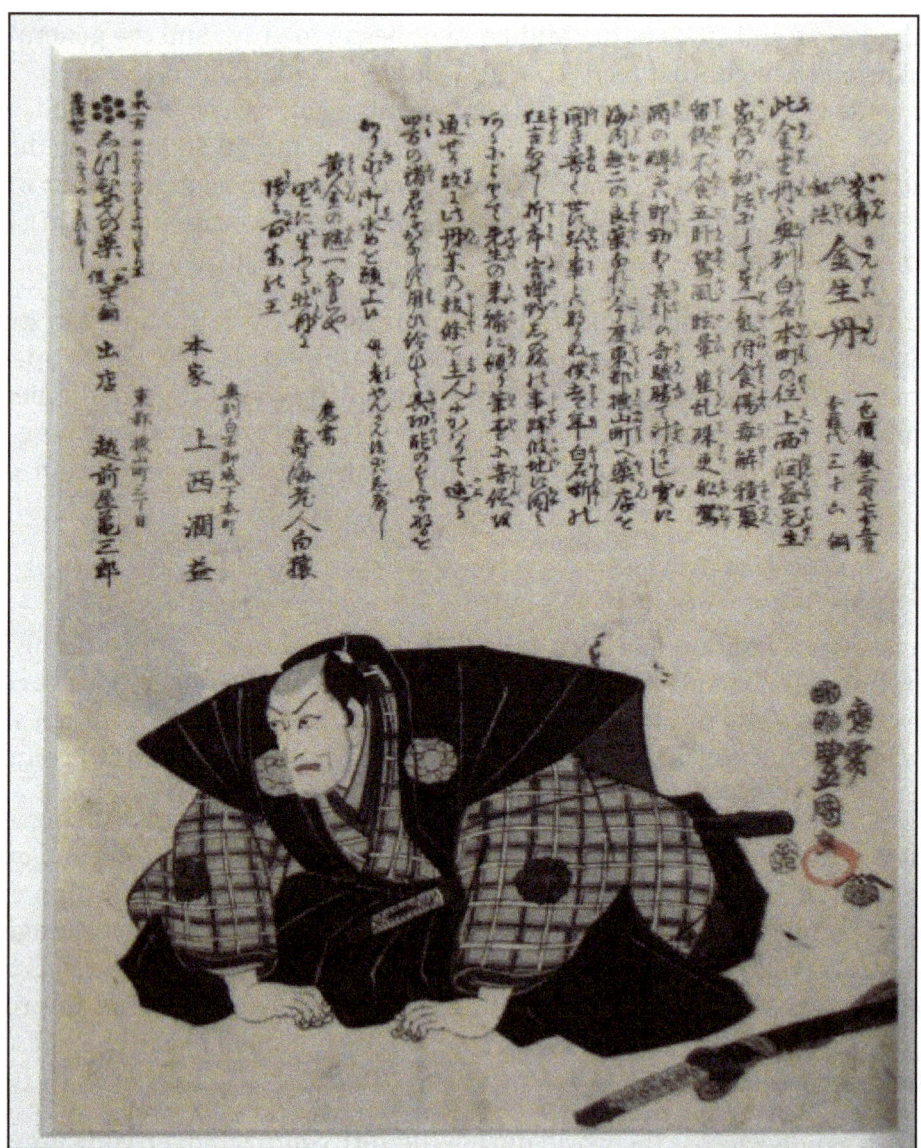

Edo period LEL flyer from 1806 for a traditional medicine called Kinseitan.

Around the same time, in France, Charles-Louis Havas extended the services of his news agency, Havas to include advertisement brokerage, making it the first French group to organize. At first, agencies were brokers for advertisement space in newspapers. N. W. Ayer & Son was the first full-service agency to assume responsibility for advertising content. N.W. Ayer opened in 1869, and was located in Philadelphia.

20th Century

A 1900 advertisement for Pears soap.

Advertising increased dramatically in the United States as industrialization expanded the supply of manufactured products. In order to profit from this higher rate of production, industry needed to recruit workers as consumers of factory products. It did so through the invention of mass marketing designed to influence the population's economic behavior on a larger scale. In the 1910s and 1920s, advertisers in the U.S. adopted the doctrine that human instincts could be targeted and harnessed – "sublimated" into the desire to purchase commodities. Edward Bernays, a nephew of Sigmund Freud, became associated with the method and is sometimes called the founder of modern advertising and public relations.

A print advertisement for the 1913 issue of the Encyclopædia Britannica.

In the 1920s, under Secretary of Commerce Herbert Hoover, the American government promoted advertising. Hoover himself delivered an address to the Associated Advertising Clubs of the World in 1925 called 'Advertising Is a Vital Force in Our National Life." In October 1929, the head of the U.S. Bureau of Foreign and Domestic Commerce, Julius Klein, stated "Advertising is the key to world prosperity." This was part of the "unparalleled" collaboration between business and government in the 1920s, according to a 1933 European economic journal.

The tobacco companies became major advertisers in order to sell packaged cigarettes. The tobacco companies pioneered the new advertising techniques when they hired Bernays to create positive associations with tobacco smoking.

Advertising was also used as a vehicle for cultural assimilation, encouraging workers to exchange their traditional habits and community structure in favor of a shared "modern" lifestyle. An important tool for influencing immigrant workers was the American Association of Foreign Language Newspapers (AAFLN). The AAFLN was primarily an advertising agency but also gained heavily centralized control over much of the immigrant press.

1916 Ladies' Home Journal version of the famous ad by Helen Lansdowne Resor of the J. Walter Thompson Agency.

At the turn of the 20th century, there were few career choices for women in business; however, advertising was one of the few. Since women were responsible for most of the purchasing done in their household, advertisers and agencies recognized the value of women's insight during the creative process. In fact, the first American advertising to use a sexual sell was created by a woman – for a soap product. Although tame by today's standards, the advertisement featured a couple with the message "A skin you love to touch".

In the 1920s psychologists Walter D. Scott and John B. Watson contributed applied psychological theory to the field of advertising. Scott said, "Man has been called the reasoning animal but he could with greater truthfulness be called the creature of suggestion. He is reasonable, but he is to a greater extent suggestible". He demonstrated this through his advertising technique of a direct command to the consumer.

On the Radio from the 1920s

Advertisement for a live radio broadcast, sponsored by a milk company, Adohr milk, and published in the Los Angeles Times on May 6, 1930

In the early 1920s, the first radio stations were established by radio equipment manufacturers and retailers who offered programs in order to sell more radios to consumers. As time passed, many non-profit organizations followed suit in setting up their own radio stations, and included: schools, clubs and civic groups.

When the practice of sponsoring programs was popularized, each individual radio program was usually sponsored by a single business in exchange for a brief mention of the business' name at the beginning and end of the sponsored shows. However, radio station owners soon realized they could earn more money by selling sponsorship rights in small time allocations to multiple businesses throughout their radio station's broadcasts, rather than selling the sponsorship rights to single businesses per show.

Commercial Television in the 1950s

In the early 1950s, the DuMont Television Network began the modern practice of selling advertisement time to multiple sponsors. Previously, DuMont had trouble finding sponsors for many of their programs and compensated by selling smaller blocks of advertising time to several businesses. This eventually became the standard for the commercial television industry in the United States. However, it was still a common practice to have single sponsor shows, such as The United States Steel Hour. In some instances the sponsors exercised great control over the content of the show – up to and including having one's advertising agency actually writing the show. The single sponsor model is much less prevalent now, a notable exception being the Hallmark Hall of Fame.

Cable Television from the 1980s

The late 1980s and early 1990s saw the introduction of cable television and particularly MTV. Pioneering the concept of the music video, MTV ushered in a new type of advertising: the consumer tunes in for the advertising message, rather than it being a by-product or afterthought. As cable and satellite television became increasingly prevalent, specialty channels emerged, including channels entirely devoted to advertising, such as QVC, Home Shopping Network, and ShopTV Canada.

On the Internet from the 1990s

With the advent of the ad server, online advertising grew, contributing to the "dot-com" boom of the 1990s. Entire corporations operated solely on advertising revenue, offering everything from coupons to free Internet access. At the turn of the 21st century, some websites, including the search engine Google, changed online advertising by personalizing ads based on web browsing behavior. This has led to other similar efforts and an increase in interactive advertising.

The share of advertising spending relative to GDP has changed little across large changes in media since 1925. In 1925, the main advertising media in America were newspapers, magazines, signs on streetcars, and outdoor posters. Advertising spending as a share of GDP was about 2.9 percent. By 1998, television and radio had become major advertising media. Nonetheless, advertising spending as a share of GDP was slightly lower – about 2.4 percent.

Guerrilla marketing involves unusual approaches such as staged encounters in public places, giveaways of products such as cars that are covered with brand messages, and interactive advertising where the viewer can respond to become part of the advertising message. This type of advertising is unpredictable, which causes consumers to buy the product or idea. This reflects an increasing trend of interactive and "embedded" ads, such as via product placement, having consumers vote through text messages, and various campaigns utilizing social network services such as Facebook or Twitter.

The advertising business model has also been adapted in recent years. In media for equity, advertising is not sold, but provided to start-up companies in return for equity. If the company grows and is sold, the media companies receive cash for their shares.

Domain name registrants (usually those who register and renew domains as an investment) sometimes "park" their domains and allow advertising companies to place ads on their sites in return for per-click payments. These ads are typically driven by pay per click search engines like Google or Yahoo, but ads can sometimes be placed directly on targeted domain names through a domain lease or by making contact with the registrant of a domain name that describes a product. Domain name registrants are generally easy to identify through WHOIS records that are publicly available at registrar websites.

Advertising Theory

Hierarchy-of-Effects Models

Various competing models of hierarchies of effects attempt to provide a theoretical underpinning to advertising practice.

- The model of Clow and Baack clarifies the objectives of an advertising campaign and for each individual advertisement. The model postulates six steps a buyer moves through when making a purchase:

    ○ Awareness,

    ○ Knowledge,

    ○ Liking,

    ○ Preference,

    ○ Conviction,

    ○ Purchase.

- Means-End Theory suggests that an advertisement should contain a message or means that leads the consumer to a desired end-state.

- Leverage Points aim to move the consumer from understanding a product's benefits to linking those benefits with personal values.

Marketing Mix

The marketing mix was proposed by professor E. Jerome McCarthy in the 1960s. It consists of four basic elements called the "four Ps". Product is the first P representing the actual product. Price represents the process of determining the value of a product. Place represents the variables of getting the product to the consumer such as distribution channels, market coverage and movement organization. The last P stands for Promotion which is the process of reaching the target market and convincing them to buy the product.

In the 1990s, the concept of four Cs was introduced as a more customer-driven replacement of four P's. There are two theories based on four Cs: Lauterborn's four Cs (consumer, cost, communication, convenience) and Shimizu's four Cs (commodity, cost, communication, channel) in the 7Cs

Compass Model (Co-marketing). Communications can include advertising, sales promotion, public relations, publicity, personal selling, corporate identity, internal communication, SNS, MIS.

Types of Advertising

An advertisement for the Wikimedia Foundation.

An advertisement for a diner. Such signs are common on storefronts.

Paying people to hold signs is one of the oldest forms of advertising, as with this human billboard.

A bus with an advertisement for GAP in Singapore. Buses and other vehicles are popular media for advertisers.

Mobile Billboard in East Coast Park, Singapore.

A DBAG Class 101 with UNICEF ads at Ingolstadt main railway station.

Virtually any medium can be used for advertising. Commercial advertising media can include wall paintings, billboards, street furniture components, printed flyers and rack cards, radio, cinema and television adverts, web banners, mobile telephone screens, shopping carts, web popups, skywriting, bus stop benches, human billboards and forehead advertising, magazines, newspapers, town criers, sides of buses, banners attached to or sides of airplanes ("logojets"), in-flight advertisements on seat-back tray tables or overhead storage bins, taxicab doors, roof mounts and passenger screens, musical stage shows, subway platforms and trains, elastic bands on disposable diapers, doors of bathroom stalls, stickers on apples in supermarkets, shopping cart handles (grabertising), the opening section of streaming audio and video, posters, and the backs of event tickets and supermarket receipts. Any place an "identified" sponsor pays to deliver their message through a medium is advertising.

Share of global adspend		
medium	**2015**	**2018**
Television advertisement	37.7%	34.8%
Desktop online advertising	19.9%	18.2%
Mobile advertising	9.2%	18.4%
Newspaper#Advertising	12.8%	10.1%
Magazines	6.5%	5.3%
Outdoor advertising	6.8%	6.6%
Radio advertisement	6.5%	5.9%
Cinema	0.6%	0.7%

A London Bus, with a film advertisement along its side.

Hot air balloon displays advertising for GEO magazine.

Television Advertising / Music in Advertising

Television advertising is one of the most expensive types of advertising; networks charge large amounts for commercial airtime during popular events. The annual Super Bowl football game in the United States is known as the most prominent advertising event on television - with an audience of over 108 million and studies showing that 50% of those only tuned in to see the advertisements. The average cost of a single thirty-second television spot during this game reached US$4 million & a 60-second spot double that figure in 2014. Virtual advertisements may be inserted into regular programming through computer graphics. It is typically inserted into otherwise blank backdrops or used to replace local billboards that are not relevant to the remote broadcast audience. More controversially, virtual billboards may be inserted into the background where none exist in real-life. This technique is especially used in televised sporting events. Virtual product placement is also possible.

Infomercials

An infomercial is a long-format television commercial, typically five minutes or longer. The word "infomercial" is a portmanteau of the words "information" and "commercial". The main objective in an infomercial is to create an impulse purchase, so that the target sees the presentation and then immediately buys the product through the advertised toll-free telephone number or website. Infomercials describe, display, and often demonstrate products and their features, and commonly have testimonials from customers and industry professionals.

Radio Advertising

Radio advertisements are broadcast as radio waves to the air from a transmitter to an antenna and a thus to a receiving device. Airtime is purchased from a station or network in exchange for airing the commercials. While radio has the limitation of being restricted to sound, proponents of radio advertising often cite this as an advantage. Radio is an expanding medium that can be found on air, and also online. According to Arbitron, radio has approximately 241.6 million weekly listeners, or more than 93 percent of the U.S. population.

Online Advertising

Online advertising is a form of promotion that uses the Internet and World Wide Web for the expressed purpose of delivering marketing messages to attract customers. Online ads are delivered by an ad server. Examples of online advertising include contextual ads that appear on search engine results pages, banner ads, in pay per click text ads, rich media ads, Social network advertising, online classified advertising, advertising networks and e-mail marketing, including e-mail spam. A newer form of online advertising is Native Ads; they go in a website's news feed and are supposed to improve user experience by being less intrusive. However, some people argue this practice is deceptive.

Domain Name Advertising

Domain name advertising is most commonly done through pay per click web search engines, however, advertisers often lease space directly on domain names that generically describe their products. When an Internet user visits a website by typing a domain name directly into their web browser, this is known as "direct navigation", or "type in" web traffic. Although many Internet users search for ideas and products using search engines and mobile phones, a large number of users around the world still use the address bar. They will type a keyword into the address bar such as "geraniums" and add ".com" to the end of it. Sometimes they will do the same with ".org" or a country-code Top Level Domain (TLD such as ".co.uk" for the United Kingdom or ".ca" for Canada). When Internet users type in a generic keyword and add .com or another top-level domain (TLD) ending, it produces a targeted sales lead. Domain name advertising was originally developed by Oingo (later known as Applied Semantics), one of Google's early acquisitions.

Product Placements

Covert advertising is when a product or brand is embedded in entertainment and media. For example, in a film, the main character can use an item or other of a definite brand, as in the movie Minority Report, where Tom Cruise's character John Anderton owns a phone with the Nokia logo clearly written in the top corner, or his watch engraved with the Bulgari logo. Another example of advertising in film is in I, Robot, where main character played by Will Smith mentions his Converse shoes several times, calling them "classics", because the film is set far in the future. I, Robot and Spaceballs also showcase futuristic cars with the Audi and Mercedes-Benz logos clearly displayed on the front of the vehicles. Cadillac chose to advertise in the movie The Matrix Reloaded, which as a result contained many scenes in which Cadillac cars were used. Similarly, product placement for Omega Watches, Ford, VAIO, BMW and Aston Martin cars are featured in recent James Bond films, most notably Casino Royale. In "Fantastic Four: Rise of the Silver Surfer", the main transport vehicle shows a large Dodge logo on the front. Blade Runner includes some of the most obvious product placement; the whole film stops to show a Coca-Cola billboard.

Press Advertising

Press advertising describes advertising in a printed medium such as a newspaper, magazine, or trade journal. This encompasses everything from media with a very broad readership base, such as a major national newspaper or magazine, to more narrowly targeted media such as local newspapers and trade journals on very specialized topics. A form of press advertising is classified advertising, which allows private individuals or companies to purchase a small, narrowly targeted ad for a low fee advertising a product or service. Another form of press advertising is the display ad, which is a larger ad (which can include art) that typically run in an article section of a newspaper.

Billboard Advertising

Billboards are large structures located in public places which display advertisements to passing pedestrians and motorists. Most often, they are located on main roads with a large amount of passing motor and pedestrian traffic; however, they can be placed in any location with large amounts of viewers, such as on mass transit vehicles and in stations, in shopping malls or office buildings, and in stadiums.

The RedEye newspaper advertised to its target market at North Avenue Beach with a sailboat billboard on Lake Michigan.

Mobile Billboard Advertising

Mobile billboards are generally vehicle mounted billboards or digital screens. These can be on dedicated vehicles built solely for carrying advertisements along routes preselected by clients, they can also be specially equipped cargo trucks or, in some cases, large banners strewn from planes. The billboards are often lighted; some being backlit, and others employing spotlights. Some billboard displays are static, while others change; for example, continuously or periodically rotating among a set of advertisements. Mobile displays are used for various situations in metropolitan areas throughout the world, including: target advertising, one-day and long-term campaigns, conventions, sporting events, store openings and similar promotional events, and big advertisements from smaller companies.

In-Store Advertising

In-store advertising is any advertisement placed in a retail store. It includes placement of a product in visible locations in a store, such as at eye level, at the ends of aisles and near checkout counters (a.k.a. POP – point of purchase display), eye-catching displays promoting a specific product, and advertisements in such places as shopping carts and in-store video displays.

Coffee Cup Advertising

Coffee cup advertising is any advertisement placed upon a coffee cup that is distributed out of an office, café, or drive-through coffee shop. This form of advertising was first popularized in Australia, and has begun growing in popularity in the United States, India, and parts of the Middle East.

Street Advertising

This type of advertising first came to prominence in the UK by Street Advertising Services to create outdoor advertising on street furniture and pavements. Working with products such as Reverse Graffiti, air dancers and 3D pavement advertising, for getting brand messages out into public spaces.

Sheltered Outdoor Advertising

This type of advertising combines outdoor with indoor advertisement by placing large mobile, structures (tents) in public places on temporary bases. The large outer advertising space aims to exert a strong pull on the observer, the product is promoted indoors, where the creative decor can intensify the impression.

Celebrity Branding

This type of advertising focuses upon using celebrity power, fame, money, popularity to gain recognition for their products and promote specific stores or products. Advertisers often advertise their products, for example, when celebrities share their favorite products or wear clothes by specific brands or designers. Celebrities are often involved in advertising campaigns such as television or print adverts to advertise specific or general products. The use of celebrities to endorse a brand can have its downsides, however; one mistake by a celebrity can be detrimental to the public relations of a brand. For example, following his performance of eight gold medals at the 2008 Olympic Games in Beijing, China, swimmer Michael Phelps' contract with Kellogg's was terminated, as Kellogg's did not want to associate with him after he was photographed smoking marijuana. Celebrities such as Britney Spears have advertised for multiple products including Pepsi, Candies from Kohl's, Twister, NASCAR, and Toyota.

Customer-Generated Advertising

This involves getting customers to generate advertising through blogs, websites, wikis and forums, for some kind of payment. Customer-generated advertising can also be used without payment being made. For example, a satisfied customer of a product may boast about their experience on social media. This message may then lead someone else to buy that product. The consumer did not do this with the intention of getting money out of their shared message, but that is what can happen. Especially with a channel as large and as effective as social media, sharing ones opinion, positive or negative can be good or bad advertising for a product.

Aerial Advertising

Using aircraft, balloons or airships to create or display advertising media. Skywriting is a notable example.

An Allegiant Air aircraft in the special Blue Man Group livery.

Purpose of Advertising

Advertising is at the front of delivering the proper message to customers and prospective customers. The purpose of advertising is to convince customers that a company's services or products are the best, enhance the image of the company, point out and create a need for products or services, demonstrate new uses for established products, announce new products and programs, reinforce the salespeople's individual messages, draw customers to the business, and to hold existing customers.

Sales Promotions and Brand Loyalty

Sales promotions are another way to advertise. Sales promotions are double purposed because they are used to gather information about what type of customers one draws in and where they are, and to jump start sales. Sales promotions include things like contests and games, sweepstakes, product giveaways, samples coupons, loyalty programs, and discounts. The ultimate goal of sales promotions is to stimulate potential customers to action.

One way to create brand loyalty is to reward consumers for spending time interacting with the brand.This method may come in many forms like rewards card, rewards programs and sampling.

Media and Advertising Approaches

Increasingly, other media are overtaking many of the "traditional" media such as television, radio and newspaper because of a shift toward the usage of the Internet for news and music as well as devices like digital video recorders (DVRs) such as TiVo.

Online advertising began with unsolicited bulk e-mail advertising known as "e-mail spam". Spam has been a problem for e-mail users since 1978. As new online communication channels became available, advertising followed. The first banner ad appeared on the World Wide Web in 1994. Prices of Web-based advertising space are dependent on the "relevance" of the surrounding web content and the traffic that the website receives.

In online display advertising, display ads generate awareness quickly. Unlike search, which requires someone to be aware of a need, display advertising can drive awareness of something new and without previous knowledge. Display works well for direct response. Display is not only used for generating awareness, it's used for direct response campaigns that link to a landing page with a clear 'call to action'.

As the mobile phone became a new mass medium in 1998 when the first paid downloadable content appeared on mobile phones in Finland, mobile advertising followed, also first launched in Finland in 2000. By 2007 the value of mobile advertising had reached $2 billion and providers such as Admob delivered billions of mobile ads.

More advanced mobile ads include banner ads, coupons, Multimedia Messaging Service picture and video messages, advergames and various engagement marketing campaigns. A particular feature driving mobile ads is the 2D barcode, which replaces the need to do any typing of web addresses, and uses the camera feature of modern phones to gain immediate access to web content. 83 percent of Japanese mobile phone users already are active users of 2D barcodes.

Some companies have proposed placing messages or corporate logos on the side of booster rockets and the International Space Station.

Unpaid advertising (also called "publicity advertising"), can include personal recommendations ("bring a friend", "sell it"), spreading buzz, or achieving the feat of equating a brand with a common noun (in the United States, "Xerox" = "photocopier", "Kleenex" = tissue, "Vaseline" = petroleum jelly, "Hoover" = vacuum cleaner, and "Band-Aid" = adhesive bandage). However, some companies oppose the use of their brand name to label an object. Equating a brand with a common noun also risks turning that brand into a generic trademark – turning it into a generic term which means that its legal protection as a trademark is lost.

From time to time, The CW Television Network airs short programming breaks called "Content Wraps", to advertise one company's product during an entire commercial break. The CW pioneered "content wraps" and some products featured were Herbal Essences, Crest, Guitar Hero II, CoverGirl, and recently Toyota.

A new promotion concept has appeared, "ARvertising", advertising on Augmented Reality technology.

Controversy exists on the effectiveness of subliminal advertising, and the pervasiveness of mass messages.

Rise in New Media

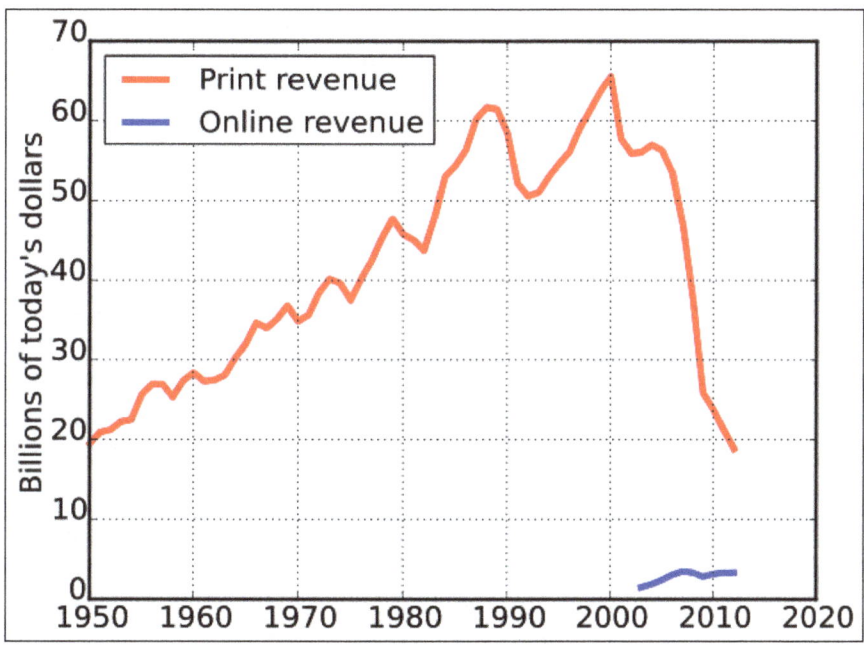

US Newspaper Advertising Revenue.

Newspaper Association of America Published Data

With the Internet came many new advertising opportunities. Popup, Flash, banner, Popunder, advergaming, and email advertisements (all of which are often unwanted or spam in the case of email) are now commonplace. Particularly since the rise of "entertaining" advertising, some people may like an advertisement enough to wish to watch it later or show a friend. In general, the advertising community has not yet made this easy, although some have used the Internet to widely distribute their ads to anyone willing to see or hear them. In the last three-quarters of 2009 mobile and internet advertising grew by 18% and 9% respectively. Older media advertising saw declines: −10.1% (TV), −11.7% (radio), −14.8% (magazines) and −18.7% (newspapers).

Niche Marketing

Another significant trend regarding future of advertising is the growing importance of the niche market using niche or targeted ads. Also brought about by the Internet and the theory of The Long Tail, advertisers will have an increasing ability to reach specific audiences. In the past, the most efficient way to deliver a message was to blanket the largest mass market audience possible. However, usage tracking, customer profiles and the growing popularity of niche content brought about by everything from blogs to social networking sites, provide advertisers with audiences that are smaller but much better defined, leading to ads that are more relevant to viewers and more effective for companies' marketing products. Among others, Comcast Spotlight is one such advertiser employing this method in their video on demand menus. These advertisements are targeted to a specific group and can be viewed by anyone wishing to find out more about a particular business or practice, from their home. This causes the viewer to become proactive and actually choose what advertisements they want to view.

Google AdSense is an example of niche marketing. Google calculates the primary purpose of a website and adjusts ads accordingly; it uses key words on the page (or even in emails) to find the general ideas of topics disused and places ads that will most likely be clicked on by viewers of the email account or website visitors.

Crowdsourcing

The concept of crowdsourcing has given way to the trend of user-generated advertisements. User-generated ads are created by people, as opposed to an advertising agency or the company themselves, often resulting from brand sponsored advertising competitions. For the 2007 Super Bowl, the Frito-Lays division of PepsiCo held the Crash the Super Bowl contest, allowing people to create their own Doritos commercial. Chevrolet held a similar competition for their Tahoe line of SUVs. Due to the success of the Doritos user-generated ads in the 2007 Super Bowl, Frito-Lays relaunched the competition for the 2009 and 2010 Super Bowl. The resulting ads were among the most-watched and most-liked Super Bowl ads. In fact, the winning ad that aired in the 2009 Super Bowl was ranked by the USA Today Super Bowl Ad Meter as the top ad for the year while the winning ads that aired in the 2010 Super Bowl were found by Nielsen's BuzzMetrics to be the "most buzzed-about". Another example of companies using crowdsourcing successfully is the beverage company Jones Soda that encourages consumers to participate in the label design themselves.

This trend has given rise to several online platforms that host user-generated advertising competitions on behalf of a company. Founded in 2007, Zooppa has launched ad competitions for brands such as Google, Nike, Hershey's, General Mills, Microsoft, NBC Universal, Zinio, and Mini Cooper. Crowdsourced remains controversial, as the long-term impact on the advertising industry is still unclear.

Global Advertising

Advertising has gone through five major stages of development: domestic, export, international, multi-national, and global. For global advertisers, there are four, potentially competing, business objectives that must be balanced when developing worldwide advertising: building a brand while speaking with one voice, developing economies of scale in the creative process, maximising local effectiveness of ads, and increasing the company's speed of implementation. Born from the evolutionary stages of global marketing are the three primary and fundamentally different approaches to the development of global advertising executions: exporting executions, producing local executions, and importing ideas that travel.

Advertising research is key to determining the success of an ad in any country or region. The ability to identify which elements and/or moments of an ad contribute to its success is how economies of scale are maximized. Once one knows what works in an ad, that idea or ideas can be imported by any other market. Market research measures, such as Flow of Attention, Flow of Emotion and branding moments provide insight into what is working in an ad in any country or region because the measures are based on the visual, not verbal, elements of the ad.

Foreign Public Messaging

Foreign governments, particularly those that own marketable commercial products or services, often promote their interests and positions through the advertising of those goods because the target audience is not only largely unaware of the forum as a vehicle for foreign messaging but also willing to receive the message while in a mental state of absorbing information from advertisements during television commercial breaks, while reading a periodical, or while passing by billboards in public spaces. A prime example of this messaging technique is advertising campaigns to promote international travel. While advertising foreign destinations and services may stem from the typical goal of increasing revenue by drawing more tourism, some travel campaigns carry the additional or alternative intended purpose of promoting good sentiments or improving existing ones among the target audience towards a given nation or region. It is common for advertising promoting foreign countries to be produced and distributed by the tourism ministries of those countries, so these ads often carry political statements and/or depictions of the foreign government's desired international public perception. Additionally, a wide range of foreign airlines and travel-related services which advertise separately from the destinations, themselves, are owned by their respective governments; examples include, though are not limited to, the Emirates airline (Dubai), Singapore Airlines (Singapore), Qatar Airways (Qatar), China Airlines (Taiwan/Republic of China), and Air China (People's Republic of China). By depicting their destinations, airlines, and other services in a favorable and pleasant light, countries market themselves to populations abroad in a manner that could mitigate prior public impressions.

Diversification

In the realm of advertising agencies, continued industry diversification has seen observers note that "big global clients don't need big global agencies any more". This is reflected by the growth of non-traditional agencies in various global markets, such as Canadian business TAXI and SMART in Australia and has been referred to as "a revolution in the ad world".

New Technology

The ability to record shows on digital video recorders (such as TiVo) allow watchers to record the programs for later viewing, enabling them to fast forward through commercials. Additionally, as more seasons of pre-recorded box sets are offered for sale of television programs; fewer people watch the shows on TV. However, the fact that these sets are sold, means the company will receive additional profits from these sets.

To counter this effect, a variety of strategies have been employed. Many advertisers have opted for product placement on TV shows like Survivor. Other strategies include integrating advertising with internet-connected EPGs, advertising on companion devices (like smartphones and tablets) during the show, and creating TV apps. Additionally, some like brands have opted for social television sponsorship.

Advertising Education

Advertising education has become popular with bachelor, master and doctorate degrees becoming available in the emphasis. A surge in advertising interest is typically attributed to the strong relationship advertising plays in cultural and technological changes, such as the advance of online social networking. A unique model for teaching advertising is the student-run advertising agency, where advertising students create campaigns for real companies. Organizations such as the American Advertising Federation establish companies with students to create these campaigns.

Criticisms

While advertising can be seen as necessary for economic growth, it is not without social costs. Unsolicited commercial e-mail and other forms of spam have become so prevalent as to have become a major nuisance to users of these services, as well as being a financial burden on internet service providers. Advertising is increasingly invading public spaces, such as schools, which some critics argue is a form of child exploitation.

One of the most controversial criticisms of advertisement in the present day is that of the predominance of advertising of foods high in sugar, fat, and salt specifically to children. Critics claim that food advertisements targeting children are exploitive and are not sufficiently balanced with proper nutritional education to help children understand the consequences of their food choices. Additionally, children may not understand that they are being sold something, and are therefore more impressionable. Michelle Obama has criticized large food companies for advertising unhealthy foods largely towards children and has requested that food companies either limit their advertising to children or advertise foods that are more in line with dietary guidelines. The other criticisms include the change that are brought by those advertisements on the society and also the deceiving ads that are aired and published by the corporations.Cosmetic and health industry are the ones which exploited the highest and created reasons of concern.

Regulation

There have been increasing efforts to protect the public interest by regulating the content and the influence of advertising. Some examples are: the ban on television tobacco advertising imposed in many countries, and the total ban of advertising to children under 12 imposed by the Swedish government in 1991. Though that regulation continues in effect for broadcasts originating within the country, the European Court of Justice ruled that Sweden was obliged to accept foreign programming, including those from neighboring countries or via satellite. Greece's regulations are of a similar nature, "banning advertisements for children's toys between 7 am and 10 pm and a total ban on advertisement for war toys".

In Europe and elsewhere, there is a vigorous debate on whether (or how much) advertising to children should be regulated. This debate was exacerbated by a report released by the Kaiser Family Foundation in February 2004 which suggested fast food advertising that targets children was an important factor in the epidemic of childhood obesity in the United States.

In New Zealand, South Africa, Pakistan, Afghanistan, Canada, and many European countries, the advertising industry operates a system of self-regulation. Advertisers, advertising agencies and the media agree on a code of advertising standards that they attempt to uphold. The general aim of such codes is to ensure that any advertising is 'legal, decent, honest and truthful'. Some self-regulatory organizations are funded by the industry, but remain independent, with the intent of upholding the standards or codes like the Advertising Standards Authority in the UK.

In the UK, most forms of outdoor advertising such as the display of billboards is regulated by the UK Town and County Planning system. Currently, the display of an advertisement without consent from the Planning Authority is a criminal offense liable to a fine of £2,500 per offense. All of the major outdoor billboard companies in the UK have convictions of this nature.

In the US, many communities believe that many forms of outdoor advertising blight the public realm. As long ago as the 1960s in the US there were attempts to ban billboard advertising in the open countryside. Cities such as São Paulo have introduced an outright ban with London also having specific legislation to control unlawful displays.

Many advertisers employ a wide-variety of linguistic devices to bypass regulatory laws (e.g. In France, printing English words in bold and French translations in fine print to deal with the Article 120 of the 1994 Toubon Law limiting the use of English). The advertisement of controversial products such as cigarettes and condoms are subject to government regulation in many countries. For instance, the tobacco industry is required by law in most countries to display warnings cautioning consumers about the health hazards of their products. Linguistic variation is often used by advertisers as a creative device to reduce the impact of such requirements.

Advertising Research

Advertising research is a specialized form of research that works to improve the effectiveness and efficiency of advertising. It entails numerous forms of research which employ different methodologies. Advertising research includes pre-testing (also known as copy testing) and post-testing of ads and/or campaigns – pre-testing is done before an ad airs to gauge how well it will perform and post-testing is done after an ad airs to determine the in-market impact of the ad or campaign. Continuous ad tracking and the Communicus System are competing examples of post-testing advertising research types.

Semiotics

Meanings between consumers and marketers depict signs and symbols that are encoded in everyday objects. Semiotics is the study of signs and how they are interpreted. Advertising has many hidden signs and meanings within brand names, logos, package designs, print advertisements, and television advertisements. Semiotics aims to study and interpret the message being conveyed in (for example) advertisements. Logos and advertisements can be interpreted at two levels - known as the surface level and the underlying level. The surface level uses signs creatively to create an image or personality for a product. These signs can be images, words, fonts, colors, or slogans. The underlying level is made up of hidden meanings. The combination of images, words, colors, and slogans must be interpreted by the audience or consumer. The "key to advertising analysis" is the signifier and the signified. The signifier is the object and the signified is the mental concept. A product has a signifier and a signified. The signifier is the color, brand name, logo design, and technology. The signified has two meanings known as denotative and connotative. The denotative meaning is the meaning of the product. A television's denotative meaning might be that it is high definition. The connotative meaning is the product's deep and hidden meaning. A connotative meaning of a television would be that it is top-of-the-line.

Apple's commercials used a black silhouette of a person that was the age of Apple's target market. They placed the silhouette in front of a blue screen so that the picture behind the silhouette could be constantly changing. However, the one thing that stays the same in these ads is that there is music in the background and the silhouette is listening to that music on a white iPod through white headphones. Through advertising, the white color on a set of earphones now signifies that the music device is an iPod. The white color signifies almost all of Apple's products.

The semiotics of gender plays a key influence on the way in which signs are interpreted. When considering gender roles in advertising, individuals are influenced by three categories. Certain characteristics of stimuli may enhance or decrease the elaboration of the message (if the product is perceived as feminine or masculine). Second, the characteristics of individuals can affect attention and elaboration of the message (traditional or non-traditional gender role orientation). Lastly, situational factors may be important to influence the elaboration of the message.

There are two types of marketing communication claims-objective and subjective. Objective claims stem from the extent to which the claim associates the brand with a tangible product or service feature. For instance, a camera may have auto-focus features. Subjective claims convey emotional, subjective, impressions of intangible aspects of a product or service. They are non-physical features of a product or service that cannot be directly perceived, as they have no physical reality. For instance the brochure has a beautiful design. Males tend to respond better to objective marketing-communications claims while females tend to respond better to subjective marketing communications claims.

Voiceovers are commonly used in advertising. Most voiceovers are done by men, with figures of up to 94% having been reported. There have been more female voiceovers in recent years but mainly for food, household products, and feminine-care products.

Gender Effects in the Processing of Advertising

According to a 1977 study by David Statt, females process information comprehensively, while males process information through heuristic devices such as procedures, methods or strategies for solving problems, which could have an effect on how they interpret advertising. According to this study, men prefer to have available and apparent cues to interpret the message where females engage in more creative, associative, imagery-laced interpretation. Later research by a Danish team found that advertising attempts to persuade men to improve their appearance or performance, whereas its approach to women is aimed at transformation toward an impossible ideal of female presentation. Advertising's manipulation of women's aspiration to these ideal types, as they are portrayed in film, in erotic art, in advertising, on stage, music video, and other media exposures, requires at least a conditioned rejection of female reality, and thereby takes on a highly ideological cast. Not everyone agrees: one critic viewed this monologic, gender-specific interpretation of advertising as excessively skewed and politicized.

More recently, research by Martin (2003) reveals that males and females differ in how they react to advertising depending on their mood at the time of exposure to the ads, and the affective tone of the advertising. When feeling sad, males prefer happy ads to boost their mood. In contrast, females prefer happy ads when they are feeling happy. The television programs in which the ads are embedded are shown to influence a viewer's mood state.

Basic Form of Advertising

Direct Marketing

A pile of advertising mail.

Direct marketing is a form of advertising which allows businesses and nonprofit organizations to communicate directly to customers through a variety of media including cell phone text messaging, email, websites, online adverts, database marketing, fliers, catalog distribution, promotional letters and targeted television, newspaper and magazine advertisements as well as outdoor advertising. Among practitioners, it is also known as direct response.

Direct marketing focuses on the customer, data, and testing. Hence, besides the actual communication, a direct marketing campaign will incorporate actionable segments and use pre- and post-campaign analytics to measure results. Characteristics that distinguish direct marketing from other types of marketing are:

- A database of names (prospects, customers, businesses, etc.), often with certain other relevant information such as contact number/address, demographic information, purchase habits/history, and company history, is used to develop a target market with common interests, traits or characteristics. Generating such a database is often considered part of the direct marketing campaign.

- Marketing messages are addressed directly to this list of customers and/or prospects. Addressability comes in a variety of forms including email addresses, phone numbers, fax numbers, postal addresses, and web browser cookies.

- Direct marketing seeks to drive a specific "call to action." For example, an advertisement may ask the prospect to call a free phone number, mail in a response or order, or click on a link to a website.

- Direct marketing emphasizes traceable, measurable responses. It also emphasizes maximizing response rates by testing while minimizing advertising expenses when engaging prospective customers, regardless of the medium used.

Direct marketing is practiced by businesses of all sizes. A direct advertising campaign aims to deliver a good return on investment by showing how many potential customers responded to a clear call to action. This is in contrast to general advertising, which eschews calls for action in favor of messages that build prospects' emotional awareness or engagement with a brand.

Popularity

A 2010 study by the Direct Marketing Association reports that in 2010, marketers—commercial and nonprofit—spent $153.3 billion on direct marketing, which accounted for 54.2% of all ad expenditures in the United States. Measured against total US sales, these advertising expenditures generated approximately $1.798 trillion in incremental sales. In 2010, direct marketing accounted for 8.3% of total US gross domestic product. In 2010, there were 1.4 million direct marketing employees in the US. Their collective sales efforts directly supported 8.4 million other jobs, accounting for a total of 9.8 million US jobs.

History

Mail order pioneer Aaron Montgomery Ward believed that using the technique of selling products directly to the customer at appealing prices could, if executed effectively and efficiently, revolutionize the market industry and therefore be used as a model for marketing products and creating customer loyalty. The term "direct marketing" was coined long after Montgomery Ward's time.

In 1872, Ward produced the first mail-order catalog for his Montgomery Ward mail order business. By buying goods and then reselling them directly to customers, Ward was consequently removing the middlemen at the general store and, to the benefit of the customer, drastically lowering the prices. The Direct Mail Advertising Association, predecessor of the present-day Direct Marketing Association, was first established in 1917. Third class bulk mail postage rates were established in 1928.

In 1967, Lester Wunderman identified, named, and defined the term "direct marketing". Wunderman—considered to be the father of contemporary direct marketing—is behind the creation of the toll-free 1-800 number and numerous loyalty marketing programs including the Columbia Record Club, the magazine subscription card, and the American Express Customer Rewards program.

Benefits

Direct marketing is attractive to many marketers because its positive results can be measured directly. For example, if a marketer sends out 1,000 solicitations by mail and 100 respond to the promotion, the marketer can say with confidence that campaign led directly to 10% direct responses. This metric is known as the 'response rate,' and it is one of many clearly quantifiable success metrics employed by direct marketers. In contrast, general advertising uses indirect measurements, such as awareness or engagement, since there is no direct response from a consumer. Measurement of results is a fundamental element in successful direct marketing.

One of the other significant benefits of Direct Marketing is, it enables promoting products or services that might not have a strong brand. Products or service with a sound value proposition, matched with an attractive offer, supported with effective communication, delivered through a suitable direct marketing channel and targeting the relevant customer segment can result in very effective cost of acquisition albeit the brand might be relatively unknown. Relative to other channels of distribution (say retailing) Direct Marketing as a practice principally relies on the proposition, offer, communication, choice of channel and the target customer and so less dependent on the brand strength.

The Internet has made it easier for marketing managers to measure the results of a campaign. This is often achieved by using a specific website landing page directly relating to the promotional material. A call to action will ask the customer to visit the landing page, and the effectiveness of the campaign can be measured by taking the number of promotional messages distributed and dividing it into the number of responses. Another way to measure the results is to compare the projected sales or generated leads for a given term with the actual sales or leads after a direct advertising campaign.

Challenges and Solutions

While many marketers recognize the financial benefits of increasing targeted awareness, some direct marketing efforts using particular media have been criticized for generating poor quality leads, either due to poor message strategy or because of poorly compiled demographic databases. This poses a problem for marketers and consumers alike, as advertisers do not wish to waste money on communicating with consumers not interested in their products.

Success of any Direct Marketing campaign, in terms of number of times the desired response may vary between the best vs. the worst of the following parameters, depends on:

- List or targeting (best targeting may yield up to 6 times the response, as compared with the worst targeting).

- Offer (best offer may yield up to 3 times the response, as compared with the worst offer).

- Timing (best timing for the campaign may yield up to 2 times the response, as compared with the worst timing).

- Ease of response (best/multiple ways offered to respond may yield up to 1.35 times the response, as compared with not-so-friendly response mechanism/s).

- Creativity (most creative messaging may yield up to 1.2 times the response, as compared to the least creative messaging).

- Media employed. The medium/media used to deliver a message can have a significant impact on responses. It is difficult to truly personalize a DRTV or radio message. One can even attempt to send a personalized message via email or text message, but a high quality direct mail envelope and letter will typically have a better chance of generated a response in this scenario.

In sum, choosing the best of all the above parameters may yield up to 58 times more response, as compared to choosing the worst of the above parameters. Addressing these helps assuage the concerns of the marketers.

Some of these concerns have been addressed by direct marketers by the use of individual "opt-out" lists, variable printing, and better-targeted list practices. Additionally, in order to avoid unwanted mailings, members of the marketing industry have established preference services that give customers more control over the marketing communications they receive in the mail.

The term "junk mail," referring to unsolicited commercial ads delivered via post office or directly deposited in consumers' mail boxes, can be traced back to 1954. The term "spam," meaning "unsolicited commercial e-mail," can be traced back to March 31, 1993, although in its first few months it merely referred to inadvertently posting a message so many times on UseNet that the repetitions effectively drowned out the normal flow of conversation.

To address the concerns of unwanted emails or spam, in 2003, The US Congress enacted the Controlling the Assault of Non-Solicited Pornography and Marketing (CAN-SPAM) Act to curb unwanted email messages. Can-Spam gives recipients the ability to stop unwanted emails, and set out tough penalties for violations. Additionally, ISPs and email service providers have developed increasingly effective Email Filtering programs. These filters can interfere with the delivery of email marketing campaigns, even if the person has subscribed to receive them, as legitimate email marketing can possess the same hallmarks as spam. There are a range of email service providers that provide services for legitimate opt-in emailers to avoid being classified as spam.

Consumers have expressed concerns about the privacy and environmental implications of direct marketing. In response to consumer demand and increasing business pressure to increase the effectiveness of reaching the right customer with direct marketing, companies specialize in targeted direct advertising to great effect, reducing advertising budget waste and increasing the effectiveness of delivering a marketing message with better geo-demography information, delivering the advertising message to only the customers interested in the product, service, or event on offer. Additionally, members of the advertising industry have been working to adopt stricter codes regarding online targeted advertising.

Channels

Any medium that can be used to deliver a communication to a customer can be employed in direct marketing, including.

Email Marketing

Sending marketing messages through email or email marketing is one of the most widely used direct-marketing methods. One reason for email marketing's popularity is that it is relatively inexpensive to design, test, and send an email message. It also allows marketers to deliver messages around the clock, and to accurately measure responses.

Online Tools

With the expansion of digital technology and tools, direct marketing is increasingly taking place through online channels. Most online advertising is delivered to a focused group of customers and has a trackable response.

- Display Ads are interactive ads that appear on the Web next to content on Web pages or Web services. Formats include static banners, pop ups, videos, and floating units. Customers can click on the ad to respond directly to the message or to find more detailed information. According to research by eMarketer, expenditures on online display ads rose 24.5% between 2010 and 2011.

- Search: 49% of US spending on Internet ads goes to search, in which advertisers pay for prominent placement among listings in search engines whenever a potential customer enters a relevant search term, allowing ads to be delivered to customers based upon their already-indicated search criteria. This paid placement industry generates more than $10 billion for search companies. Marketers also use search engine optimization to drive traffic to their sites.

- Social Media Sites, such as Facebook and Twitter, also provide opportunities for direct marketers to communicate directly with customers by creating content to which customers can respond.

Mobile

Through mobile marketing, marketers engage with prospective customers and donors in an interactive manner through a mobile device or network, such as a cellphone, smartphone, or tablet. Types of mobile marketing messages include: SMS (short message service)—marketing communications are sent in the form of text messages, also known as texting. MMS (multi-media message service)—marketing communications are sent in the form of media messages.

In October 2013, the Federal Telephone Consumers Protection Act made it illegal to contact an individual via cell phone without prior express written consent for all telephone calls using an automatic telephone dialing system or a prerecorded voice to deliver a telemarketing message to wireless numbers and residential lines. An existing business relationship does not provide an exception to this requirement.

Mobile Applications: Smartphone-based mobile apps contain several types of messages. Push Notifications are direct messages sent to a user either automatically or as part of a campaign. They include transactional, marketing, geo-based, and more. Rich Push Notifications are full HTML Push Notifications. Mobile apps also contain Interactive ads that appear inside the mobile application or app; Location-Based Marketing: marketing messages delivered directly to a mobile device based on the user's location; QR Codes (quick-response barcodes): This is a type of 2D barcode with an encoded link that can be accessed from a smartphone. This technology is increasingly being used for everything from special offers to product information. Mobile Banner Ads: Like standard banner ads for desktop Web pages but smaller to fit on mobile screens and run on the mobile content network .

Telemarketing

Another common form of direct marketing is telemarketing, in which marketers contact customers by phone. The primary benefit to businesses is increased lead generation, which helps businesses increase sales volume and customer base. The most successful telemarketing service providers focus on generating more "qualified" leads that have a higher probability of getting converted into actual sales.

In the United States, the National Do Not Call Registry was created in 2003 to offer consumers a choice whether to receive telemarketing calls at home. The FTC created the National Do Not Call Registry after a comprehensive review of the Telemarketing Sales Rule (TSR). The do-not-call provisions of the TSR cover any plan, program, or campaign to sell goods or services through interstate phone calls.

The 2012 modification, which went into effect on October 16, 2013, stated that prior express written consent will be required for all autodialed and/or pre-recorded calls/texts sent/made to cell phone; and for pre-recorded calls made to residential land lines for marketing purposes.

Further, a consumer who does not wish to receive further prerecorded telemarketing calls can "opt out" of receiving such calls by dialing a telephone number (required to be provided in the prerecorded message) to register his or her do-not-call request. The provisions do not cover calls from political organizations or charities.

Canada has its own National Do Not Call List (DNCL). In other countries it is voluntary, such as the New Zealand Name Removal Service.

Voicemail Marketing

Voicemail marketing emerged from the market prevalence of personal voice mailboxes, and business voicemail systems. Voicemail marketing presented a cost effective means by which to reach people directly, by voice. Abuse of consumer marketing applications of voicemail marketing resulted in an abundance of "voice-spam," and prompted many jurisdictions to pass laws regulating consumer voicemail marketing. More recently, businesses have utilized guided voicemail (an application where pre-recorded voicemails are guided by live callers) to accomplish personalized business-to-business marketing formerly reserved for telemarketing. Because guided voicemail is used to contact only businesses, it is exempt from Do Not Call regulations in place for other forms of voicemail marketing.

Voice-mail courier is a similar form of voice-mail marketing with both business-to-business and business-to-consumer applications.

Broadcast Faxing

Broadcast faxing, in which faxes are sent to multiple recipients, is now less common than in the past.

This is partly due to laws in the United States and elsewhere which regulate its use for consumer marketing. In 2005, President Bush signed into law S.714, the Junk Fax Prevention Act of 2005 (JFPA), which allows marketers to send commercial faxes to those with whom they have an established business relationship (EBR), but imposes some new requirements. These requirements include providing an opt-out notice on the first page of faxes and establishing a system to accept opt-outs at any time of the day. Roughly 2% of direct marketers use fax, mostly for business-to-business marketing campaigns.

Couponing

Couponing is used in print and digital media to elicit a response from the reader. An example is a coupon which the reader receives through the mail and takes to a store's check-out counter to receive a discount.

Digital Coupons: Manufacturers and retailers make coupons available online for electronic orders that can be downloaded and printed. Digital coupons are available on company websites, social media outlets, texts, and email alerts. There are an increasing number of mobile phone applications offering digital coupons for direct use.

Daily Deal Sites offer local and online deals each day, and are becoming increasingly popular. Customers sign up to receive notice of discounts and offers, which are sent daily by email. Purchases are often made using a special coupon code or promotional code. The largest of these sites, Groupon, has over 83 million subscribers.

Direct Response Marketing

Direct Response Marketing is designed to generate an immediate response from consumers, where each consumer response (and purchase) can be measured, and attributed to individual advertisements. This form of marketing is differentiated from other marketing approaches, primarily because there are no intermediaries such as retailers between the buyer and seller, and therefore the buyer must contact the seller directly to purchase products or services. Direct-response marketing is delivered through a wide variety of media, including DRTV, radio, mail, print advertising, telemarketing, catalogues, and the Internet.

Direct Response Mail Order

Mail order in which customers respond by mailing a completed order form to the marketer. Mail order direct response has become more successful in recent years due to internet exposure.

Direct Response Television

Direct marketing via television (commonly referred to as DRTV) has two basic forms: long form (usually half-hour or hour-long segments that explain a product in detail and are commonly referred to as infomercials) and short form, which refers to typical 30-second or 60-second commercials that ask viewers for an immediate response (typically to call a phone number on screen or go to a website). TV-response marketing—i.e. infomercials—can be considered a form of direct marketing, since responses are in the form of calls to telephone numbers given on-air. This allows marketers to reasonably conclude that the calls are due to a particular campaign, and enables them to obtain customers' phone numbers as targets for telemarketing. One of the most famous DRTV commercials was for Ginsu Knives by Ginsu Products, Inc. of RI. Several aspects of ad, such as its use of adding items to the offer and the guarantee of satisfaction were much copied, and came to be considered part of the formula for success with short-form direct-response TV ads (DRTV).

Forms of direct response marketing on television include standard short form television commercials, infomercials and home shopping networks. Short-form direct-response commercials have time lengths ranging from 30 seconds to 2 minutes. Long form infomercials are typically 30 minutes long. An offshoot of the infomercial is the home shopping industry. In this medium, items can potentially be offered with reduced overhead.

Direct Response Radio

In direct response radio, ads contain a call to action with a specific tracking mechanism. Often, this tracking mechanism is a "call now" prompt with a toll-free phone number or a unique Web URL. Results of the ad can be tracked in terms of calls, orders, customers, leads, sales, revenue, and profits that result from the airing of those ads.

Direct Response Magazines and Newspapers

Magazine and newspaper ads often include a direct response call-to-action, such as a toll-free number, a coupon redeemable at a brick-and-mortar store, or a QR code that can be scanned by a mobile device—these methods are all forms of direct marketing, because they elicit a direct and measurable action from the customer.

Other Direct Response Media

Other media, such as magazines, newspapers, radio, social media, search engine marketing and e-mail can be used to elicit the response. A survey of large corporations found e-mail to be one of the most effective forms of direct response.

Direct Mail

The term advertising, or direct mail, is used to refer to communications sent to potential customers or donors via the postal service and other delivery services. Direct mail is sent to customers based on criteria such as age, income, location, profession, buying pattern, etc. Direct mail includes advertising circulars, catalogs, free-trial CDs, pre-approved credit card applications, and other unsolicited merchandising invitations delivered by mail to homes and businesses. Bulk mailings are a particularly popular method of promotion for businesses operating in the financial services, home computer, and travel and tourism industries.

In many developed countries, direct mail represents such a significant amount of the total volume of mail that special rate classes have been established. In the United States and United Kingdom, for example, there are bulk mail rates that enable marketers to send mail at rates that are substantially lower than regular first-class rates. In order to qualify for these rates, marketers must format and sort the mail in particular ways—which reduces the handling (and therefore costs) required by the postal service. In the US, marketers send over 90 billion pieces of direct mail per year.

Advertisers often refine direct mail practices into targeted mailing, in which mail is sent out following database analysis to select recipients considered most likely to respond positively. For example, a person who has demonstrated an interest in golf may receive direct mail for golf-related products or perhaps for goods and services that are appropriate for golfers. This use of database analysis is a type of database marketing. The United States Postal Service calls this form of mail "advertising mail" (admail for short).

Insert Media

Another form of direct marketing, insert media are marketing materials that are inserted into other communications, such as a catalog, newspaper, magazine, package, or bill. Coop or shared mail, where marketing offers from several companies are delivered via a single envelope, is also considered insert media.

Out-of-Home

Out-of-home direct marketing refers to a wide array of media designed to reach the consumer outside the home, including billboards, transit, bus shelters, bus benches, aerials, airports, in-flight, in-store, movies, college campus/high schools, hotels, shopping malls, sport facilities, stadiums, taxis—that contain a call-to-action for the customer to respond.

Direct Selling

Direct selling is the sale of products by face-to-face contact with the customer, either by having salespeople approach potential customers in person, or through indirect means such as Tupperware parties.

Grassroots/Community Marketing

The Door-to-Door Distribution

Ethical Conduct

The ICC Consolidated Code of Advertising and Marketing relates to all direct marketing activities in their entirety, whatever their form, medium or content. It sets the standards of ethical conduct to be followed by marketers, practitioners or other contractors providing services for direct marketing purposes or in the media.

The Offer

The fulfilment of any obligation arising from a direct marketing activity should be prompt and efficient.

Whenever an offer is made, all the commitments to be fulfilled by the marketer, the operator and the consumer should be made clear to consumers, either directly or by reference to sales conditions available to them at the time of the offer.

Presentation

When the presentation of an offer also features products not included in the offer, or where additional products need to be purchased to enable the consumer to use the product on offer, this should be made clear in the original offer.

High-pressure tactics which might be construed as harassment should be avoided, and, marketers should ensure that they respect local culture and tradition to avoid offensive questions.

Right of Withdrawal

Where consumers have a right of withdrawal (the consumer's right to resend any goods to the seller, or to cancel the order for services, within a certain time limit and thus annulling the sale), the marketer should inform them of the existence of this right, how to obtain further information about it, and how to exercise it. Where there is an offer to supply products to the consumer on the basis of "free examination", "free trial", "free approval" and the like, it should be made clear in the offer who will bear the cost of returning products and the procedure for returning them should be as simple as possible. Any time limit for the return should be clearly disclosed.

Identity of the Marketer

The identity of the marketer and/or operator and details of where and how they may be contacted should be given in the offer, so as to enable the consumer to communicate directly and effectively with them. This information should be available as a permanent reference which the consumer can keep, i.e. via a separate document offline, an online document, email or SMS; it should not, for example, appear only on an order form which the consumer is required to return. At the time of delivery of the product, the marketer's full name, address and telephone number should be supplied to the consumer.

Respecting Consumer Wishes

Where consumers have indicated the wish not to receive direct marketing communications by signing on to a preference service, or in any other way, this should be respected. Marketers who are communicating with consumers internationally should, where possible ensure that they avail themselves of the appropriate preference service in the markets to which they are addressing their communications and respect consumers' wishes not to receive such communications General Provisions, article 19, data protection and privacy. Where a system exists, en-abling consumers to indicate a wish not to receive unaddressed mail (e.g. mailbox stickers), this should be respected.

Responsibility

Overall responsibility for all aspects of direct marketing activities, whatever their kind or content, rests with the marketer. However, responsibility also applies to other participants in direct marketing activities and that needs to be taken into account. As well as marketers, these may include:operators, telemarketers or data controllers, or their subcontractors, who contribute to the activity or communication; publishers, media-owners or contractors who publish, transmit or distribute the offer or any other communication.

Brand

Ferrari is the world's most powerful brand according to Brand Finance.

A brand is a set of marketing and communication methods that help to distinguish a company from competitors and create a lasting impression in the minds of customers. The key components that form a brand's toolbox include a brand's identity, brand communication (such as by logos and trademarks), brand awareness, brand loyalty, and various branding (brand management) strategies. Brand equity is the measurable totality of a brand's worth and is validated by assessing the effectiveness of these branding components. In a fleeting market where traditional linear models of business are being replaced by more radical interconnected models, brand equity is one marketing technique that remains firmly rooted in prosperity. To reach such an invaluable brand prestige requires a commitment to a particular way of doing business. A corporation who exhibits a strong brand culture is dedicated on producing intangible outputs such as customer satisfaction, reduced price sensitivity and customer loyalty. A brand is in essence a promise to its customers that they can expect long-term security, a competitive frame of reference and consistent delivery of functional as well as emotional benefits. When a customer is familiar with a brand or favours it incomparably to its competitors, this is when a corporation has reached a high level of brand equity.

A brand (or marque for car model) is a name, term, design, symbol, or other feature that distinguishes one seller's product from those of others. Brands are used in business, marketing, and advertising. Initially, livestock branding was adopted to differentiate one person's cattle from another's by means of a distinctive symbol burned into the animal's skin with a hot branding iron.

In accounting, a brand defined as an intangible asset is often the most valuable asset on a corporation's balance sheet. Brand owners manage their brands carefully to create shareholder value, and brand valuation is an important management technique that ascribes a money value to a brand,

and allows marketing investment to be managed (e.g.: prioritized across a portfolio of brands) to maximize shareholder value. Although only acquired brands appear on a company's balance sheet, the notion of putting a value on a brand forces marketing leaders to be focused on long term stewardship of the brand and managing for value.

The word "brand" is often used as a metonym referring to the company that is strongly identified with a brand.

Marque or make are often used to denote a brand of motor vehicle, which may be distinguished from a car model. A concept brand is a brand that is associated with an abstract concept, like breast cancer awareness or environmentalism, rather than a specific product, service, or business. A commodity brand is a brand associated with a commodity.

History

The word "brand" derives from the Old Norse "brandr" meaning "to burn" - recalling the practice of producers burning their mark (or brand) onto their products.

The oldest generic brand, in continuous use in India since the Vedic period (ca. 1100 B.C.E to 500 B.C.E), is the herbal paste known as Chyawanprash, consumed for its purported health benefits and attributed to a revered rishi (or seer) named Chyawan. This product was developed at Dhosi Hill, an extinct volcano in northern India.

Roman glassmakers branded their works, with Ennion being the most prominent.

The Italians used brands in the form of watermarks on paper in the 13th century. Blind Stamps, hallmarks, and silver-makers' marks are all types of brand.

Although connected with the history of trademarks and including earlier examples which could be deemed "protobrands" (such as the marketing puns of the "Vesuvinum" wine jars found at Pompeii), brands in the field of mass-marketing originated in the 19th century with the advent of packaged goods. Industrialization moved the production of many household items, such as soap, from local communities to centralized factories. When shipping their items, the factories would literally brand their logo or insignia on the barrels used, extending the meaning of "brand" to that of a trademark.

Bass & Company, the British brewery, claims their red-triangle brand as the world's first trademark. Tate & Lyle of Lyle's Golden Syrup makes a similar claim, having been recognized by Guinness World Records as Britain's oldest brand, with its green-and-gold packaging having remained almost unchanged since 1885. Another example comes from Antiche Fornaci Giorgi in Italy, which has stamped or carved its bricks (as found in Saint Peter's Basilica in the Vatican City) with the same proto-logo since 1731.

Cattle-branding has been used since Ancient Egypt. The term "maverick," originally meaning an un-branded calf, came from a Texas pioneer rancher, Sam Maverick, whose neglected cattle often got loose and were rounded up by his neighbors. Use of the word maverick spread among cowboys and came to apply to unbranded calves found wandering alone.

Factories established during the Industrial Revolution introduced mass-produced goods and needed to sell their products to a wider market - to customers previously familiar only with locally produced goods. It quickly became apparent that a generic package of soap had difficulty competing with familiar, local products. The packaged-goods manufacturers needed to convince the market that the public could place just as much trust in the non-local product. Pears soap, Campbell's soup, soft drink Coca-Cola, Juicy Fruit chewing gum, Aunt Jemima pancake mix, and Quaker Oats oatmeal were among the first products to be "branded" in an effort to increase the consumer's familiarity with their merits. Other brands which date from that era, such as Uncle Ben's rice and Kellogg's breakfast cereal, furnish illustrations of the trend.

Around 1900, James Walter Thompson published a house ad explaining trademark advertising. This was an early commercial explanation of what we now know as branding. Companies soon adopted slogans, mascots, and jingles that began to appear on radio and early television. By the 1940s, manufacturers began to recognize the way in which consumers were developing relationships with their brands in a social/psychological/anthropological sense.

Manufacturers quickly learned to build their brands' identity and personality such as youthfulness, fun or luxury. This began the practice we now know as "branding" today, where the consumers buy "the brand" instead of the product. This trend continued to the 1980s, and is now quantified in concepts such as brand value and brand equity. Naomi Klein has described this development as "brand equity mania". In 1988, for example, Philip Morris purchased Kraft for six times what the company was worth on paper; it was felt that what they really purchased was its brand name.

April 2, 1993, or Marlboro Friday, is often considered the "death" of the brand – the day Philip Morris declared that they were cutting the price of Marlboro cigarettes by 20% in order to compete with bargain cigarettes. Marlboro cigarettes were noted at the time for their heavy advertising campaigns and well-nuanced brand image. In response to the announcement, Wall Street stocks nose-dived for a large number of branded companies: Heinz, Coca-Cola, Quaker Oats, PepsiCo, Tide, and Lysol. Many thought the event signalled the beginning of a trend towards "brand blindness" (Klein 13), questioning the power of "brand value".

Concepts

Effective branding can result in higher sales of not only one product, but of other products associated with that brand. If a customer loves Pillsbury biscuits and trusts the brand, he or she is more likely to try other products offered by the company - such as chocolate-chip cookies, for example. Brand development, often the task of a design team, takes time to produce. Brand is the personality that identifies a product, service or company (name, term, sign, symbol, or design, or combination of them) and how it relates to key constituencies: customers, staff, partners, investors etc.

Some people distinguish the psychological aspect (brand associations like thoughts, feelings, perceptions, images, experiences, beliefs, attitudes, and so on that become linked to the brand) of a brand from the experiential aspect. The experiential aspect consists of the sum of all points of contact with the brand and is known as the brand experience. The brand experience is a brand's action perceived by a person. The psychological aspect, sometimes referred to as the brand image, is a symbolic construct created within the minds of people, consisting of all the information and expectations associated with a product, with a service or with the company(ies) providing them.

People engaged in branding seek to develop or align the expectations behind the brand experience, creating the impression that a brand associated with a product or service has certain qualities or characteristics that make it special or unique. A brand can therefore become one of the most valuable elements in an advertising theme, as it demonstrates what the brand owner is able to offer in the marketplace. The art of creating and maintaining a brand is called brand management. Orientation of an entire organization towards its brand is called brand orientation. Brand orientation develops in response to market intelligence.

Careful brand management seeks to make products or services relevant to a target audience. Brands should be seen as more than the difference between the actual cost of a product and its selling price – they represent the sum of all valuable qualities of a product to the consumer.

A widely known brand is said to have "brand recognition". When brand recognition builds up to a point where a brand enjoys a critical mass of positive sentiment in the marketplace, it is said to have achieved brand franchise. Brand recognition is most successful when people can state a brand without being explicitly exposed to the company's name, but rather through visual signifiers like logos, slogans, and colors. For example, Disney successfully branded its particular script font (originally created for Walt Disney's "signature" logo), which it used in the logo for go.com.

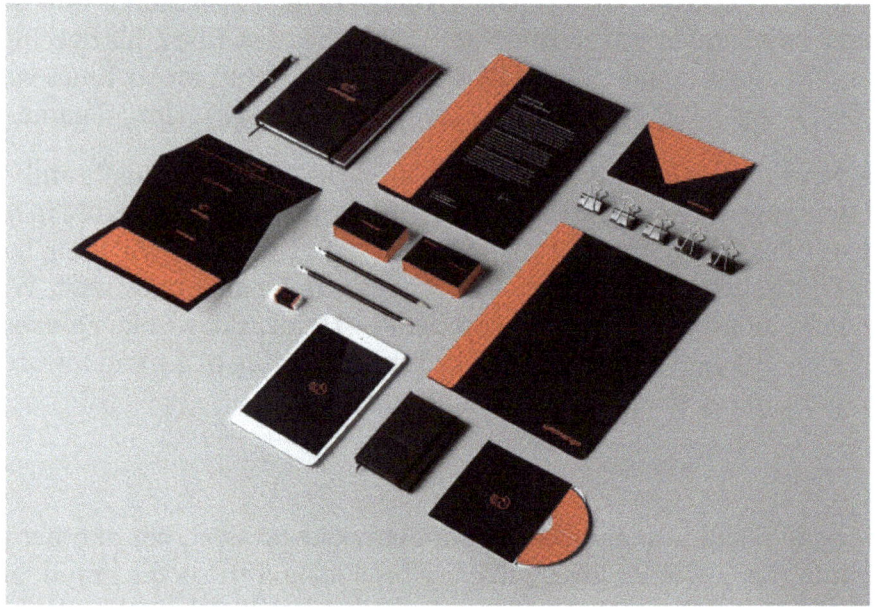

Visual Identity (example) created by Przemek Kowal.

Consumers may look on branding as an aspect of products or services, as it often serves to denote a certain attractive quality or characteristic. From the perspective of brand owners, branded products or services can command higher prices. Where two products resemble each other, but one of the products has no associated branding (such as a generic, store-branded product), potential purchasers may often select the more expensive branded product on the basis of the perceived quality of the brand or on the basis of the reputation of the brand owner.

Corporate Brand Identity

Brand identity is the embodiment behind a corporation's reason for existence. Simply, the brand identity is a set of individual components, such as a name, a design, a set of imagery, a slogan, a vision, etc. which set the brand aside from others. In order for a company to exude a strong sense of brand identity, it must have an in-depth understanding of its target market, competitors and the surrounding business environment. Brand identity includes both the core identity and the extended identity. The core identity reflects consistent long-term associations with the brand; whereas the extended identity involves the intricate details of the brand that help generate a constant motif.

According to Kotler et al. (2009), a brand's identity may deliver four levels of meaning:

1. Attributes

2. Benefits

3. Values

4. Personality

A brand's attributes are a set of labels with which the corporation wishes to be associated. For example, a brand may showcase its primary attribute as environmental friendliness. However, a brand's attributes alone are not enough to persuade a customer into purchasing the product. These attributes must be communicated through benefits, which are more emotional translations. If a brand's attribute is being environmentally friendly, customers will receive the benefit of feeling that they are helping the environment by associating with the brand. Aside from attributes and benefits, a brand's identity may also involve branding to focus on representing its core set of values. If a company is seen to symbolise specific values, it will, in turn, attract customers who also believe in these values. For example, Nike's brand represents the value of a "just do it" attitude. Thus, this form of brand identification attracts customers who also share this same value. Even more extensive than its perceived values is a brand's personality. Quite literally, one can easily describe a successful brand identity as if it were a person. This form of brand identity has proven to be the most advantageous in maintaining long-lasting relationships with consumers, as it gives them a sense of personal interaction with the brand Collectively, all four forms of brand identification help to deliver a powerful meaning behind what a corporation hopes to accomplish, and to explain why customers should choose one brand over its competitors.

Brand Awareness

Brand awareness is a key component in understanding the effectiveness both of a brand's identity and of its communication methods. When potential customers need to make a purchasing decision, they rely on their brand awareness to trigger their memories. Successful brands are those that consistently generate a high level of brand awareness, as this can often be the pivotal factor in securing customer transactions. The two forms of brand awareness are brand recognition and brand recollection. Each form reflects a different stage in a customer's cognitive ability to address the brand in a given circumstance.

Brand recognition is the initial phase of brand awareness and validates whether or not a customer remembers being pre-exposed to the brand. When customers experience brand recognition, they are triggered by either a visual or verbal cue. For example, when looking to satisfy a category need such as toilet paper, the customer would firstly be presented with multiple brands to choose from. Once the customer is visually or verbally faced with a brand, he/she may remember being introduced to the brand before. This would be classified as brand recognition, as the customer can retrieve the particular memory node that referred to the brand, once given a cue. Often, this form of brand awareness assists customers in choosing one brand over another when faced with a low-involvement purchasing decision.

Unlike brand recognition, brand recollection is not triggered by a visual or verbal cue. Instead, brand recollection "...requires that the consumers correctly retrieve the brand from memory". Rather than being given a choice of multiple brands to satisfy a need, consumers are faced with a need first, and then must recall a brand from their memory to satisfy that need. This level of brand awareness is stronger than brand recognition, as the brand must be firmly cemented in the consumer's memory to enable unassisted remembrance. Thus, brand recollection is a confirmation that previous branding touchpoints have successfully fermented in the minds of its consumers.

Brand awareness involves a customers' ability to recall and recognize brands, logos and advertisements. It helps the customers to understand to which product or service category the particular brand belongs and what products and services sell under the brand name. It also ensures that customers know which of their needs are satisfied by the brand through its products (Keller). Brand awareness is of critical importance in competitive situations, since customers will not consider a brand if they are not aware of it.

Various levels of brand awareness require different levels and combinations of brand recognition and recall:

- Most companies aim for "Top-of-Mind". Top-of-mind awareness occurs when a brand pops into a consumer's mind when asked to name brands in a product category. For example, when someone is asked to name a type of facial tissue, the common answer, "Kleenex", will represent a top-of-mind brand.

- Aided awareness occurs when consumers see or read a list of brands, and express familiarity with a particular brand only after they hear or see it as a type of memory aide.

- Strategic awareness occurs when a brand is not only top-of-mind to consumers, but also has distinctive qualities which consumers perceive as making it better than other brands in the particular market. The distinction(s) that set a product apart from the competition is/are also known as the unique selling point or USP.

Marketing-mix modeling can help marketing leaders optimize how they spend marketing budgets to maximize the impact on brand awareness or on sales. Managing brands for value creation will often involve applying marketing-mix modeling techniques in conjunction with brand valuation.

Brand Elements

Brands typically comprise various elements, such as:

- Name: the word or words used to identify a company, product, service, or concept.

- Logo: the visual trademark that identifies a brand.

- Tagline or catchphrase: "The Quicker Picker Upper" is associated with Bounty paper towels.

- Graphics: the "dynamic ribbon" is a trademarked part of Coca-Cola's brand.

- Shapes: the distinctive shapes of the Coca-Cola bottle and of the Volkswagen Beetle are trademarked elements of those brands.

- Colors: Owens Corning produces the only brand of fiberglass insulation that can be pink.

- Sounds: a unique tune or set of notes can denote a brand. NBC's chimes provide a famous example.

- Scents: the rose-jasmine-musk scent of Chanel No. 5 is trademarked.

- Tastes: Kentucky Fried Chicken has trademarked its special recipe of eleven herbs and spices for fried chicken.

- Movements: Lamborghini has trademarked the upward motion of its car doors.

Demonstrating touch points associated with purchase experience stages.

Brand Communication

Although brand identity is regarded as the most fundamental asset to a brand's equity, the worth of a brand's identity would become obsolete without ongoing brand communication. Integrated marketing communications (IMC) relates to how a brand transmits a clear consistent message to its stakeholders. Five key components comprise IMC:

- Advertising,

- Sales promotions,

- Direct marketing,

- Personal selling,

- Public relations.

The effectiveness of a brand's communication is determined by how accurately the customer perceives the brand's intended message through its IMC. Although IMC is a broad strategic concept, the most crucial brand communication elements are pinpointed to how the brand sends a message and what touch points the brand uses to connect with its customers.

One can analyse the traditional communication model into several consecutive steps:

- Firstly, a source/sender wishes to convey a message to a receiver. This source must encode the intended message in a way that the receiver will potentially understand.

- After the encoding stage, the forming of the message is complete and is portrayed through a selected channel. In IMC, channels may include media elements such as advertising, public relations, sales promotions, etc.

- It is at this point where the message can often deter from its original purpose as the message must go through the process of being decoded, which can often lead to unintended misinterpretation.

- Finally, the receiver retrieves the message and attempts to understand what the sender was aiming to render. Often, a message may be incorrectly received due to noise in the market, which is caused by "...unplanned static or distortion during the communication process".

- The final stage of this process is when the receiver responds to the message, which is received by the original sender as feedback.

When a brand communicates a brand identity to a receiver, it runs the risk of the receiver incorrectly interpreting the message. Therefore a brand should use appropriate communication channels to positively "...affect how the psychological and physical aspects of a brand are perceived".

In order for brands to effectively communicate to customers, marketers must "...consider all touch points, or sources of contact, that a customer has with the brand". Touch points represent the channel stage in the traditional communication model, where a message travels from the sender to the receiver. Any point where a customer has an interaction with the brand - whether watching a television advertisement, hearing about a brand through word of mouth, or even noticing a branded license plate - defines a touch point. According to Dalen et al. (2010), every touch point has the "...potential to add positive - or suppress negative - associations to the brand's equity" Thus a brand's IMC should cohesively deliver positive messages through appropriate touch points associated with its target market. One methodology involves using sensory stimuli touch points to activate customer emotion. For example, if a brand consistently uses a pleasant smell as a primary touch point, the brand has a much higher chance of creating a positive lasting effect on its customers' senses as well as memory. Another way a brand can ensure that it is utilising the best communication channel, is by focusing on touch points that suit particular areas associated with customer experience. As suggested Figure 2, certain touch points link with a specific stage in customer-brand-involvement. For example, a brand may recognise that advertising touch points are most effective during the pre-purchase experience stage therefore they may target their advertisements to new customers rather than to existing customers. Overall, a brand has the ability to strengthen brand equity by using IMC branding communications through touch points.

Brand communication is important in ensuring brand success in the business world and refers to how businesses transmit their brand messages, characteristics and attributes to their consumers. One method of brand communication which companies can exploit involves electronic word-of-mouth (eWOM). EWoM is a relatively new approach identified to communicate with consumers. One popular method of eWOM involves social networking sites (SNSs) such as Twitter. A study found that consumers classed their relationship with a brand as closer if that brand was active on a specific social media site (Twitter). Research further found that the more consumers "retweeted" and communicated with a brand, the more they trusted the brand. This suggests that a company could look to employ a social-media campaign to gain consumer trust and loyalty as well as in the pursuit of communicating brand messages.

McKee (2014) also looked into brand communication and states that when communicating a brand, a company should look to simplify its message as this will lead to more value being portrayed as well as an increased chance of target consumers recalling and recognising the brand.

In 2012 Riefler stated that if the company communicating a brand is a global organisation or has future global aims, that company should look to employ a method of communication which is globally appealing to their consumers, and subsequently choose a method of communication with will be internationally understood. One way a company can do this involves choosing a product or service's brand name, as this name will need to be suitable for the marketplace that it aims to enter.

It is important that if a company wishes to develop a global market, the company name will also need to be suitable in different cultures and not cause offense or be misunderstood. It has also been found that when communicating a brand a company needs to be aware that they must not just visually communicate their brand message and should take advantage of portraying their message through multi-sensory information. One article suggests that other senses, apart from vision, need to be targeted when trying to communicate a brand with consumers. For example, a jingle or background music can have a positive effect on brand recognition, purchasing behaviour and brand recall.

Therefore, when looking to communicate a brand with chosen consumers, companies should investigate a channel of communication which is most suitable for their short-term and long-term aims and should choose a method of communication which is most likely to be adhered to by their chosen consumers. The match-up between the product, the consumer lifestyle, and the endorser is important for effectiveness of brand communication.

Global Brand Variables

Brand Name

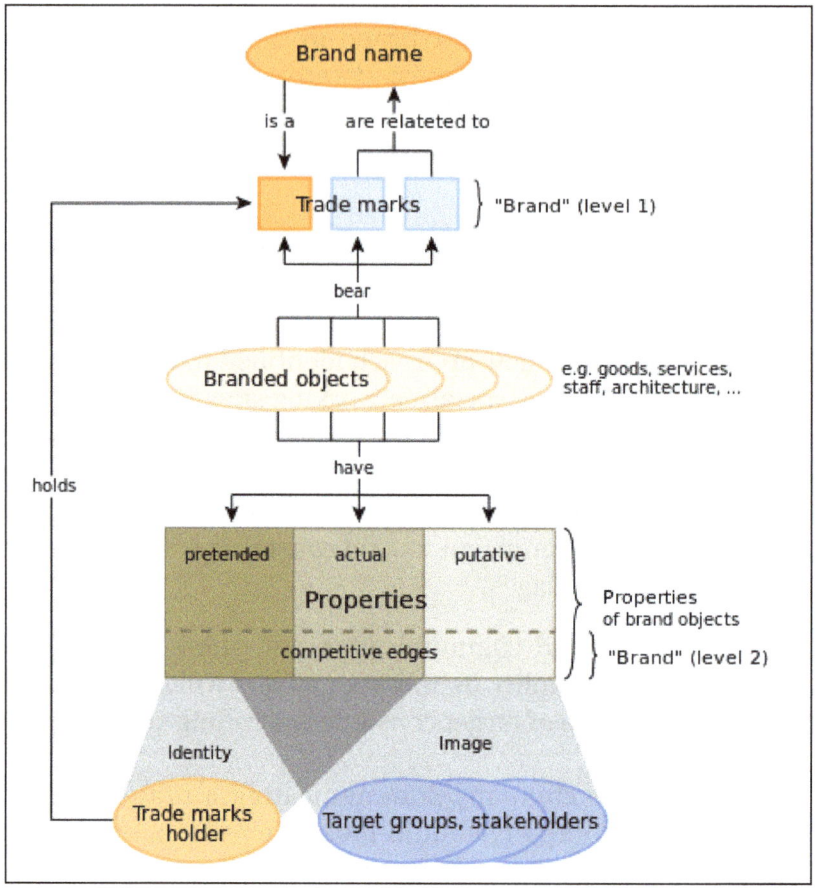

Relationship between trade marks and brand.

The term "brand name" is quite often used interchangeably with "brand", although it is more correctly used to specifically denote written or spoken linguistic elements of any product. In this context a "brand name" constitutes a type of trademark, if the brand name exclusively identifies the brand owner as the commercial source of products or services. A brand owner may seek to protect proprietary rights in relation to a brand name through trademark registration - such trademarks are called "Registered Trademarks". Advertising spokespersons have also become part of some brands, for example: Mr. Whipple of Charmin toilet tissue and Tony the Tiger of Kellogg's Frosted Flakes. Putting a value on a brand by brand valuation or using marketing mix modeling techniques is distinct to valuing a trademark.

Types of Brand Names

Brand names come in many styles. A few include:

- Initialism: a name made of initials, such as "UPS" or "IBM".

- Descriptive: names that describe a product benefit or function, such as "Whole Foods" or "Toys R' Us".

- Alliteration and rhyme: names that are fun to say and which stick in the mind, such as "Reese's Pieces" or "Dunkin' Donuts".

- Evocative: names that can evoke a vivid image, such as "Amazon" or "Crest".

- Neologisms: completely made-up words, such as "Wii" or "Häagen-Dazs".

- Foreign word: adoption of a word from another language, such as "Volvo" or "Samsung".

- Founders' names: using the names of real people, (especially a founder's name), such as "Hewlett-Packard", "Dell", "Disney", "Stussy" or "Mars".

- Geography: naming for regions and landmarks, such as "Cisco" or "Fuji Film".

- Personification: taking names from myths, such as "Nike"; or from the minds of ad execs, such as "Betty Crocker".

- Punny: some brands create their name by using a silly pun, such as "Lord of the Fries", "Wok on Water" or "Eggs Eggscetera".

- Combination: combining multiple words together to create one, such as "Microsoft" ("microcomputer" and "software"), "Comcast" ("communications" and "broadcast"), "Evernote" ("forever" and "note"), "Vodafone" ("voice", "data", "telephone").

The act of associating a product or service with a brand has become part of pop culture. Most products have some kind of brand identity, from common table salt to designer jeans. A brandnomer is a brand name that has colloquially become a generic term for a product or service, such as Band-Aid, Nylon, or Kleenex—which are often used to describe any brand of adhesive bandage; any type of hosiery; or any brand of facial tissue respectively. Xerox, for example, has become synonymous with the word "copy".

Brand Line

A brand line allows the introduction of various subtypes of a product under a common, ideally already established, brand name. Examples would be the individual Kinder Chocolates by Ferrero SA, the subtypes of Coca-Cola, or special editions of popular brands.

Brand Identification

Open Knowledge Foundation created in December 2013 the BSIN (Brand Standard Identification Number). BSIN is universal and is used by the Open Product Data Working Group of the Open Knowledge Foundation to assign a brand to a product. The OKFN Brand repository is critical for the Open Data movement.

Brand Identity

The outward expression of a brand – including its name, trademark, communications, and visual appearance – is brand identity. Because the identity is assembled by the brand owner, it reflects how the owner wants the consumer to perceive the brand – and by extension the branded company, organization, product or service. This is in contrast to the brand image, which is a customer's mental picture of a brand. The brand owner will seek to bridge the gap between the brand image and the brand identity. Brand identity is fundamental to consumer recognition and symbolizes the brand's differentiation from competitors.

Brand identity is what the owner wants to communicate to its potential consumers. However, over time, a product's brand identity may acquire (evolve), gaining new attributes from consumer perspective but not necessarily from the marketing communications an owner percolates to targeted consumers. Therefore, businesses research consumer's brand associations.

Visual Brand Identity

The visual brand identity manual for Mobil Oil (developed by Chermayeff & Geismar & Haviv), one of the first visual identities to integrate logotype, icon, alphabet, color palette, and station architecture.

A brand can also be used to attract customers by a company, if the brand of a company is well established and has goodwill. The recognition and perception of a brand is highly influenced by its visual presentation. A brand's visual identity is the overall look of its communications. Effective visual brand identity is achieved by the consistent use of particular visual elements to create distinction, such as specific fonts, colors, and graphic elements. At the core of every brand identity is a brand mark, or logo. In the United States, brand identity and logo design naturally grew out of the Modernist movement in the 1950s and greatly drew on the principles of that movement – simplicity (Mies van der Rohe's principle of "Less is more") and geometric abstraction. These principles can be observed in the work of the pioneers of the practice of visual brand identity design, such as Paul Rand, Chermayeff & Geismar & Haviv, and Saul Bass. As part of a company's brand identity, a logo should complement the company's message strategy. An effective logo is simple, memorable, and works well in any medium including both online and offline applications.

Color is a particularly important element of visual brand identity and color mapping provides an effective way of ensuring color contributes to differentiation in a visually cluttered marketplace (O'Connor, 2011).

Brand Trust

Brand trust is the intrinsic 'believability' that any entity evokes. In the commercial world, the intangible aspect of brand trust impacts the behavior and performance of its business stakeholders in many intriguing ways. It creates the foundation of a strong brand connect with all stakeholders, converting simple awareness to strong commitment. This, in turn, metamorphoses normal people who have an indirect or direct stake in the organization into devoted ambassadors, leading to concomitant advantages like easier acceptability of brand extensions, perception of premium, and acceptance of temporary quality deficiencies.

The Brand Trust Report is a syndicated primary research that has elaborated on this metric of brand trust. It is a result of action, behavior, communication and attitude of an entity, with the most trust results emerging from its action component. Action of the entity is most important in creating trust in all those audiences who directly engage with the brand, the primary experience carrying primary audiences. However, the tools of communications play a vital role in the transferring the trust experience to audiences which have never experienced the brand, the all important secondary audience.

Brand Parity

Brand parity is the perception of the customers that some brands are equivalent. This means that shoppers will purchase within a group of accepted brands rather than choosing one specific brand. When brand parity operates, quality is often not a major concern because consumers believe that only minor quality differences exist.

Expanding Role of Brand

Branding was meant to make identifying and differentiating a product easier, while also providing the benefit of letting the name sell a second rate product. Over time, brands came to embrace a performance or benefit promise, for the product, certainly, but eventually also for the company behind the brand. Today, brand plays a much bigger role. Brands have been co-opted as powerful symbols in larger debates about economics, social issues, and politics. The power of brands to communicate a complex message quickly and with emotional impact and the ability of brands to attract media attention, make them ideal tools in the hands of activists. Cultural conflict over a brand's meaning have also been shown to influence the diffusion of an innovation.

Branding Strategies

Company Name

Often, especially in the industrial sector, it is just the company's name which is promoted (leading to one of the most powerful statements of branding: saying just before the company's downgrading. This approach has not worked as well for General Motors, which recently overhauled how its corporate brand relates to the product brands. Exactly how the company name relates to product and services names is known as brand architecture. Decisions about company names and product names and their relationship depends on more than a dozen strategic considerations.

In this case, a strong brand name (or company name) is made the vehicle for a range of products (for example, Mercedes-Benz or Black & Decker) or a range of subsidiary brands (such as Cadbury Dairy Milk, Cadbury Flake, or Cadbury Fingers in the UK).

Individual Branding

Each brand has a separate name (such as Seven-Up, Kool-Aid, or Nivea Sun (Beiersdorf), which may compete against other brands from the same company (for example, Persil, Omo, Surf, and Lynx are all owned by Unilever).

Multiproduct Branding Strategy

Multiproduct branding strategy is when a company uses one name across all their products in a product class. When the company's trade name is used, multiproduct branding is also known as corporate branding, family branding or umbrella branding. Examples of companies that use corporate branding are Microsoft, Samsung, Apple, and Sony as the company's brand name is identical to their trade name. Other examples of multiproduct branding strategy include Virgin and Church & Dwight. Virgin, a multination conglomerate uses the punk inspired, handwritten red logo with the iconic tick for all its products ranging from airlines, hot air balloons, telecommunication to healthcare. Church & Dwight, a manufacturer of household products displays the Arm & Hammer family brand name for all its products containing baking soda as the main ingredient. Multiproduct branding strategy has many advantages. It capitalises on brand equity as consumers that have a good experience with the product will in turn pass on this positive opinion to supplementary objects in the same product class as they share the same name. Consequently, the multiproduct branding strategy makes product line extension possible.

Product Line Extension

Product line extension is the procedure of entering a new market segment in its product class by means of using a current brand name. An example of this is the Campbell Soup Company, predominately a producer of canned soups. They utilize a multiproduct branding strategy by way of soup line extensions. They have over 100 soup flavours putting forward varieties such as regular Campbell soup, condensed, chunky, fresh-brewed, organic, and soup on the go. This approach is seen as favourable as it can result in a lower promotion costs and advertising due to the same name being used on all products, therefore increasing the level of brand awareness. Although, line extension has potential negative outcomes with one being that other items in the company's line may be disadvantaged because of the sale of the extension. Line extensions work at their best when they deliver an increase in company revenue by enticing new buyers or by removing sales from competitors.

Subbranding

Subbranding is used by certain multiproduct branding companies. Subbranding merges a corporate, family or umbrella brand with the introduction of a new brand in order to differentiate part of a product line from others in the whole brand system. Subbranding assists to articulate and construct offerings. It can alter a brand's identity as subbranding can modify associations of the parent brand. Examples of successful subbranding can be seen through Gatorade and Porsche. Gatorade, a manufacturer of sport-themed food and beverages effectively introduced Gatorade G2, a low-calorie line of Gatorade drinks. Likewise, Porsche, a specialised automobile manufacturer successfully markets its lower-end line, Porsche Boxster and higher-end line, Porsche Carrera.

Brand Extension

Brand extension is the system of employing a current brand name to enter a different product class. Having a strong brand equity allows for brand extension. Nevertheless, brand extension has its disadvantages. There is a risk that too many uses for one brand name can oversaturate the market resulting in a blurred and weak brand for consumers. Examples of brand extension can be seen through Kimberly-Clark and Honda. Kimberly-Clark is a corporation that produces personal and health care products being able to extend the Huggies brand name across a full line of toiletries for toddlers and babies. The success of this brand extension strategy is apparent in the $500 million in annual sales generated globally. Similarly, Honda using their reputable name for automobiles has spread to other products such as motorcycles, power equipment, engines, robots, aircraft, and bikes.

Co-Branding

Co-branding is a variation of brand extension. It is where a single product is created from the combining of two brand names of two manufacturers. Co-branding has its advantages as it lets firms enter new product classes and exploit a recognized brand name in that product class. An example of a co-branding success is Whitaker's working with Lewis Road Creamery to create a co-branded beverage called Lewis Road Creamery and Whittaker's Chocolate Milk. This product was a huge success in the New Zealand market with it going viral.

Multibranding Strategy

Multibranding strategy is when a company gives each product a distinct name. Multibranding is best used as an approach when each brand in intended for a different market segment. Multibranding is used in an assortment of ways with selected companies grouping their brands based on price-quality segments. Procter & Gamble (P&G), a multinational consumer goods company that offers over 100 brands, each suited for different consumer needs. For instance, Head & Shoulders that helps consumers relieve dandruff in the form of a shampoo, Oral-B which offers inter-dental products, Vicks which offers cough and cold products, and Downy which offers dryer sheets and fabric softeners. Other examples include Coca-Cola, Nestlé, Kellogg's, and Mars.

This approach usually results in higher promotion costs and advertising. This is due to the company being required to generate awareness among consumers and retailers for each new brand name without the benefit of any previous impressions. Multibranding strategy has many advantages. There is no risk that a product failure will affect other products in the line as each brand is unique to each market segment. Although, certain large multiband companies have come across that the cost and difficulty of implementing a multibranding strategy can overshadow the benefits. For example, Unilever, the world's third-largest multination consumer goods company recently streamlined its brands from over 400 brands to centre their attention onto 14 brands with sales of over 1 billion euros. Unilever accomplished this through product deletion and sales to other companies. Other multibrand companies introduce new product brands as a protective measure to respond to competition called fighting brands or fighter brands.

Fighting Brands

The main purpose of fighting brands is to challenge competitor brands. For example, Qantas, Australia's largest flag carrier airline, introduced Jetstar to go head-to-head against the low-cost carrier, Virgin Australia (formerly known as Virgin Blue). Jetstar is an Australian low-cost airline for budget conscious travellers, but it receives many negative reviews due to this. The launching of Jetstar allowed Qantas to rival Virgin Australia without the criticism being affiliated with Qantas because of the distinct brand name.

Private Branding Strategy

Private branding is also known as reseller branding, private labelling, store brands, or own brands have increased in popularity. Private branding is when a company manufactures products but it is sold under the brand name of a wholesaler or retailer. Private branding is popular because it typically produces high profits for manufacturers and resellers. The pricing of private brand product are usually cheaper compared to competing name brands. Consumers are commonly deterred by these prices as it sets a perception of lower quality and standard but these views are shifting.

In Australia, their leading supermarket chains, both Woolworths and Coles are saturated with store brands (or private labels). For example, in the United States, Paragon Trade Brands, Ralcorp Holdings, and Rayovac are major suppliers of diapers, grocery products, and private label alkaline batteries, correspondingly. Costco, Walmart, RadioShack, Sears, and Kroger are large retailers that have their own brand names. Similarly, Macy's, a mid-range chain of department stores offers a wide catalogue of private brands exclusive to their stores, from brands such as First Impressions which supply newborn and infant clothing, Hotel Collection which supply luxury linens and mattresses, and Tasso Elba which supply European inspired menswear. They use private branding strategy to specifically target consumer markets.

Mixed Branding Strategy

Mixed branding strategy is where a firm markets products under its own name(s) and that of a reseller because the segment attracted to the reseller is different from its own market. For example, Elizabeth Arden, Inc., a major American cosmetics and fragrance company, uses mixed branding strategy. The company sells its Elizabeth Arden brand through department stores and line of skin care products at Walmart with the "skin simple" brand name. Companies such as Whirlpool, Del

Monte, and Dial produce private brands of home appliances, pet foods, and soap, correspondingly. Other examples of mixed branding strategy include Michelin, Epson, Microsoft, Gillette, and Toyota. Michelin, one of the largest tire manufacturers allowed Sears, an American retail chain to place their brand name on the tires. Microsoft, a multinational technology company is seriously regarded as a corporate technology brand but it sells its versatile home entertainment hub under the brand Xbox to better align with the new and crazy identity. Gillette catered to females with Gillette for Women which has now become known as Venus. The launch of Venus was conducted in order to fulfil the feminine market of the previously dominating masculine razor industry. Similarly, Toyota, an automobile manufacturer used mixed branding. In the U.S., Toyota was regarded as a valuable car brand being economical, family orientated and known as a vehicle that rarely broke down. But Toyota sought out to fulfil a higher end, expensive market segment, thus they created Lexus, the luxury vehicle division of premium cars.

Attitude Branding and Iconic Brands

Attitude branding is the choice to represent a larger feeling, which is not necessarily connected with the product or consumption of the product at all. Marketing labeled as attitude branding include that of Nike, Starbucks, The Body Shop, Safeway, and Apple Inc.. In the 2000 book No Logo, Naomi Klein describes attitude branding as a "fetish strategy".

A great brand raises the bar – it adds a greater sense of purpose to the experience, whether it's the challenge to do your best in sports and fitness, or the affirmation that the cup of coffee you're drinking really matters. – Howard Schultz (president, CEO, and chairman of Starbucks)·

The color, letter font and style of the Coca-Cola and Diet Coca-Cola logos in English were copied into matching Hebrew logos to maintain brand identity in Israel.

Iconic brands are defined as having aspects that contribute to consumer's self-expression and personal identity. Brands whose value to consumers comes primarily from having identity value are said to be "identity brands". Some of these brands have such a strong identity that they become more or less cultural icons which makes them "iconic brands". Examples are: Apple, Nike, and Harley-Davidson. Many iconic brands include almost ritual-like behaviour in purchasing or consuming the products.

There are four key elements to creating iconic brands (Holt 2004):

1. "Necessary conditions" – The performance of the product must at least be acceptable, preferably with a reputation of having good quality.

2. "Myth-making" – A meaningful storytelling fabricated by cultural insiders. These must be seen as legitimate and respected by consumers for stories to be accepted.

3. "Cultural contradictions" – Some kind of mismatch between prevailing ideology and emergent undercurrents in society. In other words, a difference with the way consumers are and how they wish they were.

4. "The cultural brand management process" – Actively engaging in the myth-making process in making sure the brand maintains its position as an icon.

"No-Brand" Branding

Recently, a number of companies have successfully pursued "no-brand" strategies by creating packaging that imitates generic brand simplicity. Examples include the Japanese company Muji, which means "No label" in English (from 無印良品 – "Mujirushi Ryohin" – literally, "No brand quality goods"), and the Florida company No-Ad Sunscreen. Although there is a distinct Muji brand, Muji products are not branded. This no-brand strategy means that little is spent on advertisement or classical marketing and Muji's success is attributed to the word-of-mouth, a simple shopping experience and the anti-brand movement. "No brand" branding may be construed as a type of branding as the product is made conspicuous through the absence of a brand name. "Tapa Amarilla" or "Yellow Cap" in Venezuela during the 1980s is another good example of no-brand strategy. It was simply recognized by the color of the cap of this cleaning products company.

Derived Brands

In this case the supplier of a key component, used by a number of suppliers of the end-product, may wish to guarantee its own position by promoting that component as a brand in its own right. The most frequently quoted example is Intel, which positions itself in the PC market with the slogan (and sticker) "Intel Inside".

Brand Extension and Brand Dilution

The existing strong brand name can be used as a vehicle for new or modified products; for example, many fashion and designer companies extended brands into fragrances, shoes and accessories, home textile, home decor, luggage, (sun-) glasses, furniture, hotels, etc.

Mars extended its brand to ice cream, Caterpillar to shoes and watches, Michelin to a restaurant guide, Adidas and Puma to personal hygiene. Dunlop extended its brand from tires to other rubber products such as shoes, golf balls, tennis racquets, and adhesives. Frequently, the product is no different from what else is on the market, except a brand name marking. Brand is product identity.

There is a difference between brand extension and line extension. A line extension is when a current brand name is used to enter a new market segment in the existing product class, with new varieties or flavors or sizes. When Coca-Cola launched "Diet Coke" and "Cherry Coke", they stayed within the originating product category: non-alcoholic carbonated beverages. Procter & Gamble (P&G) did likewise extending its strong lines (such as Fairy Soap) into neighboring products (Fairy Liquid and Fairy Automatic) within the same category, dish washing detergents.

The risk of over-extension is brand dilution where the brand loses its brand associations with a market segment, product area, or quality, price or cachet.

Social Media Brands

In 'The Better Mousetrap: Brand Invention in a Media Democracy' (2012), author and brand strategist Simon Pont posits that social media brands may be the most evolved version of the brand form, because they focus not on themselves but on their users. In so doing, social media brands are arguably more charismatic, in that consumers are compelled to spend time with them, because the time spent is in the meeting of fundamental human drivers related to belonging and individualism. "We wear our physical brands like badges, to help define us – but we use our digital brands to help express who we are. They allow us to be, to hold a mirror up to ourselves, and it is clear. We like what we see."

Multi-Brands

Alternatively, in a market that is fragmented amongst a number of brands a supplier can choose deliberately to launch totally new brands in apparent competition with its own existing strong brand (and often with identical product characteristics); simply to soak up some of the share of the market which will in any case go to minor brands. The rationale is that having 3 out of 12 brands in such a market will give a greater overall share than having 1 out of 10 (even if much of the share of these new brands is taken from the existing one). In its most extreme manifestation, a supplier pioneering a new market which it believes will be particularly attractive may choose immediately to launch a second brand in competition with its first, in order to pre-empt others entering the market. This strategy is widely known as multi-brand strategy.

Individual brand names naturally allow greater flexibility by permitting a variety of different products, of differing quality, to be sold without confusing the consumer's perception of what business the company is in or diluting higher quality products.

Once again, Procter & Gamble is a leading exponent of this philosophy, running as many as ten detergent brands in the US market. This also increases the total number of "facings" it receives on supermarket shelves. Sara Lee, on the other hand, uses it to keep the very different parts of the business separate—from Sara Lee cakes through Kiwi polishes to L'Eggs pantyhose. In the hotel business, Marriott uses the name Fairfield Inns for its budget chain (and Choice Hotels uses Rodeway for its own cheaper hotels).

Cannibalization is a particular problem of a multi-brand strategy approach, in which the new brand takes business away from an established one which the organization also owns. This may be acceptable (indeed to be expected) if there is a net gain overall. Alternatively, it may be the price the organization is willing to pay for shifting its position in the market; the new product being one stage in this process.

Private Labels

Private label brands, also called own brands, or store brands have become popular. Where the retailer has a particularly strong identity (such as Marks & Spencer in the UK clothing sector) this "own brand" may be able to compete against even the strongest brand leaders, and may outperform those products that are not otherwise strongly branded.

Individual and Organizational Brands

With the development of brand, it has been widely used, no longer limited to a product or service. There are kinds of branding that treat individuals and organizations as the products to be branded.

Personal Branding,

Employer Branding,

Crowd Sourcing Branding.

These are brands that are created by "the public" for the business, which is opposite to the traditional method where the business create a brand.

Personalised Branding

Many businesses have started to use elements of personalisation in their branding strategies, offering the client or consumer the ability to choose from various brand options or have direct control over the brand. Examples of this include the #ShareACoke campaign by Coca-Cola which printed people's names and place names on their bottles encouraging people. AirBNB has created the facility for users to create their own symbol for the software to replace the brand's mark known as The Bélo.

Nation Branding (Place Branding and Public Diplomacy)

Nation branding is a field of theory and practice which aims to measure, build and manage the reputation of countries (closely related to place branding). Some approaches applied, such as an increasing importance on the symbolic value of products, have led countries to emphasise their distinctive characteristics. The branding and image of a nation-state "and the successful transference of this image to its exports – is just as important as what they actually produce and sell."

Destination Branding

Destination branding is the work of cities, states, and other localities to promote to themselves. This work is designed to promote the location to tourists and drive additional revenues into a tax base. These activities are often undertaken by governments, but can also result from the work of community associations. The Destination Marketing Association International is the industry leading organization.

Doppelgänger Brand Image (DBI)

A doppelgänger brand image or "DBI" is a disparaging image or story about a brand that it circulated in popular culture. DBI targets tend to be widely known and recognizable brands. The purpose of DBIs is to undermine the positive brand meanings the brand owners are trying to instill through their marketing activities.

The term stems from the combination of the German words doppel (double) and gänger (walker).

Doppelgänger brands are typically created by individuals or groups to express criticism of a brand and its perceived values, through a form of parody, and are typically unflattering in nature.

Due to the ability of Doppelgänger brands to rapidly propagate virally through digital media channels, they can represent a real threat to the equity of the target brand. Sometimes the target organization is forced to address the root concern or to re-position the brand in a way that defuses the criticism.

Examples Include:

- Joe Chemo campaign organized to criticize the marketing of tobacco products to children and their harmful effects.

- Version of the Coca-Cola logo crafted to protest their sponsorship of the 2022 FIFA World Cup in Qatar and associated human rights abuses.

- Parody of the Pepsi logo as an obese man to highlight the relationship between soft drink consumption and obesity.

- The FUH2 campaign protesting the Hummer SUV as a symbol of corporate and consumer irresponsibility toward public safety and the environment.

In the 2006 article "Emotional Branding and the Strategic Value of the Doppelgänger Brand Image", Thompson, Rindfleisch, and Arsel suggest that a doppelgänger brand image can be a benefit to a brand if taken as an early warning sign that the brand is losing emotional authenticity with its market.

Publicity

Publicity (from French publicité, from public 'public') is the movement of information to the general public from the media. The subjects of publicity includes people (for example, politicians and performing artists), goods and services, organizations, and works of art or entertainment.

Publicity is gaining public visibility or awareness for a product, service or your company via the media. It is the publicist that carries out publicity, while PR is the strategic management function that helps an organization communicate, establish and maintain communication with the public.

This can be done internally, without the use of media.

From a marketing perspective, publicity is one component of promotion and marketing. The other elements of the promotional mix are advertising, sales promotion, direct marketing and personal selling. Examples of promotional tactics include:

- Announce an appointment.

- Arrange a speech or talk.

- Arrange for a testimonial.

- Art people

- Conduct a poll or survey.

- Event sponsorship.

- Invent then present an award.

- Issue a commendation.

- Issue a report.

- Make an analysis or prediction.

- Organize a tour of your business or projects.

- Stage a debate.

- Take a stand on a controversial subject.

The advantages of publicity are low cost and credibility (particularly if the publicity is aired in between news stories like on evening TV news casts). New technologies such as weblogs, web cameras, web affiliates, and convergence (phone-camera posting of pictures and videos to websites) are changing the cost-structure. The disadvantages are lack of control over how your releases will be used, and frustration over the low percentage of releases that are taken up by the media.

Publicity draws on several key themes including birth, love, and death. These are of particular interest because they are themes in human lives which feature heavily throughout life. In television series, several couples have emerged during crucial ratings and important publicity times as a way to make constant headlines. Also known as a publicity stunt, the pairings may or may not be according to the fact.

"Publicity is not merely an assembly of competing messages: it is a language in itself which is always being used to make the same general proposal," writes the art critic John Berger. "It proposes to each of us that we transform ourselves, or our lives by buying. .publicity is not paid for something more."

Publicity is often referred to as the result of public relations in terms of providing favourable information to media and any third party outlets; these may including bloggers, mainstream media, as well as new media forms such as podcasts. All this is done to provide a message to consumers without having to pay for direct time or space. This in return creates awareness and carries out more credibility as well. After the message has been distributed, the publicist in charge of the information will lose control on how the message is used and interpreted, much different to the way it works in Advertising. According to Grunig, public relations is often reduced to publicity. He also states how publicity is a form of activity in which should be associated with the sales promotion effort of a company, in order to help aid advertising and personal salesmanship as well. Kent also stated that the doing of publicity can help attract attention whilst also supplying information regarding a specific organization or individual client and any event, activity or attribute associated with them.

The use of publicity is also known to be an important strategic element and promotional tool due to its effect of intentional exposure over a consumer, this helps publicity gain a beneficial advantage over other marketing aspects such as Advertising alongside its high credibility. Favourable publicity is also created through reputation management in which organizations try strive to control via the web. Furthermore, despite the fact that publicity, both good or bad, can be beneficial for an organization, company or client, much of it is paid for despite claims that publicity is often free. Despite publicity being an influential benefit within the marketing sector, one disadvantage which highly affects publicity, is the lack of ability in which publicity cannot be repeated as such compared to advertising.

Publicists

A publicist is a person whose job is to generate and manage publicity for a product, public figure, especially a celebrity, or for a work such as a book or movie or band. Publicists could work in large companies and in little companies.

Though there are many aspects to a publicist's job, their main function is to persuade the press to report about their client in the most positive way possible. Publicists are adept at identifying and pulling out "newsworthy" aspects of products and personalities to offer to the press as possible reportage ideas. Publicists offer this information to reporters in the specific format of a magazine, newspaper, TV or radio show, or online outlet. The third aspect of a publicist's job is to shape "stories" about their clients at a time that fits within a media outlet's news cycle.

Publicists are most often categorized under a marketing arm of a company. Marketing is anything that a company does to get their product into the hands of a customer who will pay for it. Publicity, specifically, uses the objective opinion of a reporter to tell that story. A seasoned publicist knows how to present a newsworthy story in a way that suggests editorial coverage in a certain direction. This is what is generally referred to as "spin," though it is not a negative connotation, only a very keen ability to present a story in a way that fits for a media outlet at the right time.

A publicist generally serves as a bridge between the relationship of a client and the public and said to use any possible technique inorder to get favourable mentions within the media in regards to the information that they are willing to release. Although day-to-day duties vary depending on what each clients needs consist of, the main focal point for a publicist is promotion. When it comes to a crisis situation, Publicists often find themselves taking a more optimistic view in regards to seeing them as an opportunity to help get their organization or clients name into the media. Furthermore, Toth goes on to describe how Press Agents, another form of publicists, are willing to intrigue news outlets, mainstream media and web blogs with "bad news" (celebrity drug addictions, divorces, scandals, sordid affairs etc.) inorder to "sell" a story and help gain further coverage for their clients as well. This is supported by the Press Agentry/Publicity model in which is often used within the fashion, sporting and entertainment industry at which point follows the presumption that even bad news can be good publicity.

Effectiveness of Publicity

"So where the bloody hell are you?" advertising campaign.

The theory, Any press is good press, has been coined to describe situations where bad behaviour by people involved with an organization or brand have actually resulted in positive results, due to the fame and press coverage accrued by such events.

One example would be the Australian Tourism Board's "So where the bloody hell are you?" advertising campaign that was initially banned in the UK, but the amount of publicity this generated resulted in the official website for the campaign being swamped with requests to see the banned ad. This event had caused former British Prime Minister, Tony Blair, to show his support once setting foot in Australia by responding "and here I am, in the Australian parliament building at what I think is something like four o'clock in the morning in the UK. And so I'm thinking, so where the bloody hell am I?"

As previously mentioned, Publicity is known to contain high credibility, making it more influential amongst other market-driven communications. This in its self can affect consumers thoughts by catching them 'off-guard' applying differentiation between advertising. The use of publicity may also influence a consumers attitude towards an advertisement or brand because of its high credibility value in order to assess the trustworthiness or further information within a marketplace. The effect of positive publicity is also said to complement advertising in predictable ways, as opposed to the effects of negative publicity in which seem to be mitgated through advertising, eventually adding to the creation of brand familiarity. Furthermore, publicity highly disputes the idea of trying to persuade a consumers feelings towards the brand and focus more towards how they feel, think and remember things in relation to the brand or client. Edward Bernays had one quoted "it is important that any effort to influence or effect the American public that is not in the public interest be killed by the light of pitiless publicity and analysis".

Negative Publicity

The main focus for publicity is to create awareness for an organization, brand or individual. Despite this, publicity can also create a negative effect resulting in negative publicity. One of the most important factors in relation to influencing a consumers buying decision falls down to how a company, brand or individual deal with the negative publicity surrounding themselves. The power of negative publicity may also result in major loss of revenue or market shares within a business. Negative publicity can also play a part in damaging a consumers perception of a brand or its products. Its high credibility and greater influence compared to other company-controlled communications also play a part in negative publicity occurring and the potential damage it may have upon a corporate image. Crises involved with an organization may also result in negative publicity as well.

Furthermore, negative publicity is seen to affect everything from the product and evaluation of a brand to the present firm net value and sale. Often when an awareness of a company, brand or individual is high, the negative publicity provided is deemed to hurt possible sales, where as company, brands and individuals whom of maintain a low awareness rate may use the negative publicity as a beneficial feature inorder to get their name across to the public. The extensive range of media outlets, including both traditional and new media also provide companies new opportunities in which to market their products or services. This however, restricts or reduces the management of negative publicity that may be spread across involving their products or services offered. In order for organizations to try salvage any negative publicity surrounding their brand, corporate social responsibility (CSR) is one solution in which can help protect the image of that certain company or help restore the effects caused. In favour of CSR remaining effective, company's however, must adopt the CSR approach early or potential risks such as falsified intentions may develop within a consumer.

Despite the damaging effect negative publicity may cause, there is a possibility that negative publicity may infact gain more attention as opposed to publicity of a positive manner. Regardless of the nature within negative publicity, and its ability to turn most people away, any slight hint of negative publicity can in fact build interest amongst the consumer and product/service offered to which positive effects are shown. Negative publicity surrounding a company can also influence product evaluations which in return increases the likelihood of purchase and sales as well. As identified by Monga & John, negative publicity is not always harmful, and consumers whom identify a brand with strong attitudes are highly unlikely to be affected by the negative publicity formed.

References

- Peeter Verlegh, Hilde Voorveld, and Martin Eisend, eds. *Advances in Advertising Research (Vol. VI): The Digital, the Classic, the Subtle, and the Alternative* (Springer, 2015)

- McKee, S., 2014. Branding Made Simple. [online] Bloomberg Business. Available at: <http://www.bloomberg.com/bw/articles/2014-10-13/branding-made-simple> [Accessed 6 Feb. 2015]

- Divola, Barry (2004). *Searching for Kingly Critter: a deliciously different tale of obsession and nostalgia.* Published by ABC Books, Sydney. OCLC 156420816. ISBN 073331399X

- Shimizu, Koichi (2014) "Advertising Theory and Strategies", (Japanese) 18th edition, Souseisha Book Company (ISBN 4-7944-2132-X C3034) pp. 63–102

- Shimizu, Koichi (2003) "Symbiotic Marketing Strategy", (Japanese) 4th edition, Souseisha Book Company. (ISBN 4-7944-2158-3 C3034) pp. 25–62

- McChesney, Robert, *Educators and the Battle for Control of U.S. Broadcasting, 1928–35*, Rich Media, Poor Democracy, ISBN 0-252-02448-6 (1999)

- Clow, Kenneth E.; Baack, Donald (2007). Integrated Advertising, Promotion, and Marketing Communications 3rd edition. Pearson Education. pp. 165–71. ISBN 0-13-186622-2

Marketing Environment: Exploring Business

Marketing environment is a term that refers to the different factors and forces that are in play and influence the marketing operations of businesses. It can be further grouped into specific categories like internal environment, external environment, macroenvironment, microenvironment, etc. This chapter provides the reader with detailed explanations of each sub-type of marketing environment and their particular components.

Marketing activities are influenced by several factors inside and outside a business firm. These factors or forces influencing marketing decision-making are collectively called marketing environment. It comprises all those forces which have an impact on market and marketing efforts of the enterprise. According to Philip Kotler, marketing environment refers to "external factors and forces that affect the company's ability to develop and maintain successful transactions and relationships with its target customers".

The marketing programme of a firm is influenced and shaped by a firm's inwardly need to begin its business planning by looking outwardly at what its customers require, rather than inwardly at what it would prefer to produce. The firm must be aware of what is going on in its marketing environment and appreciate how change in its environment can lead to changing patterns of demand for its products.

It also needs to assess marketing opportunities and threats present in the surroundings. An environment can be defined as everything which surrounds and impinges on a system. Systems of many kinds have environments with which they interact. Marketing can be seen as a system which must respond to environmental change.

Just as the human body may have problems, it fails to adjust to environmental change. Similarly, businesses may fail if they do not adapt to external changes such as new sources of competition or changes in consumers' preferences.

Scanning the Environment

Marketing activities do not take place in a vacuum, isolated from all external forces. In fact all marketing operations are conducted in a highly complex, dynamic and changing environment. According to Philip Kotler, "A company's marketing environment consists of the factors and forces outside marketing that affect management's ability to build and maintain successful relationships with target customers".

The marketing environment offers both opportunities and threats. Successful companies know the vital importance of constantly watching and adapting to the changing environment. A company's marketers take the major responsibility for identifying significant changes in the environment.

More than any other groups in the company, marketers must be the trend trackers and opportunity seekers. Although every manager in an organisation needs to observe the outside environment, marketers have two special aptitudes. They have disciplined methods – marketing intelligence and marketing research – for collection of information about the marketing environment.

They also spend time in the customer and competitor environment. By conducting systematic environmental scanning, marketers are able to revise and adapt marketing strategies to meet new challenges and opportunities in the market place.

Marketing as a function is basically all about matching the offerings of the organisation to the outside world, in particular, the market-place. Not surprisingly, many functions within marketing, such as selling, product development and market research, concern themselves with issues, problems and opportunities outside the organisation, and focus on responding to outside events and circumstances. Kotler identifies in this external role the need for marketers to develop an 'outside- in' perspective, an ability to work on external cues and stimuli to the profit of the whole organisation.

Environment scanning is a constant, important activity of successful companies. This process includes gathering, filtering and analyzing information related to the marketing environment. It also includes monitoring the changes taking place in the environment and forecasting future status of each factor.

Such analysis helps to spot opportunities and threats in the environment, and pinpoints the ones that are specifically relevant to the company. The company's marketing people have the responsibility for scanning and identifying significant changes or trends in the marketing environment.

As we know that marketing research and marketing intelligence system are the methods used by companies for environment scanning and gathering vital information about changes. Customers' behaviour and competitors' activities are also important factors to be watched in the environment. Successful companies know the vital importance of constantly scanning and adapting to the changing environment. The environment continues to change at a rapid pace.

Importance of Environment Analysis

The following are the benefits of environment analysis:

- It helps in marketing analysis.
- It can assess the impact of opportunities and threats on the business.
- It facilitates the company to increase general awareness of environmental changes.

- It is possible to develop effective marketing strategies on the basis of analysis.

- It helps to capitalize the opportunities rather than losing out to competitors.

- It facilitates to understand the elements of the environment.

- It helps to develop best strategies, in the light of analyzing "what is going around the company".

Need for Environment Analysis

Environmental analysis attempts to give an extensive insight as to the current market conditions as well as of impact of external factors that are uncontrollable by the marketers. These variables play an important role in convincing potential customers regarding changes in market trends, market conditions etc.

Facilitating the corporation's strategic response to the changes taking place in environmental factors is the ultimate purpose of environment analysis. The firm has to come up with alternative programmes and strategies in line with environmental realities. This is possible only with proper environment analysis.

It helps strategic response by highlighting opportunities, the pursuit of which will help the firm to attain its objectives. It helps to assess the attractiveness and probability position of these opportunities, and helps to prepare a shortlist of those which are relevant to the firm and which can be pursued by it.

Components of Marketing Environment

The marketing environment is made up of the internal and external environment of the business. While internal environment can be controlled, the business has very less or no control over the external environment.

Internal Environment

The internal environment of the business includes all the forces and factors inside the organisation which affect its marketing operations. These components can be grouped under the Five Ms of the business, which are:

- Men

- Money

- Machinery

- Materials

- Markets

The internal environment is under the control of the marketer and can be changed with the changing external environment. Nevertheless, the internal marketing environment is as important for the business as the external marketing environment. This environment includes the sales department, marketing department, the manufacturing unit, the human resource department, etc.

External Environment

The external environment constitutes factors and forces which are external to the business and on which the marketer has little or no control. The external environment is of two types:

Micro Environment

The micro component of the external environment is also known as the task environment. It comprises of external forces and factors that are directly related to the business. These include suppliers, market intermediaries, customers, partners, competitors and the public:

- Suppliers include all the parties which provide resources needed by the organisation.

- Market intermediaries include parties involved in distributing the product or service of the organisation.

- Partners are all the separate entities like advertising agencies, market research organisations, banking and insurance companies, transportation companies, brokers, etc. which conduct business with the organisation.

- Customers comprise of the target group of the organisation.

- Competitors are the players in the same market who targets similar customers as that of the organisation.

- Public is made up of any other group that has an actual or potential interest or affects the company's ability to serve its customers.

Macro Environment

The macro component of the marketing environment is also known as the broad environment. It constitutes the external factors and forces which affect the industry as a whole but don't have a direct effect on the business. The macro environment can be divided into 6 parts.

Demographic Environment

The demographic environment is made up of the people who constitute the market. It is characterised as the factual investigation and segregation of the population according to their size, density, location, age, gender, race, and occupation.

Economic Environment

The economic environment constitutes factors which influence customers' purchasing power and spending patterns. These factors include the GDP, GNP, interest rates, inflation, income distribution, government funding and subsidies, and other major economic variables.

Physical Environment

The physical environment includes the natural environment in which the business operates. This includes the climatic conditions, environmental change, accessibility to water and raw materials, natural disasters, pollution etc.

Technological Environment

The technological environment constitutes innovation, research and development in technology, technological alternatives, innovation inducements also technological barriers to smooth operation. Technology is one of the biggest sources of threats and opportunities for the organisation and it is very dynamic.

Political-legal Environment

The political & Legal environment includes laws and government's policies prevailing in the country. It also includes other pressure groups and agencies which influence or limit the working of industry and/or the business in the society.

Social-cultural Environment

The social-cultural aspect of the macro environment is made up of the lifestyle, values, culture, prejudice and beliefs of the people. This differs in different regions.

Importance of Marketing Environment

Every business, no matter how big or small, operates within the marketing environment. Its present and future existence, profits, image, and positioning depend on its internal and external environment. The business environment is one of the most dynamic aspects of the business. In order to operate and stay in the market for long, one has to understand and analyze the marketing environment and its components properly.

Essential for Planning

An understanding of the external and internal environment is essential for planning for the future. A marketer needs to be fully aware of the current scenario, dynamism, and future predictions of the marketing environment if he wants his plans to succeed.

Understanding Customers

A thorough knowledge of the marketing environment helps marketers acknowledge and predict what the customer actually wants. In-depth analysis of the marketing environment reduces (and even removes) the noise between the marketer and customers and helps the marketer to understand the consumer behaviour better.

Tapping Trends

Breaking into new markets and capitalizing on new trends requires a lot of insight about the marketing environment. The marketer needs to research about every aspect of the environment to create a foolproof plan.

Threats and Opportunities

A sound knowledge of the market environment often gives a first mover advantage to the marketer as he makes sure that his business is safe from the future threats and taps the future opportunities.

Understanding the Competitors

Every niche has different players fighting for the same spot. A better understanding of the marketing environment allows the marketer to understand more about the competitions and about what advantages do the competitors have over his business and vice versa.

Internal Environment

An organization's *internal environment* is composed of the elements within the organization, including current employees, management, and especially corporate culture, which defines employee behavior. Although some elements affect the organization as a whole, others affect only the manager. A manager 's philosophical or leadership style directly impacts employees. Traditional managers give explicit instructions to employees, while progressive managers empower employees to make many of their own decisions. Changes in philosophy and/or leadership style are under the control of the manager.

An organization's mission statement describes what the organization stands for and why it exists. It explains the overall purpose of the organization and includes the attributes that distinguish it from other organizations of its type.

A mission statement should be more than words on a piece of paper; it should reveal a company's philosophy, as well as its purpose. This declaration should be a living, breathing document that provides information and inspiration for the members of the organization. A mission statement should answer the questions, "What are our values?" and "What do we stand for?" This statement provides focus for an organization by rallying its members to work together to achieve its common goals.

But not all mission statements are effective in America's businesses. Effective mission statements lead to effective efforts. In today's quality-conscious and highly competitive environments, an effective mission statement's purpose is centered on serving the needs of customers. A good mission statement is precise in identifying the following intents of a company:

- Customers — who will be served
- Products/services — what will be produced
- Location — where the products/services will be produced
- Philosophy — what ideology will be followed

Company policies are guidelines that govern how certain organizational situations are addressed. Just as colleges maintain policies about admittance, grade appeals, prerequisites, and waivers, companies establish policies to provide guidance to managers who must make decisions about circumstances that occur frequently within their organization. Company policies are an indication of an organization 's personality and should coincide with its mission statement.

The formal structure of an organization is the hierarchical arrangement of tasks and people. This structure determines how information flows within the organization, which departments are responsible for which activities, and where the decision-making power rests.

Some organizations use a chart to simplify the breakdown of its formal structure. This organizational chart is a pictorial display of the official lines of authority and communication within an organization.

The organizational culture is an organization's personality. Just as each person has a distinct personality, so does each organization. The culture of an organization distinguishes it from others and shapes the actions of its members.

Four main components make up an organization's culture:
- Values
- Heroes
- Rites and rituals
- Social network

Values are the basic beliefs that define employees ' successes in an organization. For example, many universities place high values on professors being published. If a faculty member is published in a professional journal, for example, his or her chances of receiving tenure may be enhanced. The university wants to ensure that a published professor stays with the university for the duration of his or her academic career — and this professor 's ability to write for publications is a value.

The second component is heroes. A *hero* is an exemplary person who reflects the image, attitudes, or values of the organization and serves as a role model to other employees. A hero is sometimes the founder of the organization (think Sam Walton of Wal-Mart). However, the hero of a company doesn't have to be the founder; it can be an everyday worker, such as hard-working paralegal Erin Brockovich, who had a tremendous impact on the organization.

Rites and rituals, the third component, are routines or ceremonies that the company uses to recognize high-performing employees. Awards banquets, company gatherings, and quarterly meetings can acknowledge distinguished employees for outstanding service. The honorees are meant to exemplify and inspire all employees of the company during the rest of the year.

The final component, the *social network,* is the informal means of communication within an organization. This network, sometimes referred to as the company grapevine, carries the stories of both heroes and those who have failed. It is through this network that employees really learn about the organization 's culture and values.

A byproduct of the company's culture is the organizational climate. The overall tone of the workplace and the morale of its workers are elements of daily climate. Worker attitudes dictate the positive or negative "atmosphere" of the workplace. The daily relationships and interactions of employees are indicative of an organization's climate.

Resources are the people, information, facilities, infrastructure, machinery, equipment, supplies, and finances at an organization 's disposal. People are the paramount resource of all organizations. Information, facilities, machinery equipment, materials, supplies, and finances are supporting, nonhuman resources that complement workers in their quests to accomplish the organization 's mission statement. The availability of resources and the way that managers value the human and nonhuman resources impact the organization 's environment.

Philosophy of management is the manager 's set of personal beliefs and values about people and work and as such, is something that the manager can control. McGregor emphasized that a manager 's philosophy creates a self-fulfilling prophecy. Theory X managers treat employees almost as children who need constant direction, while Theory Y managers treat employees as competent adults capable of participating in work-related decisions. These managerial philosophies then have a subsequent effect on employee behavior, leading to the self-fulfilling prophecy. As a result, organizational philosophies and managerial philosophies need to be in harmony.

The number of coworkers involved within a problem-solving or decision-making process reflects the manager's *leadership style*. *Empowerment* means delegating to subordinates decision-making authority, freedom, knowledge, autonomy, and skills. Fortunately, most organizations and managers are making the move toward the active participation and teamwork that empowerment entails.

When guided properly, an empowered workforce may lead to heightened productivity and quality, reduced costs, more innovation, improved customer service, and greater commitment from the employees of the organization. In addition, response time may improve, because information and decisions need not be passed up and down the hierarchy. Empowering employees makes good sense because employees closest to the actual problem to be solved or the customer to be served can make the necessary decisions more easily than a supervisor or manager removed from the scene.

The following points highlight the seven factors that determine internal environment of a business firm.

The factors are: (1) Value System, (2) Mission and Objectives, (3) Organisation Structure, (4) Corporate Culture and Style of Functioning of Top Management, (5) Quality of Human Resources, (6) Labour Unions, and (7) Physical Resources and Technological Capabilities.

Factors Affecting Internal Environment of a Business

Value System

The value system of an organisation means the ethical beliefs that guide the organisation in achieving its mission and objective. The value system of a business organisation also determines its behaviour towards its employees, customers and society at large. The value system of the promoters of a business firm has an important bearing on the choice of business and the adoption of business policies and practices. Due to its value system a business firm may refuse to produce or distribute liquor for it may think morally wrong to promote the consumption of liquor.

The value system of a business organisation makes an important contribution to its success and its prestige in the world of business. For instance, the value system of J.R.D. Tata, the founder of Tata group of industries, was its self-imposed moral obligation to adopt morally just and fair business policies and practices which promote the interests of consumers, employees, shareholders and society at large. This value system of J.R.D. Tata was voluntarily incorporated in the articles of association of TISCO, a premier Tata company.

Infosys Technologies which won the first national corporate governance award in 1999 attributes its success to its high value system which guides its corporate culture. To quote one of its reports, "our corporate culture is to achieve our objectives in environment of fairness, honesty, transparency and courtesy towards our customers, employees, vendors and society at large" Thus value system of a business firm has an important bearing on its corporate culture and determines its behaviour towards its employees, shareholders and society as a whole.

Mission and Objectives

The objective of all firms is assumed to be maximization of long-run profits. But mission is different from this narrow objective of profit maximization. Mission is defined as the overall purpose or reason for its existence which guides and influences its business decision and economic activities.

The-choice of a business domain, direction of its development, choice of a business strategy and policies are all guided by the overall mission of the company. For example, to become a world-class company and to achieve global dominance has been the mission of 'Reliance Industries of India'. Similarly "to become a research based international pharma company" has been stated as mission of Ranbaxy Laboratories of India.

Organisation Structure

Organisation structure means such things as composition of board of directors, the number of independent directors, the extent of professional management and share -holding pattern. The nature of organisational structure has a significant influence over decision making process in an organisation. An efficient working of a business organisation requires that its organisation structure should be conducive to quick decision making. Delays in decision making can cost a good deal to a business firm.

The board of directors is the highest decision making body in a business organisation. It takes general policy decisions regarding direction of growth of business of the firm and supervises its overall functioning. Therefore, the managerial capability of the board of directors is of crucial importance for the functioning of a business firm and for achievement of its overall mission and objectives.

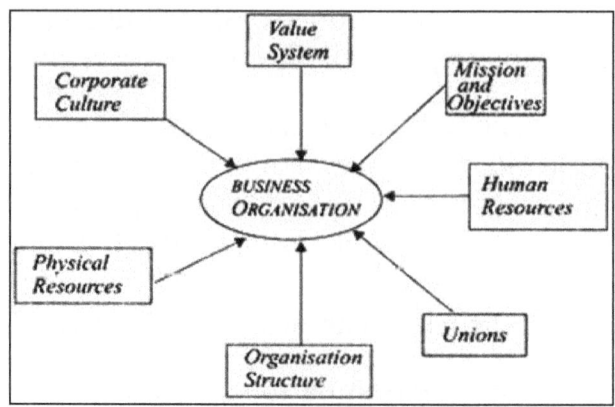

Internal Environment.

For efficient and transparent working of the board of directors in India it has been suggested that the number of independent directors be increased. Many private corporate firms in India are managed by family members of their promoters which is not conducive to the efficient working of these firms.

It is therefore highly desirable to increase the extent of professional management of private corporate companies. The share holding pattern has also an important implication for business management. In some Indian companies the majority of shares is held by the promoters of the company themselves.

In some others share-holding pattern is quite diversified among the public. In India financial institutions such as UTI, LIC, GIC, IDBI, IFC etc. have large share holdings in prominent Indian corporate companies and the nominees of these financial institutions play a critical role in making major business policy decisions of these corporate companies.

Technically, shareholders elect directors who make up the board of directors. The directors then appoint company's top managers who take various business decisions. However, most of the shareholders delegate the voting rights to the management or do not attend the general body meeting.

Thus, most of the shareholders regard ownership of the company as a purely financial investment. However, in recent years in developed countries like the United States the shareholders have come to wield a great influence.

The bankruptcy of business giants such as Enron, World Com. in the United States have created great awareness as well as mistrust among shareholders. In the last few years there has been frequent law suits filed by shareholders against directors and managers for ignoring the interests of shareholders or in fact cheating them by not declaring dividends. That is why there is worldwide debate on proper corporate governance of business firms.

Corporate Culture and Style of Functioning of Top Management

Corporate culture and style of functioning of top managers is important factor for determining the internal environment of a company. Corporate culture is generally considered as either closed and threatening or open and participatory.

In a closed and threatening type of corporate culture the business decisions are taken by top-level managers, while middle level and work-level managers have no say in business decision making. There is lack of trust and confidence in subordinate officials of the company and secrecy pervades throughout in the organisation. As a result, among lower level managers and workers there is no sense of belongingness to the company.

On the contrary, in an open and participatory culture, business decisions are taken at lower levels of management, and top management has a high degree of trust and confidence in the subordinates. Free communication between the top level management and lower-level managers is the rule in this open and participatory type of corporate culture. In this open and participatory system the participation of workers in managerial tasks is encouraged.

Closely related to corporate culture is the style of functioning of top management. Some top managers believe in just giving orders and want them to be strictly followed without holding consultations with lower level managers. This style of functioning is not conducive to the adaptability and flexibility in dealing with the changing external environment of business.

Quality of Human Resources

Quality of employees (i.e. human resources) of a firm is an important factor of internal environment of a firm. The success of a business organisation depends to a great extent on the skills, capabilities, attitudes and commitment of its employees. Employees differ with regard to these characteristics.

It is difficult for the top management to deal directly with all the employees of the business firm. Therefore, for efficient management of human resources, employees are divided into different groups. The manager may pay little attention to the technical details of the job done by a group and encourage group cooperation in the interests of a company. Due to the importance of human resources for the success of a company these days there is a special course for managers how to select and manage efficiently human resources of a company.

Labour Unions

Labour unions are other factor determining internal environment of a firm. Unions collectively bargain with top managers regarding wages, working conditions of different categories of employees. Smooth working of a business organisation requires that there should be good relations between management and labour union.

Each side must implement the terms of agreement reached. Sometimes, a business organisation requires restructuring and modernisation. In this regard, the terms and conditions reached with the labour union must be implemented in both letter and spirit if cooperation of workers is to be ensured for the reconstruction and modernisation of business.

Physical Resources and Technological Capabilities

Physical resources such as plant and equipment, and technological capabilities of a firm determine its competitive strength which is an important factor determining its efficiency and unit cost of production. R and D capabilities of a company determine its ability to introduce innovations which enhance productivity of workers.

It is however important to note that rapid technological progress, especially unprecedented growth of information technology in recent years has increased the relative importance of 'intellectual capital and human resources as compared to physical resources of a company. The growth of Bill Gates Microsoft Company and Murthy's Infosys Technologies is mostly due to the quality of human resources and intellectual capital than to any superior physical resources.

External Environment

All outside factors that may affect an organization make up the external environment. The external environment is divided into two parts:

Directly interactive: This environment has an immediate and firsthand impact upon the organization. A new competitor entering the market is an example.

Indirectly interactive: This environment has a secondary and more distant effect upon the organization. New legislation taking effect may have a great impact. For example, complying with the Americans with Disabilities Act requires employers to update their facilities to accommodate those with disabilities.

Directly interactive forces include owners, customers, suppliers, competitors, employees, and employee unions. Management has a responsibility to each of these groups. Here are some examples:

- Owners expect managers to watch over their interests and provide a return on investments.

- Customers demand satisfaction with the products and services they purchase and use.

- Suppliers require attentive communication, payment, and a strong working relationship to provide needed resources.

- Competitors present challenges as they vie for customers in a marketplace with similar products or services.

- Employees and employee unions provide both the people to do the jobs and the representation of work force concerns to management.

The second type of external environment is the *indirectly interactive* forces. These forces include sociocultural, political and legal, technological, economic, and global influences. Indirectly interactive forces may impact one organization more than another simply because of the nature of a particular business. For example, a company that relies heavily on technology will be more affected by software updates than a company that uses just one computer. Although somewhat removed, indirect forces are still important to the interactive nature of an organization.

The *sociocultural* dimension is especially important because it determines the goods, services, and standards that society values. The sociocultural force includes the demographics and values of a particular customer base.

Demographics are measures of the various characteristics of the people and social groups who make up a society. Age, gender, and income are examples of commonly used demographic characteristics.

Values refer to certain beliefs that people have about different forms of behavior or products. Changes in how a society values an item or a behavior can greatly affect a business.

The *political and legal dimensions* of the external environment include regulatory parameters within which an organization must operate. Political parties create or influence laws, and business owners must abide by these laws. Tax policies, trade regulations, and minimum wage legislation are just a few examples of political and legal issues that may affect the way an organization operates.

The *technological dimension* of the external environment impacts the scientific processes used in changing inputs (resources, labor, money) to outputs (goods and services). The success of many organizations depends on how well they identify and respond to external technological changes.

For example, one of the most significant technological dimensions of the last several decades has been the increasing availability and affordability of management information systems (also known as MIS). Through these systems, managers have access to information that can improve the way they operate and manage their businesses.

The economic dimension reflects worldwide financial conditions. Certain economic conditions of special concern to organizations include interest rates, inflation, unemployment rates, gross national product, and the value of the U.S. dollar against other currencies.

A favorable economic climate generally represents opportunities for growth in many industries, such as sales of clothing, jewelry, and new cars. But some businesses traditionally benefit in poor economic conditions. The alcoholic beverage industry, for example, traditionally fares well during times of economic downturn.

The *global dimension* of the environment refers to factors in other countries that affect U.S. organizations. Although the basic management functions of planning, organizing, staffing, leading, and controlling are the same whether a company operates domestically or internationally, managers encounter difficulties and risks on an international scale. Whether it be unfamiliarity with language or customs or a problem within the country itself (think mad cow disease), managers encounter global risks that they probably wouldn't have encountered if they had stayed on their own shores.

The external environment consists of the micro environment and macro environment.

Macro Environment

The general environment within the economy that influences the working, performance, decision making and strategy of all business groups at the same time is known as Macro Environment. It is dynamic in nature. Therefore it keeps on changing.

It constitutes those outside forces that are not under the control of the firm but have a powerful impact on the firm's functioning. It consists of individuals, groups, organizations, agencies and others with which the firm deals during the course of its business.

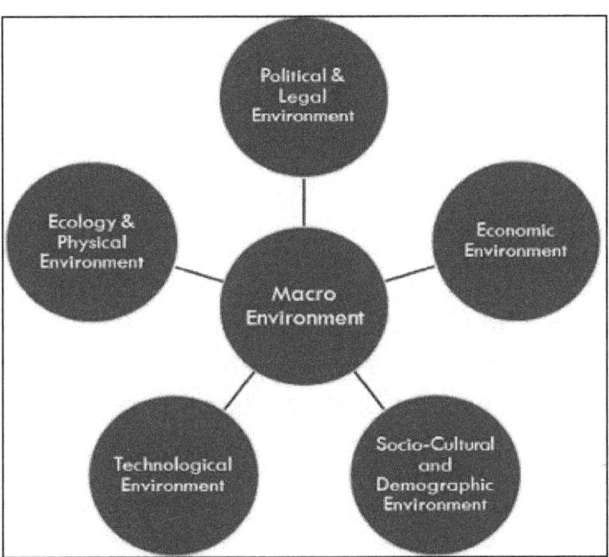

The study of Macro Environment is known as PESTLE Analysis. PESTLE stands for the variables that exist in the environment, i.e. Population & Demographic, Economic, Socio-Cultural, Technological, Legal & Political and Environmental. These variables, consider both economic and non-economic factors like social concerns, government policies, family structure, population size, inflation, GDP aspects, income distribution, ethnic mix, political stability, taxes, and duties, etc.

The macro environment in which a company or sector operates influences its performance, and the amount of the influence depends on how much of the company's business is dependent on the health of the overall economy. Cyclical industries, for example, are heavily influenced by the macro environment, while consumer staples are less influenced. The macro environment can also greatly affect consumers directly, affecting their ability and willingness to spend. Consumers' reactions to the broad macro environment are closely monitored by businesses and economists as a gauge for an economy's health. Effects from some of the market's key factors influencing the macro environment include the following:

Gross Domestic Product

GDP is a measure of a country's output and production of goods and services. The Bureau of Economic Analysis releases a quarterly report on GDP growth that provides a broad overview of the output of goods and services across all sectors. GDP is often the lead influencing factor of corporate profits for the economy, which is another measure of an economy's comprehensive productivity.

Inflation

Inflation is a key factor watched by economists, investors and consumers. It affects the spending strength of the U.S. dollar and is a factor closely regulated through monetary policy by the Federal Reserve. The target rate for annual inflation from the Federal Reserve is 2%. Inflation higher than 2% significantly affects the purchasing power of the dollar, making each unit less valuable as inflation rises.

Employment

Employment levels in the United States are measured by the Bureau of Labor Statistics, which releases a monthly report on increases in business payrolls and the status of the unemployment rate. The U.S. unemployment rate is 4.1% as of March 15, 2018. The Federal Reserve also seeks to regulate employment levels through monetary policy stimulus and credit measures that can ease borrowing rates for businesses to help improve capital spending and business growth, also resulting in employment growth.

Monetary Policy

The Federal Reserve's monetary policy initiatives are a key factor influencing the macro environment in the United States. Monetary policy measures are typically centered around access to credit and federal interest rate limits, one of the main levers of the Federal Reserve's monetary policy tools. The Federal Reserve sets a federal funds rate for which federal banks borrow from each other, and this rate is used as a base rate for all credit rates in the broader market. The tightening of monetary policy indicates rates are rising, making credit borrowing less appealing.

The company is not alone in doing business. It is surrounded by and operates in a larger context. This context is called the Macro Environment. It consists of all the forces that shape opportunities, but also pose threats to the company.

The Macro Environment consists of 6 different forces. These are: Demographic, Economic, Political, Ecological, Socio-Cultural, and Technological forces. This can easily be remembered: the DESTEP model, also called DEPEST model, helps to consider the different factors of the Macro Environment.

Demographic Forces in the Macro Environment

Demographic forces relate to people. The name refers to the term Demography. The latter refers to the study of human populations. This includes size, density, age, gender, occupation and other statistics. Why are people important? Because, on the whole, their needs is the reason for businesses to exist. In other words, people are the driving force for the development of markets. The large and diverse demographics both offer opportunities but also challenges for businesses. Especially in times of rapid world population growth, and overall demographic changes, the study of people is crucial for marketers. The reason is that changing demographics mean changing markets. Further, changing markets mean a need for adjusted marketing strategies.

Therefore, marketers should keep a close eye on demographics. This may include all kinds of characteristics of the population, such as size, growth, density, age- and gender structure, and so on.

Some of the most important demographic trends that affect markets are:

World Population Growth

The world population is growing at an explosive rate. Already in 2011, it reached 7 million, while being expected to reach 8 billion by the year 2030. By the end of the century, it is likely to double. However, the strongest growth occurs where wealth and stability is mostly absent. More than 70% of the expected world population growth in the next 40 years is expected to take place outside of the 20 richest nations on earth. This changes requirements for effective marketing strategies and should be kept in mind.

Changing Age Structure

The changing age structure of world population is another critical factor influencing marketing. In the future, there will be countries with far more favourable age structures than others. For example, India has one of the youngest populations on earth and is expected to keep that status. By 2020, the median age in India will be 28 years. In contrast, the countries of the European Union and the USA have to face an aging population already today. This may lead to harmful reductions in dynamism and challenges regarding the supply of young workers who, at the same time, have to support a growing population of elderly people.

Changing Family Structures

Also, families are changing which means that the marketing strategies aimed at them must undergo an adjustment. For example, new household formats start emerging in many countries. While in traditional western countries a typical household consisted of husband, wife and children, nowadays there are more married couples without children, as well as single parent and single households. Another factor comes from the growing number of women working full time, particularly in European nations. Together with further forces, changing family structures require the marketing strategy to be changed.

Geographic Shifts in Population

One – and the most important – element of geographic shifts is migration. By 2050, global migration is expected to double. This has a major impact on both the location and the nature of demand for products and services. The reason is that the place people can be reached has changed, as have their needs because of the new situations. Other important factors are the ethnic diversity that provides new opportunities, as well as urbanisation.

Economic Forces in the Macro Environment

The Economic forces relate to factors that affect consumer purchasing power and spending patterns. For instance, a company should never start exporting to a country before having examined how much people will be able to spend. Important criteria are: GDP, GDP real growth rate, GNI, Import Duty rate and sales tax/ VAT, Unemployment, Inflation, Disposable personal income, and Spending patterns.

Socio-Cultural Forces in the Macro Environment

The Socio-Cultural forces link to factors that affect society's basic values, preferences and behavior. The basis for these factors is formed by the fact that people are part of a society and cultural group that shape their beliefs and values. Many cultural blunders occur due to the failure of businesses in understanding foreign cultures. For instance, symbols may carry a negative meaning in another culture. To understand these forces, Hofstede's cultural dimensions can be used: Power Distance, Individualism versus Collectivism, Masculinity versus Femininity, Uncertainty Avoidance etc.

Technological Forces in the Macro Environment

Technological forces form a crucial influence in the Macro Environment. They relate to factors that create new technologies and thereby create new product and market opportunities.

A technological force everybody can think of nowadays is the development of wireless communication techniques, smartphones, tablets and so further. This may mean the emerge of opportunities for a business, but watch out: every new technology replaces an older one. Thus, marketers must watch the technological environment closely and adapt in order to keep up. Otherwise, the products will soon be outdated, and the company will miss new product and market opportunities.

Ecological Forces in the Macro Environment

Ecological, or natural forces in the Macro Environment are important since they are about the natural resources which are needed as inputs by marketers or which are affected by their marketing activities. Also, environmental concerns have grown strongly in recent years, which makes the ecological force a crucial factor to consider. For instance, world, air and water pollution are headlines every marketer should be aware of. In other words, you should keep track of the trends in the ecological environment.

Important trends in the ecological environment are the growing shortage of raw materials and the care for renewable resources. In addition, increased pollution, but also increased intervention of government in natural resource management is an issue.

Because of all these concerns and the increased involvement of society in ecological issues, companies more than ever before need to consider and implement environmental sustainability. This means that they should contribute to supporting the environment, for instance by using renewable energy sources. Thereby, businesses do not only support the maintenance of a green planet, but also respond to consumer demands for environmentally friendly and responsible products.

Political Forces in the Macro Environment

Every business is limited by the political environment. This involves laws, government agencies and pressure groups. These influence and restrict organisations and individuals in a society. Therefore, marketing decisions are strongly influenced and affected by developments in the political environment.

Before entering a new market in a foreign country, the company should know everything about the legal and political environment. How will the legislation affect the business? What rules does it need to obey? What laws may limit the company's ability to be successful? For example, laws covering issues such as environmental protection, product safety regulations, competition, pricing etc. might require the firm to adapt certain aspects and strategies to the new market.

As we have seen, the company is surrounded by a complex environment. The Macro Environment consists of a large variety of different forces. All of these may shape opportunities for the company, but could also pose threats. Therefore, it is of critical importance that marketers understand and have an eye on development in the Macro Environment, to make their business grow in the long term.

Components of Macro Environment

The following are the components of Macroenvironment:

    (a) Demographic Environment.

    (b) Economic Environment.

    (c) Physical Environment.

    (d) Technological Environment.

    (e) Political Environment.

    (f) Legal Environment.

    (g) Social and Cultural Environment.

Demographic Environment

Demographics are statistics that companies keep on business clients and consumers. These marketing statistics may include the sizes of businesses so companies can better differentiate between small, mid-sized or large companies. But they are more commonly used to identify differences in personal attributes among consumers. There are many different types of demographics companies use for various purposes.

Identification

Common demographics include age, gender, race and ethnic origin. Companies also track demographics like education, household size and occupation. Most demographics are defined or delineated by specific ranges. For example, the age demographic may divided into ranges such as 18 to 24; 25 to 34; 35 to 54; and 55 years and over. People within these age groups have different values. Their preferences for certain products or services may vary as well. Similarly, statisticians may divide income statistics into groups to differentiate those in the lower middle, middle and upper class.

Obtaining the Data

Companies can obtain demographic information from the U.S. Census Bureau. They usually list various demographics by state and city. Marketers can also obtain more localized demographic information from area or county Chambers of Commerce. These entities typically break data down by various census tracts or smaller regions in metropolitan areas. Companies that want demographic data related to their industry often purchase reports from marketing research companies like Nielsen, Forrester Research or The NPD Group. These companies usually conduct regular surveys to garner this information. For example, a consumer products company may want age breakdowns on the heaviest buyers or users of laundry detergents. Businesses can obtain more company-specific data by conducting their own phone or Internet surveys. Warranty cards are another tool that can be used for collecting demographic data.

Local uses of Data

Companies use local demographic data to better define their key customers. Certain data are more relevant to various businesses. For example, a high-end woman's specialty retailer, which offers premium or higher-priced clothing, may focus on women over 35 with incomes above $75,000 per year. A fast food restaurant offering children's meals may be interested in learning the percentage of families in their area who have kids. Hence, it may start by studying household size data along with age breakouts of kids 12 and under.

Market Segmentation

Companies also use demographic data to identify key buying groups on a regional or national basis. For example, a small financial management firm may be interested in expanding to markets with large populations of people over 55. Hence, top management may study available data in contiguous markets first to determine where to locate the new offices.

There are a number of demographics that can affect a business. Demographics are various traits that can be used to determine product preferences or buying behaviors of consumers. Most companies identify their key customers through these various traits. They then target consumers with like characteristics in their advertisements and promotions. Targeting consumers with similar demographic characteristics helps maximize a company's sales and profits.

Income Influence

Income is one demographic variable that can affect businesses. A company's products usually appeal to certain income groups. For example, premium products such as high-end woman's clothing usually appeal to women with higher incomes. Conversely, people with comparatively lower incomes are more sensitive to price and, therefore, may prefer purchasing discount products. People with lower incomes have less disposable income. Value is a major determinant in the products they purchase. Hence, a company may best reach lower-income people through discount retailers and wholesalers and attract higher-income buyers in specialty retail shops.

Age Variables

Age is another demographic element that impacts businesses. A company's products and services are more likely to appeal to certain age groups. Younger people under 35 are often the first consumers to purchase high-tech products like cell phones, electronic books and video games. The millennial generation is increasing buying power and growing market share while baby boomers remain a large and viable group as well. For example, there are about 76 million baby boomers in the United States, according to "Entrepreneur" online. This is the single largest population segment. These people were born between 1946 and 1964, according to "Elderly Journal" online. Baby Boomers spent $400 billion more than any other age group, according to a a June 2009 report by "Entrepreneur." Small business owners can target this specific age group.

Geographic Region

People's buying preferences also vary by geographic region, which is another type of demographic. Those who meet buyers' needs and requirements in certain geographic regions can earn higher sales and profits. For example, people often prefer certain food and drink flavors in certain markets. Companies that sell the flavors consumers desire in various areas are more likely to profit. Those who do not offer these flavors may risk losing customers to other competitors.

Obtaining Demographic Information

One of the best ways to collect consumer demographic data is through market research surveys. These surveys can be conducted by phone, mail, Internet or in person. The key is collecting as much demographic information as possible. Other demographic variables, besides age, income and geography, include household size, education, occupation, gender, race and employment status. Most marketing research professionals include demographic questions at the end of their surveys. Warranty cards are another way to collect this information from customers.

The Importance of Demographics to Marketing

Business owners are always looking for an edge in marketing products and services to generate more revenue and profit margins. Demographics are a key factor in getting that edge. The term demographics refers to a statistical analysis of people or a group. What that really means to a business owner is that it enables her to find the group of people who fit the mold of the ideal customer. Find those who need what you have, and you will be more successful in selling. Demographics finds those people. Learn the value of different segments of demographic groups.

Generational Groups

It is important to understand which generation your target market belongs to. Baby Boomers have very different buying habits compared to those of the X-Generation or Millenials. Not only do different generations have different buying habits from each other, but they also have different ways of speaking and alternative ways of buying. If you aren't marketing to Millenials online, you aren't capturing the greatest potential share of this demographic.

Age Ranges

Age ranges may seem like they are another way to say generational groups, but it goes a bit farther than that. Ranges can actually transcend generations. For example, a life insurance agent can target married couples having their first baby. This is not a generational thing, but is more likely an age range target for couples between the ages of 20 and 50. This age range spans several generations and is contingent on the common thread of having a baby.

Ethnic Background

People from different cultures have different tastes and have different buying habits from one another. For example, if a kitchen remodeling contractor expands his business to a community in which it is culturally acceptable to negotiate every purchase, the contractor will need to prepare himself for the sales process and potentially altering his pricing to ensure that he gets clients and still makes a profit. It is also important to understand and respect the different holidays and cultural traditions of specific ethnic demographics.

Family Structure

Knowing whether a person is married, single or divorced, is also an important demographic to understand. While single parents still buy life insurance, the key demographic that we looked at in the age section was that of married couples. Family structure affects buying habits and also affects the sales process. If the husband is the decision maker and you are speaking to the wife, you have the wrong person in front of you. Marketing needs to target the couple and to lean toward the most common decision-maker for that purchase. For example, married couples who own homes might buy home theater systems, but the husband might direct the sale, with his football season parties in mind.

Income and Investments

Knowing whether or not you are targeting a group that can afford your products and services is important. You don't want to market a luxury car to someone who can barely afford a used clunker. When you know the income range of clients, you can also find data to support how those groups spend money on both the higher and lower end of the spectrum.

Focusing on a Niche

All of the above topics of demographic data are a foundation. Many businesses are using contemporary technology via social media and online analytics programs to closely target the demographic down to a focused niche. An example would be single women who own dogs; this demographic might be more likely to spend money on the dog as if it were a child, rather than a pet. This is a good target for pet service and supply providers. Niches can look at political affiliations, hobbies and favorite sports teams. Pretty much anything you can think of regarding buyer preferences is available data. The theory of this marketing strategy is that the more focused your demographic is, the better you can speak to their emotions and get them to buy.

Economic Environment

Economic Environment refers to all those economic factors, which have a bearing on the functioning of a business. Business depends on the economic environment for all the needed inputs. It also depends on the economic environment to sell the finished goods. Naturally, the dependence of business on the economic environment is total and is not surprising because, as it is rightly said, business is one unit of the total economy.

Economic environment influences the business to a great extent. It refers to all those economic factors which affect the functioning of a business unit. Dependence of business on economic environment is total — i.e. for input and also to sell the finished goods. Trained economists supplying the Macro economic forecast and research are found in major companies in manufacturing, commerce and finance which prove the importance of economic environment in business. The following factors constitute economic environment of business:

(a) Economic system,

(b) Economic planning,

(c) Industry,

(d) Agriculture,

(e) Infrastructure,

(f) Financial & fiscal sectors,

(g) Removal of regional imbalances,

(h) Price & distribution controls,

(i) Economic reforms,

(j) Human resource, and

(k) Per capita income and national income.

The state became the encourager of savings and also an important investor and the owner of capital. Since the state was to be the primary agent of economic change, it followed that private sector activities had to be strictly regulated and controlled to conform to the objectives of state policy.

The growth strategy also meant, in the early years of planning, a relative neglect of public investments in agriculture. This negligence of agriculture sector was supported by the general view that the increase labour in the developing countries could only be absorbed in the industry, and that during the early stages of industrialization, it was necessary for agriculture to contribute in the establishment of modern industry by offering inexpensive work force. A faster development of industry was the central objective of planning. The above is a thumbnail sketch of the growth strategy followed by the planners in the past four decades.

The importance of Environmental Economics lies on the fact that absolutely all economic activities performed by mankind are intrinsically linked to the environment, which provides all sorts of resources and also acts as a sink for our waste. Therefore, in order to keep paving the path of economic growth, it is mandatory to acknowledge, value, and consider the goods and services provided by the Earth's environmental systems, to sustain the supply of resources and energy without breaking the equilibrium of the fragile natural environment.

Environmental Economics combines the study of environmental science with its interactions with human economic markets. It encompasses the understanding of the capacities and vulnerabilities of the planet, to adapt and respond to different challenges; considering natural resources as fundamental assets for the global economy, it explores the common interaction of economic analysis with market failure, externalities, property rights, and valuing the environment as a capital asset.

The economic environment of business is affected by internal and external factors. An internal factor that affects the business environment is the cost of labor, materials, processes and procedures. Internal factors can be improved through company projects. On the other hand, external factors can also affect a company's business environment and the business has less control over these factors. The primary influences on a business are: political, economical, social, legal, technological and environmental.

Political Factors

The political environment affects the economic environment of businesses. Legislators at the local, state and federal levels may provide incentives or tax breaks to companies or they can impose regulations that restrict business transactions. In the latter case, for example, if a political body states that a company must include a certain chemical in its product, the cost of the product differs. The company passes those costs on to the customer in the form of higher prices. The customer must determine whether he wants to purchase that product. If he does not purchase the product, then the company does not receive the revenue. If a large number of customers decide not to purchase the product, the company may need to layoff employees.

Economic Factors

The larger economic environment of a society is a factor that can affect a company's business environment. During a recession, consumers spend less on optional items such as cars and appliances. As a result, the business environment suffers. On the other hand, if the economic environment is one of prosperity, consumers are more likely to spend money, not just on necessities, but larger items as well.

Social Factors

Social factors that affect the economic environment of a business are the cultural influences of the time. For example, a fashion designer that creates bell bottom, striped pants will not succeed in an environment where straight-leg, solid colored pants are desired. A social environment that tends to be more conservative will not support styles that appear to be trendy. The fashion designer's business will suffer if he does not change the clothing style. The same would apply to the manufacturers that produce and stores that sell these wares.

Legal Factors

Often, a business will need to change how it operates for legal reasons. This is often done when a company's lawyers anticipate a change in legislation, or it may be due to lawsuits, already filed or anticipated. For example, if a part in a machine is found to be defective, the company may need to issue a recall. If other companies in the same industry are being sued over something like a data breach of confidential information, a business may need to change how information is collected and stored.

Technological Factors

Innovation and technology affect business environments. As technology advances, a business is forced to keep pace. For example, when computers were first invented, they were the size of a room. Users were forced to employ punch cards to perform basic functions. Today, computers that are much more powerful can fit into the palm of a hand. Businesses that do not keep up with technology risk increased costs of production and higher prices. If the company's cost to produce a product or service outpaces competitors, the company may soon find itself out of business.

Environmental Factors

The environment can have a direct and indirect affect on how a business operates. Businesses in the food industry are routinely affected by the environment. Droughts or disease can affect pricing models and even the ability of food processors, grocery stores and restaurants in obtaining sufficient supplies to meet consumer demands. Indirect environmental factors can affect any business by creating changes in societal expectations and government laws and regulations in efforts to protect the environment. For example, in 2016, California citizens voted for a law to ban the use of single-use plastic bags, affecting the majority of retailers in that state.

Physical/Natural Environment

The physical environment is a key component of the business environment in which you intend to operate or in which you already run your business irrespective of whether it's conventional or online, small or big. It refers to the availability of resources that you need to run your business efficiently. These resources may generally include among others inputs like materials, services, land, climate, water, physical plants and facilities. Every business needs these resources to get started or to have its work done efficiently and effectively.

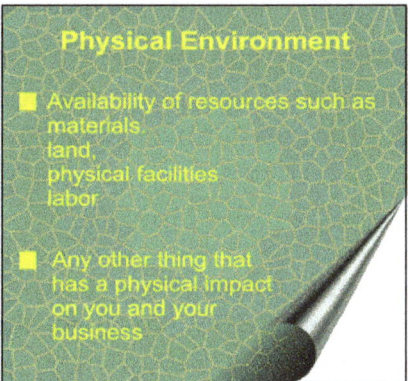

Your physical environment comprises of both natural and man-made resources. Features like land, water, climate, wildlife and vegetation are natural components of the physical environment in which we live and operate our businesses. On the other hand, dams, roads, premises and much more, are man-made resources that affect your business.

Physical environment may also refer to the physical location, space and any other thing that physically impacts on you and your business. For instance, light, temperature and distractions in your office can affect your performance. If you are working in an office with little light, it can make you get stressed up. If it's extremely hot in your workplace, it can make you get so tired that you find it difficult to work comfortably and effectively. What about a noisy and polluted place? What effect can it have on your health and your business? Think about it.

The importance of understanding the physical environment in which the business operates-

1 – Good for planning purposes:

The success of your business depends largely on good planning. You need to have a business plan if you intend to start any business. Additionally, you need a marketing plan and an activity plan as well. One of the most important aspects you should consider at any planning level is the physical environment.

Understanding your physical environment enables you to plan well for your business from an informed point of view. If you already have a business, discovering about the physical environment helps you to grow a successful business. When the resources you need for your business become scarce in the environment, it's hard for you to continue with your business operations normally. Many times, one has to borrow funds from banks, micro-finance institutions or other money lenders to acquire resources so that the business can survive.

For instance, Uganda was naturally endowed with abundant rainfall, good climate and fertile soils. This is why Winston Churchill named it in 1908 the "Pearl of Africa". These words still ring in the heads of Ugandans and they're proud of it because of the good natural physical environment God gave to Uganda.

However, due to the uncontrolled disastrous activities by Ugandans themselves, rainfall has become as scarce as in desert countries. The once fertile soils are no long productive without adding fertilizers or manure. As a result, the climate has changed greatly countrywide.

2 – To know the resources you need for your business:

The resources you need vary from business to business. For instance, if you want to set up a laser engraving business, you will have to get engravable materials, technical people, and office space in a good location, a laser engraver and constant power supply. You will also need designing software, skills and knowledge in designing / engraving and a computer to start your business.

But if you want to set up a juice manufacturing business, you will have to get different resources. You will need fruits as your raw materials, juice making equipment, electricity, transport and much more.

You therefore need to consider so important the physical environment in which you intend to set up your business. First ask yourself what you can offer by yourself. Secondly, consider outsourcing what you cannot offer either locally or abroad. It's always beneficial if your physical environment can offer what you need for your business.

Natural factors such as climate, soil, forests, minerals, rivers and ocean have tremendous influence on the functioning and growth of commerce and industry. The impact of natural environment of business may be described under the following heads:

- Source of Raw Materials: Natural and physical environment provides the raw materials required for the functioning of industries. For example, iron and steel industry cannot function without ore and other necessary minerals. In fact, the mines, flora, fauna, land mass, nature of soil, etc. serve as the basis of production function.

- Mainstay of Agriculture: People and business both require several types of agricultural items for their survival and growth. Agriculture largely depends on nature. Cultivation of crops and raising of livestock are directly dependent on soil. The types of crops that can be grown in an area depend upon climate and soil.

- Location of Industry: Heavy industry has to be located near the source of raw materials. For example. India's iron and steel industry is concentrated in the regions which are rich in the deposits of iron ore and coal. Extractive industries such as mining, oil drilling, stone quarrying, etc. depend on the availability of minerals deposited by nature. Industrialists don not like to set up factories in areas which are climate affect the location of certain industries like cotton textiles and watch manufacturing.

- Employment Generation: Existence of minerals and other natural resources alone does not guarantee economic prosperity of people. Proper exploration and utilisation is necessary. Exploitation and utilization of natural resources provides jobs to millions.

- Foreign Exchange Earner: A country can export its surplus natural resources like minerals and oils and thereby earn valuable foreign exchange. Arabian countries have become affluent by exploiting their oil resources gifted by nature. In fact the genesis of international trade lies in the natural environment. Trade between nation is the outcome of geographical differences. Due to natural factors some regions are more suitable for production of certain goods, *e.g.,* tea and coffee in India, Petroleum in Middle East, dairy products in Denmark and so on.

- Basis of Transportation and Communication: Business depends upon transportation and communication facilities which in turn are largely dependent on geographical factors. Uneven land surface, deserts, oceans and forests are barriers in transportation and communication, Though modern technology has enabled man to overcome these barriers, the costs increase tremendously. Even today business activities do not flourish in areas which by nature lack efficient transportation and communication systems.

- Key to Human Life: Business can prosper only when people are healthy and happy. Nature serves not only as a store house of raw materials, it also provides the physical and biological conditions within which people can live in a healthy and happy manner. Almost every commodity which we consume and produce has existed originally in the natural environment. Nature is also the source of almost all the energy used in production and distribution. Nature has is a symbiotic link between man and nature. In fact, earth is so crucial to mankind that out Vedas and seers suggest worship to the Mother Earth.

- Demand Pattern: Demand pattern depends upon topographical and weather conditions. For example, jeeps may be in greater demand than cars in hilly areas with a difficult terrain. Similarly, woolens are in demand in cool areas while coolers and air conditioners are more in demand in high temperature regions. Natural environment may also call for modifications in product mix, packaging and storage systems.

Technological Environment

Technological environment is associated with the external factors that impact on business operators. It also relates to the development of technology which affects business by way of new inventions of productions and other improvements in techniques to perform the business. The changing technological environment may pose threats or present opportunities.

The competitive nature of business environment and globalization has made it imperative for manufacturing organizations mostly towork hard towards identifying business strategies that will give them an edge over their competitor(s).

Before an organization can begin its strategic formulation and implementation, it must scan the external environment to identify possible opportunities and threats and its internal environment for strengths and weaknesses. It is against the backdrop that environmental conditions and factors have the potentials to influence strategic decisions. Strategic planning is an organization's process of defining its strategy or direction and making decision on allocating its various business analytical techniques. What can be used in strategic planning include SWOT analysis (i.e. Strength, Weakness, Opportunities and Threats), PEST analysis (i.e. Political, Economic, Social and Technological), STEER analysis (i.e. Socio-Cultural, Technological, Economic, Ecological and Regulatory Factors) and EPISTEL (i.e.Environment, Political, Information, Social, Technological, Economic and Legal). Industrialization and economic development have been two of the critical interrelated and prominent objective pursued by many developing nations of the world.

One of the most pervasive factors in the environment is technology. Managers are generally concerned with two components of the technological environment; the process of innovation and the process of technology transfer. The process of innovation refers to their efforts in the basic sciences to develop new technologies, processes, methods and products . While the process of technology transfer involves taking the new technology from the laboratory to the market, that is the transfer of science to useful products and applications.

Theoretical and empirical investigations have emphasized the crucial role that technological innovation and entrepreneurship lay in fostering the development of today's industrialized nations. These types of investigation are now seen as crucial to the development of the third world, and they are accordingly recognized as important components of technology policy and indigenous socio-economic planning. The present emphasis on indigenous technical innovation and entrepreneurship stems from the failure of past attempts to stimulate Third World development by borrowing or transferring advanced technology from developed nations.

In most third world countries, governments are criticized for paying not more than lip service to the need for accelerated growth and for not 'harnessing the abilities of their own citizens for technological innovation and entrepreneurship'. Critics also lament that these countries depend too much on exogenous and often exploitative technology and they point out the inappropriate choices of technology made by many developing countries.

According to Inegbenebor, the desire of most developing countries, is to have a self-reliant and resilient economy capable of generating an internally self-sustaining growth. For many decades,developing countries were exporters of raw materials and importers of finished goods from the colonial metropolis. Having recently gained political independence, these countries want to quickly transform their economies in order to achieve economic independence as well.

Generally, the word "Technology" is associated with the industrial arts, applied science engineering and with physical things . It has been defined as the systematized practical knowledge, skills, methods, activities and artifacts by means of which man pushes back his limitations and extend his capability.

The technological environment in the manufacturing sector itself has changed dynamically from mechanized powered systems to the present day trend towards the application of advanced manufacturingtechnology which is seen in new products, machines, tools, materials and better mode of services. Among the benefits of technology are greater productivity, higher living standards, more leisure time and greater variety of products.

Technological impact on management practice is great. It is a vital element in planning both in the design of products and services and in their development, production and distribution.

Technology can come as an important tool within the company, improving the operations and functions or it can be the very reason why a company exists. Such is the scale of impact of technology on business. Heads of companies are on constant lookout for updates and developments in the technological environment. This helps them not just to improve the efficiency of the way the organization works but to be aware of the transformational phase and come up with groundbreaking strategies to drive growth. Management students during their academic course are thought how technological environment can influence business environment. This write-up tries to provide few instances and helps readers realize how technology constantly transforms businesses.

New Technology – New Products – New Business

During the 1990s, the world of photography started to see a shift from film photography to digital photography. Three big names in the field of film photography then were Fujifilm, Konica and Kodak. The change in technology affected these businesses greatly. Experts state that Fujifilm was more successful in adapting to the new digital technology and today it manufactures digital cameras and lenses. Though Kodak manufactured digital cameras during the 90s and 2000s it did not see great success and now it has joined hands with Flexitronics to stay in the domain. Konica on the other-hand got merged to Minolta in 2003. Today, the company is into manufacturing printers and copiers. This is a wonderful example of how technology can impact the very existence of the business.

Technology Transforming Operations

The introduction of new technology has constantly changed the way a company functions. The developments in IT has taken over almost all departments of an organization. Today, information is mostly stored in servers as opposed to decades-old method of storing in hard copies (files and registers). Thanks to the advancement in the internet, companies use digital marketing strategies to market and sell their products today. Even the research and design department of organization are subject to constant developments in technology. For instance, companies like Boeing and Siemens are investing hugely on adapting 3D printing technique for designing their products. The companies believe this can quicken the design process, reduce cost and improve effectiveness of designing.

Technology Helps Develop Business Strategies

The transformation in the way how data is collected, recorded, retrieved and utilized has helped companies come up with groundbreaking business strategies. Today, companies monitor customer taste and trends using data that is available. The development in information technology has made it possible for businesses to study customer behavior and develop strategies accordingly. Technology has not only made it possible to collect and store data but organizations are able to analyze the available data to come up with meaningful conclusions and make informed decisions. With more and more customer focus, data analytics will play a key role in growth strategies of companies.

Experts and researchers who have worked extensively trying to know the nature and extent of impact technology can have over business state that technology has disrupted business models and changed the fundamental principles. Gone are those days where companies could stick to decades old model and they have their share of customers in the market. Today, companies are working towards aligning themselves with the new-age technology. While some organizations have been successful in leveraging on technological development to grow in the market, to some businesses it has been challenging to adapt to the changes. Technology and globalization has made its impact on business of all scales. Management professionals have come out of the traditional path of using logical methods for planning and are on continuous look out for new ways to help align themselves with the market changes and get the best for their business.

Technological factors affecting businesses all over the world demands a changing behaviour with regard to traditional marketing.

The rapid development of technology requires quick reaction by businesses in order to survive in an emerging competitive environment and keep up with new trends and innovative services which other competitors might be offering.

These technological factors can include both products and processes and can present opportunities and threats but it is vital for competitive advantage and is a successful driver in globalisation. Products can be marketed in new ways and processes present immense value to the business.

Some of the following points should be considered:

- Understanding Web Terminology.

- Technology legislation.

- Internet/broadband – consumer & business markets.

- Technology infrastructure in a country (Web/Broadband/Mobile).

- Do the technologies offer consumers and businesses more innovative products and services such as Internet banking, new generation mobile telephones.

- Secure Systems: encryptions, digital certificates, SSL (secure sockets layer protocol mechanisms).

- How is distribution changed by new technologies e.g. books via the Internet, flight tickets, auctions.

- Does technology offer companies a new way to communicate with consumers e.g. Social media, Customer Relationship Management (e CRM), etc.

- Machinery.

- Equipment.

Some of these technological factors affecting businesses proved to be dramatic for some companies seriously invested in certain type of equipment only to see a more innovative and cost-effective technology emerge.

Spending money on the latest technology can be daunting for some organisations and questions such as ('Ignore it.., Ignore it for now.., Evaluate it carefully.., Adopt it enthusiastically?') always come up in their response to Innovation.

Other technological factors affecting businesses and their environment:

- Organisational change – is usually quite difficult especially when a high number of people are involved as routines will be modified. It is recommended to inform employees in advance and keep them up to date encouraging feedback when making such change.

- Business processes – integrating modern technology solicits identifying the business requirements and evaluating the business processes according to its objectives and goals. These changes should benefit the company and the consumers.

- SCA (Sustainable Competitive Advantage) – looking at technology from a positive perspective instead of a 'necessary evil'. Traditional models are changing and advantages can be achieved by investing in modern technology but just purchasing technology for the sake of having it is not enough, implementing a strategic plan is the key in order to succeed.

- Costs involved – a necessary expense in today's emerging environment. However, it's understandable that some organisations are hesitant to invest due to systems being outdated quite often, but the ones who view this investment as an opportunity to gain competitive advantage and have a well-developed strategy attached, could benefit immensely.

- Efficiency – productivity, reducing manual labour costs, cost-effective overall factor as it can simplify, speed up and enhance accuracy (or e.g. departments can interact or check a particular issue or status of an order/delivery/service from different locations in the Value Chain).

- Information Security/Contingency Planning – Technology provides a lot of advantages but we should also take into consideration the responsibilities that come with it. Businesses should take into account the rise in data breaching and various cyber-crime elements and must invest in effective ways of preventing or combating these factors. Imagine if an important process becomes unavailable suddenly or a system is hacked. Businesses must have these contingency plans in place in order to protect their valuable assets.

Mostly, technology is beneficial and businesses should try to counter the negatives in order to find the beneficial impact in its adoption.

The Impact of Technology on a Business Environment

Just a few decades ago, if you walked into an office, you'd see employees tapping away on typewriters and chatting away on landline phones. If one worker wanted to communicate with another, it meant getting up and walking to that person's desk, rather than sending a HipChat or an email. But technology continues to evolve, always impacting the way business leaders hire, market, budget and protect their investments.

Impact on Human Resources

Experts have long predicted technology will someday replace many of the jobs done by humans. However, history has shown that as jobs become obsolete, new opportunities open up. Today's students are encouraged to prepare for technology-based jobs like data analysis and computer programming, whereas four decades ago they would have been steered toward an education for an administrative or a sales position. Technology has also transformed hiring, with the internet allowing workers to complete their duties from home or another remote location. This has the added benefit of giving businesses access to a global talent pool that allows them to hire specialized, experienced workers at affordable rates.

Impact on Customer Outreach

Thanks to social media and the internet, reaching consumers is easier than ever. Using a do-it-yourself website tool and various social platforms, even the newest small business can post content that helps interested customers find them. Instead of paying third parties for advertising in print or electronic media, today's businesses are in charge of their own customer outreach. The result is a reduced cost that levels the playing field between large corporations and startups.

Impact on Operating Costs

Another area where the technological environment has evened things out is the overhead associated with running a business. Companies sell their items online, which means they don't need a brick-and-mortar storefront. The cost of starting a new business has dropped dramatically in recent years, since founders can now launch a venture from home as a side gig. There's no need to travel to land new clients, because researching and reaching out to potential customers can all be done online. And, instead of hiring a bookkeeper or an assistant, entrepreneurs find that software handles all of the early-stage functions they need.

Impact on Security

One area where the impact of technology on business has brought both positives and negatives is security. Having so much information on internet-connected servers means it's susceptible to theft. Data breaches can be devastating to a new business without the resources to handle it, with the average incident costing small businesses about $36,000. Businesses now need to put significant effort into securing their networks and all connected devices, which often means paying a monthly fee for top-tier cloud hosting and software to keep equipment safe. This has also opened up opportunities for tech specialists in the cybersecurity arena, where experts are in high demand.

Political Environment

Government actions which affects the operations of a company or business. These actions may be on local, regional, national or international level. Business owners and managers pay close attention to the political environment to gauge how government actions will affect their company.

Political Risk

Political risk refers to the "threat that social, political or economic factors in a foreign country may affect the feasibility and profitability of an organization's global operations". Political risks can be classified into two broad categories, 'macro political' and 'micro political'.

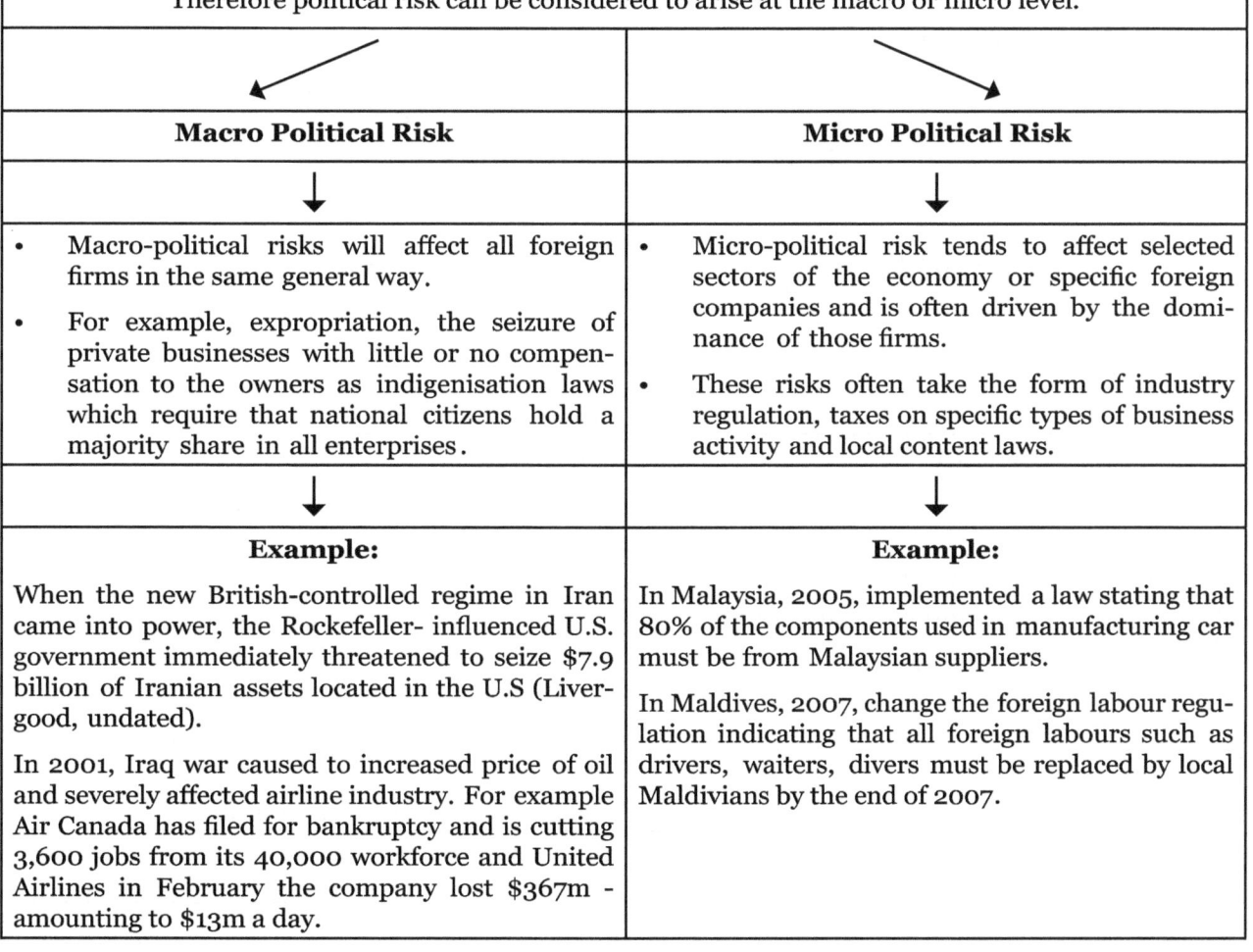

Therefore political risk can be considered to arise at the macro or micro level.	
Macro Political Risk	**Micro Political Risk**
• Macro-political risks will affect all foreign firms in the same general way. • For example, expropriation, the seizure of private businesses with little or no compensation to the owners as indigenisation laws which require that national citizens hold a majority share in all enterprises.	• Micro-political risk tends to affect selected sectors of the economy or specific foreign companies and is often driven by the dominance of those firms. • These risks often take the form of industry regulation, taxes on specific types of business activity and local content laws.
Example:	**Example:**
When the new British-controlled regime in Iran came into power, the Rockefeller- influenced U.S. government immediately threatened to seize $7.9 billion of Iranian assets located in the U.S (Livergood, undated). In 2001, Iraq war caused to increased price of oil and severely affected airline industry. For example Air Canada has filed for bankruptcy and is cutting 3,600 jobs from its 40,000 workforce and United Airlines in February the company lost $367m - amounting to $13m a day.	In Malaysia, 2005, implemented a law stating that 80% of the components used in manufacturing car must be from Malaysian suppliers. In Maldives, 2007, change the foreign labour regulation indicating that all foreign labours such as drivers, waiters, divers must be replaced by local Maldivians by the end of 2007.

Analysing Political Risk

(Rugman & Hodgetts)

Sources of Political Risk

- Political philosophies that are changing or are in competition with each other,
- Changing economic conditions,
- Social unrest,
- Armed conflict or terrorism,
- Rising nationalism,
- Impending or recent political independence,
- Vested interests of local business people,
- Competing religious groups,
- Newly created international alliances

Groups that can generate Political Risk

- Current government and its various departments and agencies;
- Opposition groups in the government that are not in power but have political influence;
- Organised interest groups such as teachers, students, workers, retired persons, etc;
- Terrorist or anarchist groups operating in the country;
- International organisations such as the World Bank or United Nations;
- Foreign governments that have entered into international alliances with the country or that are supporting the opposition within the country.

The Likely impacts of Political Risk

Type of political risk	Impact on MNE
Expropriation/confiscation	Loss of sales
	Loss of assets
	Loss of future profits
Campaign against foreign goods	Loss of sales
	Increased costs of public relations campaigns to improve public image
Mandatory labour benefit legislation	Increased operating costs
Kidnappings, terrorist threats and other forms of violence	Disrupted production Increased security costs Increased managerial costs Lower productivity
Civil wars	Destruction of property Lost sales
	Disruption of production Increased security costs Lower productivity
Currency devaluation	Reduced value of repatriated earnings
Currency revaluation	Less competitive in overseas markets and in competing against imports in home market
Increased taxations	Lower after-tax profits

Quantifying Political Risk

There are more sophisticated ways of analysing political risk, of which one is to identify and then quantify the various elements involved.

It is not only the probability of a particular political risk factor occurring but the magnitude of its potential impact on the objectives of the company that must also be taken into account.

Once, identified and assessed, any political risks can be priotrised, as in figure.

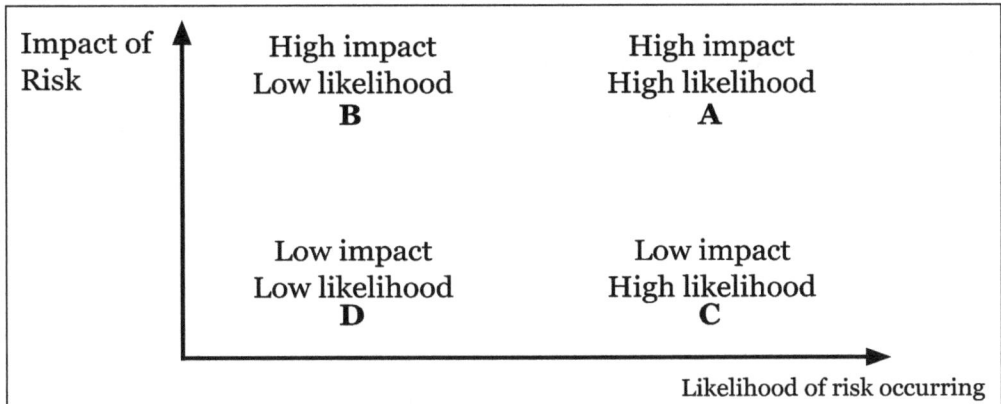

Prioritising (political) risk.

Responses to Political Risks

Once the risk has been analysed and assessed, organisation must decide if there are ways in which such risks can be managed. There are two common responses:

1. Improve relative bargaining power.

2. Adopt integrative, protective and defensive techniques.

Relative Bargaining Power

In an attempt to overcome political risk, some MNEs may seek to develop a stronger bargaining position than that of the host country itself. For example, the MNE might attempt to create a situation in which the host country loses more than it gains by taking actions against the company. This could be the case when the MNE has proprietary technology that will be lost to the host country if the company is forced to meet certain governmental regulations or where the MNE can credibly threaten to move elsewhere (with significant job losses) to avoid such regulations.

Integrative, Protective or Defensive Technique

A second approach is to use of techniques to prevent the host government interfering with the operations of MNE.

- Integrative techniques ensure that the subsidiary is as fully integrated as possible with the local economy, so that it becomes part of the host country's infrastructure. Techniques may here include:

    ◦ Developing a good relations with the host government and other local political groups.

    ◦ Producing as much of the product locally as is possible.

    ◦ Creating joint-ventures and hiring local people to manage and run the operations.

    ◦ Carrying out extensive local research and development.

    ◦ Developing good employee relations with local labour force.

These techniques raise the 'costs' to the host country economy of unwelcome interference in MNE activities.

- Proactive and defensive techniques seek to limit, in advance, the 'costs' to the MNE should the host government interfere in its activities. Such techniques may include doing as little local manufacturing as possible, locating all research and development outside the country, hiring only those local personnel who are essential, manufacturing the same product in many other different countries, etc.

A risk management strategy involves adopting a comprehensive and systematic approach to dealing with the factors causing political risk. Zonis and Wilkin cited in Wall breaks down the 'drivers' of political risk into separate categories, namely external, interaction and internal drivers.

1. External drivers of political risk involve factors whose probability cannot be influenced by the firm. Examples include political instability (riots, civil wars, coups) and weak public policy (hyper inflation, crurrency crisis).

2. Interaction drivers of political risk involve factors that are broadly related to company relationships. Examples include relationship with home country and host country governments, regional and local authorities and national and super national institutions and regulatory bodies, pressure groups, local communities etc. For example, given the importance of guanxi- type relationships to business activities in Confucian societies, politically 'risk averse' firm operating in China or Hong Kong might invest substantial resources in fostering such relationship.

3. Internal drivers of political risk involve factors which are specific to the organization and operation of the company itself. Examples might include the extent to which internal incentives structures are aligned with corporative objectives. An

executive remuneration scheme which link bonuses to turnover or market share may be less appropriate where the corporate objective is primarily profit related.

The political environment in a country affects business organizations and could introduce a risk factor that could cause them to suffer a loss. The political environment could change as a result of the actions and policies of governments at all levels, from the local level to the federal level. Businesses must plan for the variability of government policy and regulations.

Impact on the Economy

The political environment in a country affects its economic environment. The economic environment, in turn, affects the performance of a business organization. In the United States, for instance, there are significant differences in Democratic and Republican policies. This has implications for factors such as taxes and government spending, which in turn affect the country's economy. A higher level of government spending tends to stimulate the economy, for instance.

Changes in Regulation

Governments could change their rules and regulations, and this could have an effect on a business. For instance, after the accounting scandals of the early twenty-first century, the United States Securities and Exchange Commission became more focused on corporate compliance and the government introduced the Sarbanes-Oxley compliance regulations of 2002. This was a response to the social environment that called for such change to make public companies more accountable.

Political Stability

Particularly for businesses that operate internationally, a lack of political stability in any country has an effect on its operations. A hostile takeover could overthrow a government, for instance. This could lead to rioting and looting and general disorder in the environment. All this disrupts the operations of a business. Such disruptions have occurred in Sri Lanka, which went through a protracted civil war, and in Egypt and Syria, which have been subject to disturbances as people agitate for greater rights.

Mitigation of Risk

One way to manage political risk is to buy political risk insurance. Organizations that have international operations use this type of insurance to mitigate their risk exposure as a result of political instability. There are indices that provide an idea of the risk exposure an organization has in certain countries. For instance, an index of economic freedom ranks countries based on how political interference impacts business decisions in each country.

Analysis Tools

It is possible to analyse and forecast the impact of government policies on doing business. There's an established model called PEST analysis, which evaluates political, economic, social and technological factors that could affect the cost and difficulty of doing business. The political and economic sides of the analysis are directly government-related, while government policies indirectly affect the social and technological environment. An expanded form of PEST analyis, called PESTEL or PESTLE, adds legal and environmental factors to the equation. These, too, are strongly influenced by government policy.

How Political Factors Affecting Business Environment

Political factors can impact a business by making the market environment more or less friendly for that business. Typically, governments have a great deal of power over businesses and many times, there is not much that businesses can do about it.

Political factors can impact businesses in various ways. These external environmental factors can add in a risk factor which can lead to a major loss in business. These factors can change the entire results and hence, companies should be able to deal with both local as well as international political outcomes.

In addition to this, political factors not only have a direct impact but, it also impacts other factors as well which can have a significant effect on the business and its operating environment. There are certain factors that create inter-linkages in several ways like:

- Political decisions affect the socio-cultural environment of the country.

- Political decisions have an impact on the economic environment.

- Politicians can also influence the acceptance of new technologies.

- Politicians can also influence the rate of development of new technologies.

Political Factors that Affect Business Environment

With a change in administration policies, there arise political factors that can change the entire business scenario. These changes can be economic, legal or social and can include the following factors:

- Tax and economic policies: Increasing or decreasing rate of taxes is a good example of a political component. Government regulations may raise the tax rate for some businesses and can lower the same for others due to specific reasons. This decision will directly impact businesses. This is why maintaining a strategy which can deal with such situations is very important.

- Political stability: Lack of political stability within a country can significantly impact the operations of a business. This can especially be true for businesses that are operating on the global scale. For instance, a hostile takeover can take over a government. Eventually, such a situation will lead to looting, riots and general disorder within the environment. Such situations can disrupt business operations and activities which can have a major impact on its bottom line.

- Foreign Trade Regulations: Every business has a need to expand business operation to other countries. However, political background of a country can influence the desire for a business to expand its operations. Tax policies that are particularly controlled by the government can induce a particular business to expand operations in different regions whereas; other tax policies can hinder the process of business expansion for some industries. Government initiatives, which have been designed to support local businesses, might work against international companies when the question is of their competitiveness in a foreign region.

- Employment Laws: Employment laws are made to protect the rights of employees and include every aspect of employer/employee relationship. Employment law is an aspect that is very complex and involves several pitfalls as well. When businesses' are in touch with the latest developments in this law, they can manage to take their business in the right direction however, those who get it wrong needs to be completely prepared for the expensive results it will generate. In modern corporations, employees are almost 98% of the company for the accomplishments or lack thereof and any changes within employment law will, of course, have a great impact on the business operations.

Some of the other political factors affecting business:

- Bureaucracy.

- Corruption level.

- Freedom of the press.

- Tariffs.

- Trade control.

- Education Law.

- Anti-trust law.

- Employment law.

- Discrimination law.

- Data protection law.

- Environmental Law.

- Health and safety law.

- Competition regulation.

- Regulation and deregulation.

- Tax policy (tax rates and incentives).

- Government stability and related changes.

- Government involvement in trade unions and agreements.

- Import restrictions on quality and quantity of product.

- Intellectual property law (Copyright, patents).

- Consumer protection and e-commerce.

- Laws that regulate environment pollution.

The Importance of Observing the Political Environment

Firms should track their political environment. Change in the political factors can affect business strategy because of the following reasons:

- The stability of a political system can affect the appeal of a particular local market.

- Governments view business organizations as a critical vehicle for social reform.

- Governments pass legislation, which impacts the relationship between the firm and its customers, suppliers, and other companies.

- The government is liable for protecting the public interest.

- Government actions influence the economic environment.

- Government is a major consumer of goods and services.

Legal Environment

The business legal environment plays a very important role in determining the success of any businesses around the globe. The government taxes that are being imposed among other regulatory measures help to promote economic growth and to protect consumers from exploitation and other illegal factors. Prior to establishing or when in the process of running a business, accordingly.

It is imperative to understand the role of regional tax measures, legal factors affecting business and regulatory measures in the determination of how your business is affected.

Another measure to help your business adapt to legal issues in its environment is the understanding of regulatory measures and to account for all your regional economic analysis.

The legal environment of business is defined as: the attitude of the government toward business, the historical development of this attitude; current trends of public control in taxation, regulation of commerce and competition; freedom of contract, antitrust legislation and its relationship to marketing, mergers and acquisitions; and labor management relations.

Legal Factors Affecting Business Environment

Organizational Law

The organizational law is the first type of business law that we will talk about here. Any business that is organized as a legal entity is subject to the state law that governs its operation and conduct. There are different types of business entities. For example, corporations, limited partnerships, partnerships, limited liability partnerships, limited liability limited partnerships and limited liability companies all of which have different legal status and issues.

Securities Law

If a business is seeking to obtain financing through different types of investors, it may be subject to legal issues such as security law. For instance, a decision to offer promissory notes, a type of loan to your investors, will subject the legal factor affecting business to state and federal regulations and security laws.

Every company issues securities and a growing body of law suggests that non-manager interest in a limited liability company is also considered to be securities legal factors. As it is, most small businesses should not worry about business legal factors like federal and state security laws affecting them negatively. But if such a business has plans to raise capital through platforms such as public offerings or online funding.

Contract Law

If the intention is to enter an agreement with another person or entity, then contract law is binding. This also has a special area that is involved directly with factors affecting business, for example, government contracts, which is also known as government procurement laws.

Consumer Protection Laws

Some businesses act unfairly towards their consumers. For this reason, most countries have consumer protection laws that are aimed at ensuring that consumers are protected.

Weight and Measures Act: These laws ensure that the goods sold are weighed on Standard weighting equipment.

Trade Description Act: This law ensures that it is illegal to deliberately give misleading impression about products.

Consumer Credit Act: According to this Act, consumers should be given information of the credit agreement and should be made aware of the interest rates, length of loan while taking a loan.

Sale of Goods Act: This Act declares that It is illegal to sell products with flaws or problems and that any goods sold conforms to standards.

Employees Protection Laws

Different governments have passed laws to protect the interest of employees. These laws protect them against unfair discrimination at work and when applying for jobs. It ensures that no one is discriminated against on the basis of such things as race, religion, sex, age, or colour.

Antitrust Law

The initial reason of establishing this law was to check the issue of the monopoly that had affected the business sector for a long time. The law started after the civil war with an increase in petroleum, cotton and other agricultural products. The Sherman act of 1890 made a declaration that restraint of trade or other related actions by monopolies were illegal.

Objectives of the antitrust law are the Countering Unfair Competition, protecting the rights, priorities and interests of businesses and consumers by enhancing fair competition for better economic growth. There are two categories of unfair competition the traditional ones that are the likes of the counterfeits, bribes and adverts contrary to the product. The other category is by the government by certain persons in power who misuse their power to access of institutions or generally interference with the economy to a point that it is seen as sabotage to the local producers or manufacturers. The government however cannot sue or charge themselves and so they are at liberty to go free on unfair completion. Termination of monopolies could boost the productivity and quality of products produced.

According to Earl the antitrust laws are meant to deal with some four serious vices, which include:

The avoidance of entry to agreements, which hamper free and fair competition and lead to eventual unsuccessful business.

Regulation of monopolies or bigger and dominant companies from preventing small-scale companies being competitive.

Feasible competition is enhanced in the Oligopolistic industries.

Merging companies need to be monitored to concentrate on production and handle effectively the economic pressures.

This was later amended by the Robinson-Pitman Act was more of an amendment of the Clayton Act mainly dealing with the noncompetitive procedures used in the discrimination of the equity in distribution.

For example in US, capitalist like John Rockefeller had for a long time enjoyed monopoly. They had build up trust in their customers by forming different organization to ensure that they disguise people and ensure that they monopolize the market keeping the price of their services high. This ensured that they limited supply hence resulting into high price of the products in the market. After such unethical behaviors were well understood by people, there was needed to form mistrust laws to regulate such behaviors in the business sectors. The law ensured that it regulated one or more company to conspire and thus limiting the supply and controlling prices of the products. This law in most of the country came amid big blow that it caused to big business that had formed their bases in monopoly. In a country like United State, it ensured that the violators received very severe penalties. OPEC, which is an international organization that regulate oil production in the world ensure that it control the amount of oil that each country in the world produces. This ensures that there is no monopoly in the production of oil by any country.

The formation of the antitrust laws in the US made so many governmental agencies to be created to ensure that they oversee the corporate behaviors and the way business is conducted in the country. These agencies were formed to ensure that they follow the way the law is undertaken in the country. One of the most important agencies in the country is Securities and Exchange Commission (SEC). This agencies is mandated tom investigate the companies that are misbehaving and carrying out their duties against the law that is put in place.

An example of a company that has been in investigation under these agencies is Microsoft Company. SEC agency has also the ability of forming other regulations to ensure that they regulate any emergence of undue commercial behavior that may be illegal. It is capable of imposing severe injunctions on the companies that violated the law. They are can even decide to impose lawsuit ion these companies. The agency is mandated to manage other agencies that are responsible in the regulation of a specific business practice.

To show the way the way the legal business environment is affected, an example of Arthur Andersen-Enron Company is checked. The company happened to have a scandal in 2002 that made the accounting company to be put under spotlight. The scandal was discovered after an audit firm from industry regulatory committee conducted it audit. Pressure build up from Congress Party and made SEC to put in place a new watchdog to ensure that it oversee auditing process in the country. Some of the sanctions that ASEC Agency imposed to the company were that the company should not be involved in any auditing process for five years.

The idea behind the injunction was to ensure that any other company should be held in any irregularities when doing their functions. They ensured that the managers of these companies are able to follow the law at all level of their work. Such injunctions made the companies to fear if they became a law, as they would cost them a great loss by costing their long-term clients and probably eventually collapsing.

Environmental Protection Law

This is a class of law that governs how the companies should behave towards natural environment. It is a core value for the government to protect the natural environments to ensure long time health for its people (Melvin, 2010). This is done to ensure that all the companies comply on the law that protects the environment. It came to being after the companies that were involved made susceptible not to protect the environment. From the year 200, the disposal cost of toxic and nontoxic waste increased significantly.

This is because a land that the company could have used form disposal purposes became more expensive and scarce. Therefore, to ensure that it was protected from being misused, laws were put in place to ensure that the environment is maintained. Waste products disposal were to be done using regulations that were put in place. Laws to protect air pollution have been made stricter to ensure that acid rain has been minimized through stringent check of coal emissions. Laws were put in place top regulate the sea activities regulating the number of the fish that are supposed to caught from the sea. There was also enacting of oil drilling procedures to regulate the amount of the oil that ids to be processed to ensure that it is not hazard into the environment and the reservoirs are not depleted.

The law was to be put in place to ensure that there are regulation is done as some of the companies had started unethical behaviors of maximizing their returns at environmental expense and the people. This was meant to ensure that natural resources are made available to the future generation. It would also ensure that there is protection of the future economic status of the people. This is by ensuring that the companies are regulated to ensure that they do not exploit the environment hence affecting the future generation.

Legal regulations are put in place to ensure that this kind of behavior is checked. When the company are forced to pay real cost of obtaining inputs that are valuable and ensure that they dispose their waste products appropriately, the people are protected in expense of their business practice. This law ensures that such health problems that are experienced due to improper disposal of the waste products and depletion of resources that is being experienced are regulated (Alexander, et al. 2011). This cost is a part of the company operating cost that has to be considered as they comply with the law. This ensure that the company that comply to these rules enjoy management of resources making them have long time goals that have less environmental pollution as well as making sure that people health is protected.

Clean Air Act that was passed in 1990 by the congress party was one of the laws that ensured that this regulation was boosted. Through this law, the USA Environmental Agency put up limits that regulated the amount of pollution that could be released in the atmosphere (Earl, 1978). The law required that the company should be the one that incur the cost of regulating this. They were required to install cleaner burning equipment that would regulate the emissions. This harmonized the emissions rules in the entire states ion the US. The effect that this had in the business that would not comply with this rule was to close down.

International regulations has emerged of recent to ensure that different countries have come together to regulate the environment by ensuring that the business in their countries comply with different put laws. Such laws as postulated in the Kyoto protocol that is an amendment of the United Nation Treaty of the global warming has done great towards reinforcing this regulation. The countries work under the umbrella of the Kyoto protocol ensures that they reduce green house gases in their production process in their respective countries. The agreement has been ratified by 141 countries across the globe. Such treaty has affected the y the businesses in these countries are done in the pursuit of compliance of these laws.

Social and Cultural Environment

Socio-cultural forces refer to the attitudes, beliefs, norms, values, lifestyles of individuals in a society. These forces can change the market dynamics and marketers can face both opportunities and threats from them. Some of the important factors and influences operating in the social environment are the buying and consumption habits of people, their languages, beliefs and values, customs and traditions, tastes and preferences, education and all factors that affect the business.

Understanding consumer needs is central to any marketing activity and those needs will often be heavily influenced by social and cultural factors. These cover a range of values, beliefs, attitudes and customs which characterize societies or social groups. Changes in lifestyle of people affect the marketing environment.

As health problems in people have increased because of significant changes in their lifestyle, they have become concerned about their food. They prefer to eat low fat, low or no cholesterol food. This is specially true for people above 40 years. To a great extent, social forces determine what customers buy, how they buy, where they buy, when they buy, and how they use the products.

In India, social environment is continuously changing. One of the most profound social changes in recent years is the large number of women entering the job market.

They have also created or greatly expended the demand for a wide range of products and services necessitated by their absence from the home. There is a lot of change in quality-of-lifestyles and people are willing to have many durable consumer goods like T.V., fridge, washing machines etc. even when they cannot afford them because of their availability on hire-purchase or instalment basis.

Culture influences every aspect of marketing. Marketing decisions are based on recognition of needs and wants of the customer, a function of customer perceptions. These help in understanding of lifestyles and behaviour patterns as they have grown in the society's culture in which the individual has been groomed. Thus a person's perspective is generated, groomed and conditioned by culture.

Significance of Socio-cultural Environment

Each society its own culture consists of the customs, values, attitudes, beliefs, habits, languages and other of interaction between the members of the society. Any business firm which aims at entering any for its products and services must develop complete understanding of socio-cultural environment of the society involved and adapt its strategies thereto.

The question arises as to what factors constitute social environment? A long list of factors such as social institutions, social systems, social groups, social values, and attitudes are included in it. Successful business managers cannot afford to neglect the importance of these features. No business can survive and grow without social Different countries, over different time periods, attain social harmony and order of different through different ways and means. Thus socio-cultural environment differs over space, time and methods.

Three aspects may be noted in the current socio-cultural environment:

1. Changes in our life-styles and social values: For instance, changing role of women, emphasis on quality of goods instead quantity of goods, greater reliance on government, greater preference for recreation activities.

2. Major social problems: For example, concern for pollution of environment, demand for socially responsible marketing policies, head for safety in occupations and products, etc.

3. Growing consumerism: It is indicating dissatisfaction on a large scale against unfair trade practices. Consumerism is becoming increasingly important to marketing decision process. Social environment in many countries is responsible for emphasizing social responsibility of business and custoiner oriented marketing approach.

The impact of socio-cultural dimensions upon the business could be understood in many ways. In the era of globalisation, they are crossing the limits of boundaries and going to the other parts of the world. Now the need for understanding and appreciating cultural differences across various countries is essential. Work motivation, profit motivation, business goals, negotiating styles, attitudes towards the development of business relationships, gift-giving customs, significance of body gestures, meaning of colours and numbers, and the like vary from country to country. Figure brings out a summary of how major management concepts are perceived by the Japanese and Americans.

Figure: Major Concepts in the Comparative Analysis of US and Japanese Management.

Management Concepts	How Percevied in the United States	How Perceived in Japan
Company	Team in sport	Family in village
Business goal	To win	To survive
Employees	Players in a team	Children in a family
Human relations	Functional	Emotional
Competition	Cut-throat	Cooperation or sin
Profit motivation	By a11 means	Means to an end
Sense of identification	Job pride	Group prestige
Work motivation	Individual income	Group atmosphere
Production	Productivity	Training and diligence
Personnel	Efficiency	Maintenance
Promotion	According to abilities	Length af service
Pay	Service and results	Award far patience & sacrifice

Like-wise, the people of different countries having different cultural heritage behave differently. When tlie people from different cultural heritage converge in a work place, management will be required to manage diversity. Figure reveals tlie difference in the socio-cultural factors in India and Japan, and their impact on the business environment of two countries.

Figure: Contrasting Social and Cultural factors-India vs. Japan.

Social/Cultural Factors	Japan	India
Principles of government/administration	Emphasis on government by the virtuous and abrogation of, coercion, mutual trust between 1 employer and employee and acceptance of basic goodness of human nature. Results in minimum control from above, high level of delegation, highly motivated workforce	Prevalence of impersonal bureaucratic social relations, mistrust of fellow beings based on assumption of human nature as evil. Results in highly centralized administration, overemphasis of hierarchical status in decision-making, bureaucratic delays, low levels of delegation, dissatisfied workforce, and accentuation of apathy in individuals and groups

Attitude towards work and goals	High result-oriented and directed towards perfection and growth through dedicated effort	General and deep-seated apathy, dissociation of work from its results based on the belief that the results are pre-ordained. Tasks are performed without any interest. dedication or pride
Discipline and order	Highly disciplined, respect for superiors and respect for authority	Lack of discipline at all levels, basic mistrust of authority, poor superior-subordinate relationship
Group harmony	Very high based on informal affiliative patter of behaviour	Assumption of inequality of human beings, nagging suspicion of fellow beings and highly self-centered behaviour resulting in a lack of cooperation and teamwork
Emphasis on education	Very high	Generally indifferent and highly ambivalent

Critical Elements of Socio-cultural Environment

The critical elements of socio-cultural environment of business. May be classified as follows:

1   Social institutions and systems;

2   Social groups;

3   Social values and attitudes;

4   Social responsibilities of Business;

5   Role and Responsibility of government.

Social Institutions and Systems

Social Institutions

Social institutions refer to set-ups like family school, church, state, etc, which are essential to maintain the orderly arrangement of social structure. These are regarded as collective modes of behaviour. They prescribe a way of doing things. They bind the members of the group together. There are five kinds of social institutions, namely, (1) family, (2) economics, (3) religion, (4) education, and (5) state. There are also a number of secondary institutions which are derived from each of these primary institutions. The secondary institutions derived from family are marriage, divorce, monogamy, polygamy, etc. The secondary institutions of economics are property, trading, credit, banking, etc. The secondary institutions of religion are church, temple, mosque, totem, taboo, etc. The secondary institutions of education are school, college, university, etc. The secondary institutions of state are interest groups, party system, democracy, etc.

Institutions may grow as do the folkways and mores or they may be created just as laws are enacted. For example, monogamy or polyandry grew in response to some felt needs of the people. Banks grew as the need for borrowing and lending money was felt. Schools and colleges are created by deliberate choice and action. An important feature that we find in the growth of institutions is the extension of the power of the state over the other four primary institutions. The state now exercises more authority by laws and regulations. As of today, the family is being regulated and controlled by the state in various ways. A number of traditional functions of family have been taken over by the state. The state has enacted laws regulating marriage, divorce, adoption and inheritance. The authority of state has similarly been extended to economics, to education and to religion.

An institution never dies. New institutional norms may replace the old ones, but the institution goes on. For example, the modern family has replaced the norms of patriarchal family, yet family as an institution continues. When feudalism died, government did not end. The governmental and economic functions continued to be fulfilled, although according to changed norms. All the primary institutions are thousands of years old, only the institutional norms are new.

A social structure owes its stability to a proper adjustment of relationships among the different institutions. No institution works in a vacuum. Religion, education, family, government and business all interact with each other. Education creates attitudes which influence the acceptance or rejection of religious dogmas. Religion may exalt education because it enables one to know the truths of God or denounce it because it threatens the faith. Business conditions may influence the family life. Unemployment may determine the number of people who do not want to marry as an unemployed person may postpone his marriage till he gets employed in a suitable job. Postponement of marriage may affect the birth rates. The state influences the functions of institutions. It may take over some of the functions and determine their institutional norms. The businessmen, educators, energy men and the functionaries of all other institutions also seek to influence the acts of state, since any state action may obstruct or help the realization of their institutional objectives. Thus the social institutions are closely I-elated to each other. The inter-relationship of the various institutions is like that of the different parts of a wheel. The family is the hub while education, religion, government and economics are the spokes of the wheel. The rim would be the community within which the various institutions operate.

All institutions face the problem of continuously adjusting themselves to the changing society. Changes in the social environment may bring about changes in all social institutions. Inflation, for example, may have a great influence on marriage, death, crime and education. Breakdown of economic institutions may have radical effects upon political institutions. Similarly, a change in one institution may lead to a change in the other institutions. There may also take place a shifting of functions from one institution to another. Child care, formerly a function of family, has now shifted to the state. When one institution fails to meet a human need, another institution will often assume the function. No institution can avoid affecting other institutions or avoid being affected by others.

Social Systems

The concept of social system is closely related to the concept of social structure which is the means through which a social system functions. According to Loonies, the social system is composed of the patterned interaction of members. "It is constituted of the interaction of a plurality of individual actors whose relations to each other arc mutually oriented through the definition of and mediation of a pattern of structured and shared symbols and expectations." It is the patterned social relations and the social processes which determine the nature of social system. The main elements of social system are (1) belief (knowledge), (2) sentiment, (3) end, goal, or objective, (4) norms, (5) status role (position), (6) rank, (7) power, (8) sanction, and (9) facility. A brief description of these elements follows:

1   Belief and knowledge: Any proposition about any aspect of the universe that is accepted as true may be called a belief. According to D. Krech and R.S. Crutch-field. "A belief is an enduring organization of perception and cognitions about some aspect of individual's world". A belief may be true or false. It may be verifiable or not. But the people who hold it consider it to be true. Belief furnishes the cognitive basis for social action. The significance of beliefs is not determined by the objective truth or falsity of the belief. The belief that there is no God will make the social relationships of people different from the relations of those who believe in God. The Hindu social structure is founded on beliefs about the existence of God, the theory of rebirth, the doctrine of Karma and the reality of hell and heaven. The Indian caste system is based on Karma theory. It is due to the belief that the Hindu social system has been able to survive despite many invasions over it. According to Lommis, the testing and validation of the cognitive aspect of belief is also important. It will make for progress and provide dynamism to the social system.

2   Sentiment: Closely related to belief is the element of sentiment. Sentiments represent "what we feel" about the world. Sentiment is the chief element articulated in the internal pattern of a social system. The sentiments as expressed in the internal pattern result from both externally patterned and internally patterned social interaction. The sentiments of the external pattern are those which members bring from outside. Sentiments are acquired. They are the product of experience and cultural conditioning. Our cultural values and social goals influence and control our sentiments. The sentiments of love, hatred, benevolence, charity, nationalism, internationalism, etc. are created by our cultural conditioning. The sentiments may be of various kinds, intellectual, ethical, aesthetic, religious etc.

3   End, goal or objective: The end, goal or objective creates the social system. The members of a social system expect to accomplish a particular end or objective through appropriate interaction. Had there been no human needs, goals or ends, there would have been no society. The human needs, goals and ends determine the nature of the social system.

4   Norm: Norms are the standards for determining what is right and wrong, appropriate and inappropriate, just and unjust, good and bad in social relationships. Every social system is possessed of its norms which the individuals are obliged to observe. Some norms are general and may not be violated by anyone while others apply only to particular individuals and status roles within the system. Particular norms may be especially crucial for special social systems. The norm of efficiency is of great importance in the economic system. The norm of fair play is of importance in athletic activity. The concept of social system implies order. Hence, a major criterion for delineating a social system is simply the existence of consensus with respect to the appropriate ways of behaviour.

5   Status-role: Status is the position which an individual has in the society. In a social system each individual has a status. The place in a particular system which a certain individual occupies at a particular time is his status with reference to that system. The element of status is found in every social system. In the family, there are the statuses of father, mother, son, daughter, etc. Likewise, there are statuses in a club, school, union or factory. The status of an individual may be ascribed or achieved. The ascribed status is one which an individual gets at his birth. It is conferred to him by his group or society. 11 may be based on sex, age, caste or color. The achieved status is one which an individual achieves by his efforts. A man born in a low caste may, by his efforts, become the Prime Minister and achieve that status. There are some functions attached to each status which are called roles. In a social system the individuals are expected to perform their roles in accordance with their statuses.

6   Rank: Rank as used here as equivalent to "standing". It includes the importance an individual has in the system in which the rank is accorded. It is determined by the, evaluation placed upon the individual and his acts in accordance with the norms and standards of the system. A political leader enjoys higher rank than a teacher in modern society whereas in ancient times the teacher enjoyed higher rank than that of even the king.

7   Power: Power refers to the capacity to control others. A conflict may take place many conflicts among the different parts of the social system. Such conflict is harmful for the social system. For example a dispute may arise between the students and the teachers which is harmful for the efficiency of the institution. There should exist some power with the authority to control both the teachers and students. Such power is vested in the principal. Thus, each social system

gives power to some individual or body of individuals to remove tension from amongst the system. In the state the ruler, in the family the father, in the union the president has such power. This power always resides in the status role and not in the individual as such. It is the authority of office. As soon as an individual ceases to hold the office, he no longer exercises the authority of that office. An ex-principal cannot direct the students, an unfrocked priest cannot deliver the sacraments, an ex-president cannot call the parliament. Authority, therefore, implies some degree of institutionalization.

8   Sanction: Sanction refers to the rewards and penalties given out by the members of a social system as a device for inducing conformity to its norms and ends. Sanctions can be positive or negative. The positive sanctions are the rewards which may include wages, profits, interest, esteem, praise, privileges, etc. The negative sanctions are the penalties and punishments.

9   Facility: A facility has been defined as a means used to attain ends within the system. It is necessary that the individuals in a social system should be provided with adequate facilities to enable them to perform their roles efficiently. Facilities should not only exist but should also be utilized. Mere existence of facilities is of no use unless these can be utilized. The ends, goals, or objectives of a social system call be realized only through the utilization of facilities. The utilization of facilities highlights systemic ends, beliefs and norms that might otherwise remain obscure. To put it the other way, a society reveals its ends, beliefs, and norms by its failure to utilize certain available facilities. The farmers may be having the facilities of tractor and fertilizers but unless they utilize these facilities they may not be able to increase their production and save time and energy. The use of tractors may require a reorganization of land system since the facilities of a tractor cannot be utilized if the land is of very small size. There may even be some resistance to its adoption. The same can be said of the facilities available for family planning. Unless these facilities are used, goal of self-sufficiency in food cannot be achieved. If we use the nuclear energy for peaceful purposes, it shows our belief in peace, but if it is used for manufacturing nuclear bombs it would show that we are making preparation for war. Thus, it is the use of the facility rather than its intrinsic qualities which determine its significance to social systems.

Social Group

Social group is a collection of human beings. In its elementary sense, a group "is a number of units of anything in close proximity to one another". Thus we may speak of a group of houses on a street, of trees in a forest or of buses at a bus stand. In the human field it means "any collection of human beings who are brought into social relationships with one another". Some of the important definitions of social groups are:

"A group is a social unit which consists of a number of individuals who stand in (more or less) definite status and role relationships to one another and which possesses a set of values or norms of its own, regulating the behaviour of individual members at least in hatters of consequence to the group."

"A social group may be thought of as a number of persons, two or more, who have some common objects of attention, who are stimulating to each other, who have common loyalty and participate in similar activities."

Social relationships involve, as we have seen, some degree of reciprocity between the related and some degree of mutual awareness. A social group is a collection of individuals, two or more, interacting with each other, who have some common objects of attention and participate in similar activities. It may be a cricket club or a political party. It ranges from a pair or a couple to a group of millions of people. In an aggregation, the element of inter-action is lacking and so it differs from group within which observable inter-action is present. The essence of social group is not physical closeness but a consciousness of joint interaction.

Characteristics of Social Group

From the definitions of a social group as given above, it can be inferred that a social group has the following characteristics.

(i) **Reciprocal Relations:** The members of a group are inter-related to each other. A gathering of persons forms a social group only when they are interrelated. Reciprocal relations form an essential feature of a group.

(ii) **Sense of Unit:** The members of a group are united by a sense of unity and a feeling of sympathy.

(iii) **We-feeling:** The members of a group help each other and defend their interests collectively.

(iv) **Common Interests:** The interests and ideals of a group are common. It is for the realization of common interests that they meet together.

(v) **Similar Behaviour:** The members of a group behave in a similar way for the pursuit of common interests.

(vi) **Group Norms:** Every group has its own rules or norms which the members are supposed to follow.

A social group, it may be noted, is dynamic and not static. It may change its form and expand its activities from time to time. Sometimes the change may be swift and sudden, while at other times it may occur so gradually that its members are unaware of it. A group may give up one function after another until it finally ceases to exist or it may settle down to a routine and limit its activities to a mere holding of annual meeting. It may expand its organization or may die of disorganization.

Social Values and Attitudes

Social Values

Social values are cultural standards that indicate the general good deemed desirable for organised social life. These are assumptions of what is right and important for society. They provide the ultimate meaning and legitimacy for social arrangements and social behaviour. They are the abstract sentiments or ideals. An example of an important social value is "equality of opportunity". It is widely considered to be a desirable end in itself. The importance of a value in social life can hardly be exaggerated.

A social value differs from individual value. An individual value is enjoyed or sought by the individual which a man seeks from himself. Even though these values are commonly shared, they do not become social values. Social values regulate the thinking and behaving of individuals. Thus if the American culture is dominated by a belief in material progress, the Indian culture is marked by spiritualism, the forgetting of self, abandonment of personal desire and elimination of the ambition. The "Indian way" is different from the "American way". The difference in social values result in divergent social structures and patterns of expected behaviour.

Social values are different from social norms. Norms are the standards of group behaviour which incorporate value judgments and are related to the events in the real world. When a number of individuals interact, a set of standards develop that regulate their relationship and modes of beliaviour. These standards of group beliaviour are called social norms. At the same time, "A norm is a standard of behavioral expectation shared by group members against which the validity of perceptions is judged and the appropriateness of feeling and behaviour is evaluated.

Attitudes

Attitude is the state of consciousness within the individual being. It refers to certain regularities of an individual's feelings, thoughts and predispositions to act towards some aspect of his environment; It is a subjective reaction with relation to objects. All attitudes imply objects towards which they are directed, but it is the state of mind, not the object, which is denoted by the term 'attitude'. However, attitudes differ from interests. Both concepts are primarily psychological largely mould our behaviour and determine social relationships. But attitudes differ from interests in one sense that interest is objective while attitude is subjective. While interest means, "any aim or object which stimulates activity towards its attainment", the attitude is regarded as a state of mind of the individual towards a value,. Another aspect that differentiates attitudes and interests is that interests are common and alike, while attitudes are alike but not common. Interests may be identical, attitudes can never be so. MacIver Observes, "Different people cannot have a common attitude any more than they can feel a common pain. They can have only like pains and like attitudes because the subjective element is always individualized."

Attitudes determine social relationships. In fact, the origin, growth and progress of a society depend upon the interests and attitudes. Attitudes determine the structure of a society. A society is marked by particular interests and attitudes which its members follow and which determine its structure. That's why we distinguish between feudal society, bourgeois society and proletarian society. Attitudes mould social relations, the attitudinal changes and adjustments constantly go on in a society which mould re₁ n t' ions between individuals. Moreover, we find people and groups everywhere displaying characteristic attitudes.

The structure of a society, social relationships and practical utility of attitudes affect the business environment, and the managers have to take into consideration the changing social relationships and the structure of a society while formulating their strategies. The MNCs take special care of the social values and attitudes in a particular economy while planning their entry therein.

Micro Environment

When an organization starts its business in the market, its success and sustenance are shaped by a number of factors. While some of these factors are beyond the control of the company, others can be brought within its grip.

The former is known as external factors which form the macro environment and the latter encompassing the internal factors, is referred to as the micro environment. Demography, economy, Socio-Cultural factors, legal forces, political structures and technology are collectively known as macro environment. On the other hand, consumers, competitors, suppliers, dealers and distributors and the general public together constitute the micro environment of a business.

Micro environment components are within the immediate surroundings of the organization. These are the initial spheres to work on, so as to shape a strong and credible image of the company in the larger or macro environmental context.

A perfect collaboration of macro and micro environment contributes to a successful and consistent business operation. If one end is disturbed, the other end suffers by default. It is because the internal factors are components within the external ones. Hence any problem within the macro environment will gradually reflect in the micro front. At the same time, if micro environment is not under control, it will destabilise the macro environment components for the particular business.

For example, in the event of economic downfall or financial emergency in a nation, demand, and supply of any commodity is hard to hit. This in turn affects business profits and brings down its prospects. A similar scenario is also possible when suppliers or the supply chain technology of a product gets hampered. As a result, products become inaccessible to the consumers. This certainly threatens the technological and to some extent the demographic environment.

Therefore, to stand apart in any commercial venture, marketing managers need to understand the significance of each of these components and work towards maintaining a proper balance between the two environments.

Role of Micro Environment in Business

Micro environment is the first pillar to build a business empire. All marketing plans, strategies, and objectives are carried out through these components. It is, therefore, the executive arm of business where practical implementation of ideas, thoughts, and concepts are done and based on the responses of these components, a business either moves forward or may step back.

Further, it serves as a guide to future communication policies of an organization. With all such features, micro environment plays an integral role in realizing the current potential and determining the future of a business.

With a significant contribution to the overall functioning of a business, here's how the components enjoy an interface with core business development.

Components of Micro Environment

This includes the following:

   (a) The company

   (b) Company's Suppliers

(c) Marketing Intermediaries

(d) Customers

(e) Competitors

(f) Public

A brief explanations are given below:

The Company

In designing marketing plans, marketing management takes other company groups into account – Finance, Research and Development, Purchasing, Manufacturing, Accounting, Top Management etc. Marketing manager must also work closely with other company departments. Finance in concerned with funds and using funds to carry out the marketing plans.

The R&D Department focuses on designing safe and attractive product. Purchasing Department is concerned with supplies of materials whereas manufacturing is responsible for producing the desired quality and quantity of products. Accounts department has to measure revenues and costs to help marketing know-how. Together, all of these departments have impact on the marketing plans and action.

Internal Environment (Within the Co.):

The marketing management, in formulating plans, takes the other groups into account:

1. Top Management

2. Finance

3. R&D

4. Manufacturing

5. Purchasing

6. Sales Promotion

7. Advertisement etc.

Environmental forces are dynamic and any change in them brings uncertainties, threats and opportunities for the marketers. Changes in the environmental forces can be monitored through environmental scanning, that is, observation of secondary sources such as business, trade and Government, and environmental analysis, that is, interpretation of the information gathered through environmental scanning.

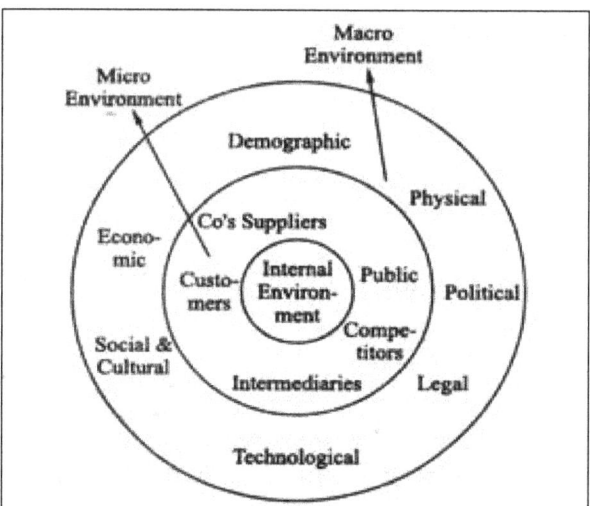

The Organisation's Marketing Environment.

Marketers try to predict what may happen in the future with the help of tools like marketing research and marketing information or marketing intelligence system, and continue to modify their marketing efforts and build future marketing strategies. The company should think about the consumer and work in harmony to provide customer value and satisfaction.

Company's Suppliers

Suppliers provide the resources needed by the company to product its goods and services. They are important links in the company's overall customer "value delivery system". Supplier developments can seriously affect marketing. Marketing managers must watch supply availability – supply shortages or delays, labour strikes and other events can cost sales in the short run and damage customer satisfaction in the long run. Marketing Managers also monitor the price trends of their key inputs. Rising supply costs may force price increases that can harm the company's sales volume.

In business-to-business marketing, one company's supplier is likely to be another company's customer and it is important to understand how suppliers, manufacturers and intermediaries work together to create value. Buyers and sellers are increasingly co-operating in their dealings with each other, rather than bargaining each transaction in a confrontational manner in order to make supply chain management most effective and value-added products are sold to the target markets.

Marketing Intermediaries

Marketing Intermediaries are businesses that help your company to promote, sell, and distribute your products and services to your customers. They can include resellers, physical distribution firms, marketing service agencies, and financial intermediaries.

Resellers

Resellers, such as Target or Best Buy, are distribution channel businesses that help your company find customers or make sales to them. There are now numerous large reseller organizations (think big box such as Target and Amazon) that have enough power to dictate terms, or even shut out other manufacturers (or even you) from larger markets and groups of customers. It is absolutely important to have great relationships with resellers. It is a give and take situation. Often times, especially with larger organizations such as Walmart, you must be willing to follow their pricing or selling guidelines in order to gain access to their customers. It may cost you money to get your product on their shelves, or be featured in their advertisements. Unless you have a long, successful relationship with these resellers, you will typically have to supply them product and services on their terms. In these situations, successful sales of your product in their stores will be what builds leverage for you in the relationship.

Physical Distribution Firms

Physical Distribution Firms help your business stock and move goods to their points of origin and to their destinations, ie: from the factory to a warehouse and then to the stores. It is often much more economical to rely on these companies, because logistics is their specialty. To build a logistics team and infrastructure is often very expensive to do from scratch, and is only really necessary when you are moving massive amounts of goods in highly specialized and time critical ways. If you are manufacturing internationally, make sure you develop a good relationship with a firm that knows the in's and out's and politics of getting product in and out of ports and dealing with customs.

Marketing Services Agencies

Agencies usually consist of marketing research firms, ad agencies, consultants, and media firms. These companies exist to help you find and target your customers. These businesses typically help to fill in the holes in your marketing staff. Research firms provide you with qualitative and quantitative data on markets and customers. Ad agencies help provide fresh, outside creative ideas for your campaigns and strategic marketing efforts. Agencies can bring multiple types of marketing experts to your business without you having to staff people for each discipline. Consultants can service the role of internal marketing staff on a temporary, campaign or project basis.

The key to using Marketing Services Agencies is to partner with them to help you with your weaknesses. Whomever you use, make sure they are filling a hole that you haven't filled yourself on staff. Make sure that they are invested in bringing you results. You must keep constant tabs on them: are they doing the right work? Are they investing your dollars properly? Are they performing at a level that meets your expectations? Are they truly concerned with achieving success for you? Do you have a good working relationship with your account executives?

Financial Intermediaries

Financial Intermediaries help you use money. They typically include banks, credit companies, insurance companies, other businesses that help you conduct financial transactions or insure against the risks associated with the buying and selling of goods and services.

Marketing Intermediaries are a crucial part of the marketing microenvironment. You must have effective partnerships with these key elements of the microenvironment if you are going to successfully give value to your customers and get value from them. Now is as good a time as any to evaluate the relationships you have with your marketing intermediaries.

Customers

Customers are the key to sales. If you don't have customers, you can't sell anything. Managers must continually study customer needs and try to anticipate how they are developing so they can meet these needs effectively now and in the future. However not all customers are the same. Managers must actively study five distinct categories of customer markets.

Consumer Markets

Consumer Markets are made up of individuals and household units. These customers buy products and services for their own personal use.

Business Markets

Customers in Business Markets typically purchase products and services that will be further processed or used in their own internal business processes. These customers are commonly referred to as B2B, or business-to-business customers.

Resellers

Customers in Reseller markets purchase products and services specifically to resell them to others for a profit. Well known resellers in the United States are "big box" stores, such as Target or Walmart.

Government Markets

Customers in Government Markets consist of government agencies that purchase products and services from private companies, and provide public services or transfer products and services to others who they deem need them. Some industries are much more dependent on Government Markets than others.

International Markets

Customers in International Markets are buyers who reside in other countries. These buyers include consumers, producers, resellers and even governments.

A business will typically sell it's products and services to multiple Customer Markets. Customer markets can also provide areas for a business to grow into. Each market requires it's own special strategic marketing to properly "sell" to it's distinct type of customer. Each Customer tastes and preferences will also change at different rates, and are effected by larger economic factors in different ways at different times. A good marketing manager will always have a good sense of what is going on in each of the Customer markets he or she is strategically marketing to.

Competitors

No single competitive marketing strategy is best for all companies. The company's marketing system is surrounded and affected by a host of competitors. Each firm should consider its own size and industry position compared to those of its competitors. These competitors have to be identified, monitored and outmanouvered to gain and maintain customer loyalty.

Industry and competition constitute a major component of the micro-environment. Development of marketing plans and strategy is based on knowledge about competitors' activities. Competitive advantage also depends on understanding the status, strength and weakness of competitors in the market.

Large firms with dominant positions in an industry can use certain strategies that smaller firms cannot afford. But being large is not enough. There are winning strategies for large firms, but there are also losing ones. And small firms can develop strategies that give them better rate of return than large firms enjoy.

Competitor Analysis is a component of Situational Analysis and is used in order to map out the external environment of a business. What kind of influence do the competitors play on the business? The opportunities and threats that emerge from this serve as input for the SWOT Analysis on which the ultimate choice of strategy is based.

In Competitor Analysis, a look at individual competitors is taken. As discussed above, opportunities and threats are very important. The competitor's weak points can serve as strong points and the same applies to the opposite. It is important to identify competitive advantages and to overcome or remedy one's own weaknesses.

The reason behind Competitor Analysis:

Conducting Competitor Analysis gives insight into the attractiveness of the market where the organisation is active. It also offers the possibility to identify opportunities and threats from external environment.

Competitor Analysis - Step by Step:

Without the clear and unambiguous structure, one can quickly forget to tie the right conclusions to the information gathered. It is therefore advisable to follow a clear structure. A step-by-step plan for conducting a good Competitor Analysis follows below.

Step 1 – Summing up one's own product portfolio Briefly describe one's own portfolio where the organisation is active.

Step 2 – Identifying the Competitors There are many different forms of competition. Such is alcohol-free beer and beer competitor, but also are drinks in general and even food competitors. It is therefore important to do a distinction between direct and indirect competitors. Direct competitors – organisations that offer comparable alternatieves Indirect competitors – organisations that do not offer the same sort of product or service but instead an alternative for the product category.

Step 3 – Choice of Competitors does an analysis have to be made of each competitor? This is a very time-consuming process with often little plus side. It is better to choose a number of important competitors and respond to them. Justify these choices with a good motivation.

Step 4 – Research the objectives & strategy what kind of strategy do the competitors follow? Which way do they go? Are the competitors aggressive or passive? Is there any attack to anticipate? In what manner does the competitor expect to growth in the coming years? Try to give an answer on these important questions. Do not hesitate to formulate and add additional questions. Research also the way the competitors bet on their marketing instruments. This gives a good insight into the present situation of the competitor. Does the competitor's present strategy have the desired effect? This also gives a first look into the strengths and the weaknesses.

Step 5 – Key factors in the market from where do the competitors gain their above-average results? Examples of this are a technological lead or qualitatively higher materials. Set a number of questions in order to determine the most important factors. Examples of this: Why does one buy at company X? Why is company X succesful? Why is company X not succesful? What do customers find important? and the likes.

Step 6 – Strength-Weakness analysis of competitors confront the key factors in the industry with the most important competitors. The outcome is a table with all strengths and weaknesses of the most important competitors in there, record also a weighting factor. Some factor is much more important than the other. After that, make an even (smaller) summarising table with scores 1 for very week and 10 for very strong and make along with it a sum-up of the most important competitors.

Step 7 – Future describe the expectation for the future. What is the competitor likely going to do?

Step 8 – Conclusion describe the most important findings and conclude with the most important opportunities and threats that serve as input for the SWOT Analysis.

Publics

In simple terms, a Public is any group of people that may have an real or potential interest in or an impact on your business's ability to achieve its objectives - whatever they may be. Why should you care about Publics? It's simple. Publics can help, or hinder your ability to get your message out to your customers, and collect value from them.

Financial Publics

Your relationships with Financial Publics are extremely important. These relationships directly influence your ability to obtain funding for your business. Financial Publics typically include banks, investment houses and stock holders. How these groups perceive you will directly affect your ability to get loans, favorable payment terms, and whether or not other Publics choose to do business with you. For example, if a brokerage perceives that you are having issues internally, or your products have deficiencies, then it may give your stock a low rating. If that happens, people may sell your stock, your market valuation will decrease, and your customers may start to buy less of your products and services.

Media Publics

Media Publics can be extremely valuable, or they can be a thorn in your side. Media Publics typically carry news, features and editorial opinions, delivering them to your customers and other Publics. They include newspapers, blogs, magazines (print and digital), radio (broadcast and internet) and television outlets (broadcast and digital). You can carry out your "relationship" with Media Publics via VNR's, PR media releases, op ed's, interviews, or open invitations to review your products and services. Do not be afraid to make friends and connect with people in the media. You can gently influence what they say about you. Having a good relationship with people in the media can make a bad situation for your company "tolerable" or a PR disaster in the eyes of your customers.

Government Publics

Management must take governmental developments into account. You should always keep an eye on the current state of any laws and regulations that effect the production of your products, the day-to-day operation of your business, or the methods you can use to sell your products and services. Marketers must often consult with government officials, their lawyers, and sometimes lobbyists. Get to know your local government, and keep tabs on what your government officials are doing.

Citizen-action Publics

The decisions you make will sometimes be questioned by citizens, consumer organizations, environmental groups, minority groups and others. Your PR department can help you stay in touch with these groups. It can keep you abreast of any concerns or problems that arise. Make it your mission to get to know the citizen groups that may affect your business and your marketing practices. Make it a point to have a friendly relationship with any of their representatives.

Local Publics

Local Publics typically include neighborhood residents and community organizations. Businesses will usually appoint a community relations officer to meet with the community, answer questions and contribute to worthwhile causes.

General Publics

A business needs to be concerned with the general public's attitude and perception towards its products and activities in the marketplace. The perception of the business, it's brands, products and services in the public directly effect consumers buying habits. Keep an eye on Twitter feeds and FaceBook posts. You will be able to get a very real sense of the general public's perception of you in the marketplace.

Internal Publics

Internal Publics are groups of people inside your own business. These groups can consist of employees, managers, volunteers, and the board of directors. Businesses typically use newsletters, memos, company meetings, intranets and other means to motivate and educate their internal publics. When your employees feel good working for you, when your board of directors are happy with your success, when your internal communications send the right messages to motivate, encourage, train, and edify your staff, this positive attitude spills over to external publics, and helps to communicate your brand message in the marketplace.

A business can construct strategic marketing plans for some or all of these major Publics alongside it's chosen customer markets. Suppose a business wants to evoke a specific response from a particular Public, such as donations of time or money (Cause Marketing). The business would have to design an messaging campaign for this Public that is enticing and persuading enough to coax the desired response.

Is it realistic for all businesses to pay attention to all of these Publics at the same time? No. Can you effectively market to all Publics. Yes and No. You have to make the judgement where to spend your time and resources. However, at some point in time you will have to deal with each of these Publics in some capacity. It is in your best interest to at least get to know them, and when appropriate, take action.

References

- Demographic-variables-affect-business-24344: smallbusiness.chron.com, Retrieved 9 July 2020

- The-internal-environment, managerial-environments, principles-of-management: cliffsnotes.com, Retrieved 9 May 2020

- Difference-between-micro-internal-and-macro-external-environment: keydifferences.com, Retrieved 2 June 2020

- Marketing-environment-study-notes-50811: yourarticlelibrary.com, Retrieved 9 July 2020

- Factors-affecting-economic-environment-business-7399326: bizfluent.com, Retrieved 29 May 2020

- Impact-technology-business-environment-7950023: bizfluent.com, Retrieved 3 March 2020

- Technological-environment-how-it-impacts-business: inurture.co.in, Retrieved 23 March 2020

- Physical-environment-operate-business: golaserengraving.com, Retrieved 29 June 2020

Permissions

Index

Lightning Source UK Ltd.
Milton Keynes UK
UKHW052207140922
408888UK00002B/51